A NOBLE RAKE

LONDON : HUMPHREY MILFORD
OXFORD UNIVERSITY PRESS

CHARLES, FOURTH LORD MOHUN, AT THIRTY

A NOBLE RAKE

THE LIFE OF
CHARLES, FOURTH LORD MOHUN

BEING A STUDY IN THE HISTORICAL BACKGROUND
OF THACKERAY'S "HENRY ESMOND"

By ROBERT STANLEY FORSYTHE, Ph.D.
PROFESSOR OF ENGLISH IN THE UNIVERSITY OF NORTH DAKOTA

CAMBRIDGE, MASSACHUSETTS : HARVARD
UNIVERSITY PRESS : MCMXXVIII

COPYRIGHT, 1928
BY THE PRESIDENT AND FELLOWS OF HARVARD COLLEGE

PRINTED AT THE HARVARD UNIVERSITY PRESS
CAMBRIDGE, MASS., U.S.A.

TO

MY WIFE

IN GRATEFUL ACKNOWLEDGEMENT
OF HER PART IN WRITING THIS BOOK

PREFACE

THE book to which the following lines serve as foreword is largely an accident. In its original form, it consisted of a brief footnote to Lord Macaulay's well-known description of William Mountford's death, and was drawn from certain passages which I had jotted down in a reading of Narcissus Luttrell's *Diary*. Some rather random investigation in the Bodleian Library and, later, in the British Museum led me to believe that I might properly expand my original note. This I did; but my longer draft, written at Florence in 1924, has grown since, as the result of further research, to the present volume. Lest it again begin to multiply its pages, I am now turning it over to the publishers.

My purpose in *A Noble Rake* is twofold. First, I aim to give a correct account of the somewhat sordid career of the mediocre profligate who served Thackeray as the original of the villain of his great romance. In the second place, I hope to show clearly how the novelist worked over the life of the historical Lord Mohun and utilized it in his book, revising here, adding there, excising elsewhere, and yet maintaining constantly such an air of the utmost veracity as to deceive the average reader into believing that the *History of Henry Esmond* is history indeed. That my work is errorless, I do not venture to think, but I am certain that I have corrected many of the mistakes of previous biographers of Lord Mohun, and have added much new material to what has been hitherto recorded concerning his life and deeds. And I believe that I am, as well, the first to point out many places wherein Thackeray has departed from the facts of history. In connection with this I ought to say that I have attempted to investigate every incident and historical person mentioned in those passages of *Esmond* wherein Lord Mohun figures. Consequently, my comments at times have dealt with Thackeray's treatment of other historical characters and of the events in which they take part.

In addition, I have felt myself justified in the elaborateness of my study by the fact that *Henry Esmond* has been almost untouched, so far as I know, by the scholarly investigator. There is only one approach to an adequate edition of the book, that of T. C. and W. Snow, and it has its faults and its oversights. Other editions which I have examined are of value only as presenting a reprint of

Thackeray's text. I offer this study, then, as supplying in part the need for a treatment of the sources of *Esmond*, and the lack of a study of the novelist's use of them.

I have not gone into the descent of Lord Mohun, inasmuch as a long genealogical disquisition seems to me to be a rather unpropitious opening to a slightly forbidding work. I expect to publish, in the near future, some notes upon the three earlier Lords Mohun of Okehampton. The impatient reader is referred, then, for the present, to Sir H. Maxwell Lyte's *History of Dunster and of the Families of Mohun and Luttrell*. So far as they go, G. E. C.'s notices, in his *Complete Peerage*, are authoritative.

I have, perhaps indiscreetly, called this book "slightly forbidding." My allusion is to its footnotes. I do not, however, pretend to be a "modern" biographer; but, rather, a combination of historian and literary student, assiduously referring to my sources. And I must confess that my own delight in antiquarian footnotes has by no means aided in deterring me from using them. I must call attention to the fact that my biographical notes deal exclusively with persons almost or wholly forgotten at present. I have not, for example, solemnly summed up the lives of the Duke of Marlborough, Lord Somers, Sir

Richard Steele, and Dean Swift, and of others nearly as well known to the modern, although I have not hesitated to touch upon what I regard as debatable questions in their careers.

There are two points which the conscientious reader will discover for himself in my footnotes and text, but which he, perhaps, will be unable to explain. The first of these is the fact that I have made no citations by page to *Henry Esmond*. This is due in part to my belief that he who desires to verify my references to the novel will find it easy to do so by locating the book and chapter to which I direct him and by glancing through the latter. This I believe to be more convenient than either securing a given edition of the novel and finding cited pages therein, or searching for my references through an edition other than the one used by me. The second point to which I would call attention is that I have adopted the contemporary spelling of "Maccartney" for the surname of Lord Mohun's friend. I have been under the necessity, therefore, as I thought, of employing two spellings, "Macartney" when I refer to Thackeray's character, "Maccartney" when I mention the historical general. Not only common contemporary usage authorizes the latter, but the fact, as well, that the Macartney of Thackeray

PREFACE xi

owes little to the lieutenant general of the wars in Flanders and Spain.

My acknowledgements for assistance in the course of this work are numerous and grateful. To the Librarian of the Bodleian and his assistants, to the officials of the Library of the British Museum, and to the Vice-Librarian of the Library of Cambridge University, I am indebted for the privilege of consulting their respective collections of books and pamphlets. To the officials of the British Public Records Office I am grateful for the assistance given me. Mrs. A. May Osler, of London, deserves my thanks also for her researches under my direction in the Public Records Office and in the British Museum. These she undertook with enthusiasm and carried through diligently and faithfully.

I can only very inadequately express my thanks to Librarian George B. Utley, and to his assistants (especially Mr. W. S. Merrill), for their many courtesies during the two years I spent at work in the Newberry Library of Chicago. My former colleague, Mr. Theodore W. Koch of Northwestern University, and his staff have also helped me on in my work. Mr. A. D. Keator of the University of North Dakota has, too, been most courteous and kind in forwarding my researches. I acknowledge with gratitude the assistance of the Libraries of the University of Chicago, of the University of Wisconsin, and of the University of Minnesota, and of the Library of Congress. I am indebted to Mr. H. M. Lydenberg, Reference Librarian of the New York Public Library, for photostats, and to Miss Anne S. Pratt, Reference Librarian of the Yale University Library, for photostats and bibliographical information. Much of my research could not have been accomplished, had it not been for the grant awarded me for 1926 by the American Council of Learned Societies. I am glad to have the honor of recording my obligation to this body for their material recognition of the potential utility of my work.

To Mr. Harold Murdock, Director of the Harvard University Press, I am most grateful, not only for his helpful advice, but for his extreme generosity in permitting me to reproduce a number of prints from his fine personal collection. I owe thanks, also, to Mr. H. M. Lydenberg for permission to reproduce certain prints in the possession of the New York Public Library. For a like courtesy, I am indebted to the officials of the British Museum; and to Mrs. Lillian A. Hall, Custodian of the Theatre Collection of the Harvard

PREFACE

College Library. For the interest which they have taken in my work and for their kind suggestions, I must thank Mr. William M. Ivins, Jr., Curator of Prints in the Metropolitan Museum of Fine Arts, New York City; Mr. Henry P. Rossiter, Curator of the Department of Prints in the Museum of Fine Arts, Boston; Mr. Walter H. Siple of the Fogg Art Museum of Harvard University; and Miss Jean E. Spaulding of the Brander Matthews Dramatic Museum of Columbia University.

My personal friends have not been backward in offering me valuable suggestions. I take pleasure in acknowledging the assistance of Professor William P. Trent of Columbia University; of Professor Thomas O. Mabbott of Northwestern University; of Professor George B. Sherburn of the University of Chicago; of Professor Aaron J. Perry of the University of Manitoba; of Dean O. P. Cockerill of the School of Law of the University of North Dakota; of Professors F. B. Kaye and A. H. Nethercot of Northwestern University; and of Mr. R. F. Almy of Cambridge, Massachusetts. To my good friend and former colleague, Mr. Bernard De Voto, of Cambridge, Massachusetts, I am deeply indebted for hearty encouragement and sound advice. Both he and Mrs. Avis De Voto have most kindly made certain investigations for me with a generous expenditure of time and effort.

My wife has not only relieved me of much of the drudgery connected with the preparation of my manuscript, but has constantly, needfully, and helpfully criticized it as to style and structure. To her, for her devotion to a very dull task, I owe much more than I can express in cold words.

R. S. F.

GRAND FORKS
May, 1928

CONTENTS

    I. Lord Mohun Enters 3
   II. A Career Begins 22
  III. A Young Man about Town and Elsewhere 48
  IV. Lord Mohun Visits Castlewood . . . 65
   V. A Duel in Leicester Fields 76
  VI. The Death of Lord Castlewood . . . 97
 VII. Colonel and Brigadier 117
VIII. Man of *Ton* 130
  IX. Statesman 145
   X. Two Duels in a Novel 176
  XI. Lawsuits 190
 XII. A Quarrel and a Challenge 201
XIII. The Last Duel 218
XIV. Fact and Fiction 233

Appendices

A. Adelaide, Duchess of Shrewsbury . . . 255
B. Lieutenant General George Maccartney 257
C. Lieutenant General Thomas Meredyth . 265
D. Pamphlets, etc., on the Hamilton-Mohun Duel 268
E. Royal Proclamations 273
F. Letters of the Earl of Sutherland and Colonel John Hamilton 277

ILLUSTRATIONS

CHARLES, FOURTH LORD MOHUN, AT THIRTY   *Frontispiece*
From Faber's mezzotint after the portrait by Kneller. (1732.)

WILLIAM, FIRST DUKE OF DEVONSHIRE   8
From Faber's mezzotint after the portrait by Kneller.

MRS. ANNE BRACEGIRDLE.   24
From the print by Harding from the engraving by Stow in Harding's *Mirrour*.

MRS. BRACEGIRDLE AS THE INDIAN QUEEN . .   32
From a rare engraving: "J. Smith ex., W. Vincent fc."

THOMAS, FIRST DUKE OF LEEDS   48
From Blooteling's engraving after the portrait by Lely.

EDWARD, SIXTH EARL OF WARWICK   76
From Richardson's engraving after the portrait by Wissing. (Published Feb. 15, 1794.)

JOHN, FIRST LORD SOMERS OF EVESHAM   92
From Faber's mezzotint, after the portrait by Kneller. (1733.)

SIR RICHARD STEELE, KNT.   108
From Faber's engraving after the portrait by Kneller. (1733.)

BOCONNOC PARK HOUSE, CORNWALL   138
From T. Jeavons's engraving of a drawing by F. W. L. Stockdale made for his *Excursions through Cornwall*. (April 1, 1822.)

JOHN, FIRST DUKE OF MARLBOROUGH   142
From Faber's mezzotint after the portrait by Kneller. (1735.)

JAMES, FOURTH DUKE OF HAMILTON   178
Frontispiece to the Memoirs of the Life and Family of the Most Illustrious James, Late Duke of Hamilton . . . London: Printed for T. Warner at the Black Boy on Pater Noster Row, 1717.

xviii   ILLUSTRATIONS

DR. JONATHAN SWIFT. 184
Frontispiece, engraved by G. Virtue, to Swift's Works. Dublin. Printed by and for George Faulkner, Printer and Bookseller, in Essex Street Opposite to the Bridge, 1735.

THE DEATH OF THE DUKE OF HAMILTON . . . 218
From a print in the British Museum.

CHARLES, FIRST DUKE OF RICHMOND 226
From Faber's mezzotint after the portrait by Kneller. (1731.)

HENRY, FIRST VISCOUNT BOLINGBROKE 236
From an engraving published December 7, 1799, by S. Harding, after a portrait in the collection of the Right Hon. Richard, Viscount Chetwynd.

A NOBLE RAKE

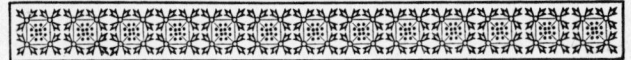

I

LORD MOHUN ENTERS

THE first mention of Charles Lord Mohun in *Esmond* occurs on Henry's arrival from Cambridge at Castlewood for his third long vacation — the summer of 1699, it would seem. Then Beatrix Esmond asks Henry if he does not wear a peruke like my Lord Mohun. "My Lord says that nobody wears their own hair."[1] We do not, however, meet his Lordship until he comes to Castlewood, escorting, with his friend Lord Firebrace, the latter's mother, Lady Sark.[2] Then Esmond describes him for us:

. . . a person of a handsome presence, with the *bel air*, and a bright, daring, warlike aspect, which, according to the chronicle of those days,[3] had already achieved

---

[1] *Henry Esmond*, bk. I, chap. 11.
[2] *Ibid.*, bk. I, chap. 12.
[3] By "the chronicle of those days," it may be that Thackeray had in mind two actual books, the scurrilous *Secret Memoirs . . . from the New Atalantis* of Mrs. Mary de la Rivière Manley, and the *Memoirs of Europe, towards the Close of the Eighth Century*, of the same writer, even though the first appeared only in 1709, and the second in 1710. Both contain some discussion of Lord Mohun's amours, for a discussion of which see *infra*, pp. 131–138.

for him the conquest of several beauties and toasts. He had fought in France as well as in Flanders; he had served a couple of campaigns with the Prince of Baden on the Danube, and witnessed the rescue of Vienna from the Turk. And he spoke of his military exploits pleasantly, and with the manly freedom of a soldier, so as to delight all his hearers at Castlewood who were little accustomed to meet a companion so agreeable.[1]

In order to present a villain who would be personally attractive enough to warrant Lord Castlewood's later jealousy of him, Thackeray has to some degree embellished both the figure and the history of Lord Mohun.[2] If his portrait by Kneller is to be trusted, Mohun was not a handsome man;[3] later in life, at any rate, he grew fat.[4] Swift says of him:

[1] *Esmond*, bk. I, chap. 12.

[2] A few of the novelist's freedoms with fact are pointed out by T. C. and W. Snow in their edition of *Esmond* (Oxford University Press, 1915), in their notes to pp. 126 and 147, on pp. 489 and 493, respectively.

[3] J. Faber, *The Kit-Cat Club, Done from the Original Paintings by Sir Godfrey Kneller*, London, 1735, Plate 23. Mrs. Manley calls Mohun handsome, but admits, however, that "he is a Favourite of hers" (*Secret Memoirs . . . from the New Atalantis*, ed. of 1720, pp. 290, 300).

[4] Art., "Mohun, Charles, fifth [*sic*] Baron," in *The Dictionary of National Biography*, xxxviii, 105 ff., by the late Professor Seccombe, who perhaps based his statement upon the testimony of Kneller's portrait. There is, however, contemporary verbal evidence that by 1706, or thereabouts, Mohun was becoming corpulent. Grove, *Lives of . . . the Dukes of Devonshire*, p. 249, n., quoting a "short character" of Lord Mohun.

LORD MOHUN ENTERS

"He was little better than a conceited talker in company."[1]

The life of Lord Mohun prior to 1699 was by no means so romantic as Thackeray would lead one to believe, although it was certainly not devoid of incident. Charles fourth[2] Lord Mohun of Okehampton, only son and younger child[3] of Charles

---

[1] Swift's notes upon Macky's *Memoirs*, reprinted by T. Scott, Swift's *Prose Works*, x, 278. It should be remembered, however, that to Swift's prejudiced mind no Whig was ever either intelligent or honest. Mrs. Manley, on the other hand, comments on Mohun's "fine sense," his "Penetration and Understanding," and his "prodigious Share of good Sense and exalted Wit" (*op. cit.*, pp. 297, 299, 300). Her praises are perhaps of no especial value, however, on account of her admission of a fondness for him (see *supra*, p. 4, n. 3). Gilbert, too, lauds Mohun's ability (*Parochial History of Cornwall*, i, 67).

[2] By various writers the last Lord Mohun is called the fifth Lord (see, for example, Seccombe, *op. cit.*; *Hist. MSS. Comm. Reports*, xv, pt. 2, 346, *MSS. of J. Eliot Hodgkin*; *Memoirs of the Celebrated Persons forming the Kit-Cat Club*, p. 120). Sir H. C. Maxwell Lyte shows, however, that the Honorable John Mohun, eldest son of the first Baron, predeceased his father in October, 1639 (*History of Dunster*, p. 487). John Mohun's brother Warwick, grandfather of the last Lord, succeeded his father, the first Lord, on March 28, 1641 (see Lyte, *loc. cit.*). In "A Catalogue of the Barons of England" in "A Catalogue of the Nobility . . ." prefixed to *A Chronicle of the Kings of England* . . . by Sir Richard Baker (8th ed., London, 1684), is given the correct descent of the Lords Mohun of Okehampton. See also G. E. C., *Complete Peerage*, v, 323, n. *a*, where John Mohun is said to have been buried at Kennington, October 31, 1639.

[3] Lyte, who says that the fourth Lord was the elder of the

third Lord Mohun, and his wife Phillippa, daughter of Arthur Earl of Anglesey, was born in London, on April 11, 1677.[1] He was baptized by the Bishop of

two children of the third Lord (*op. cit.*, p. 489) can hardly be correct in that statement, since the fourth Lord was born only a few months before his father's death, while the latter was lying ill from the wound which proved fatal. Burke, *Dormant . . . and Extinct Peerages*, p. 370, and H. L. Stephen, *State Trials Political and Social*, ii, 59, n. 1, also call the last Lord Mohun the elder of his father's children. It is barely possible that the third Lord's daughter was a posthumous child. Whatever the date of her birth was, the Honorable Elizabeth Mohun became a maid of honor to Queen Mary, not long after the latter's accession. A match between her and John Lord Cutts, the famous general of William III, which was discussed in the summer of 1693, was not carried through; Lord Cutts was married to a Miss Pickering of Cambridgeshire, in February, 1696/7 (Luttrell, *A Brief Relation of State Affairs*, iii, 143; iv, 180). Miss Mohun's recovery from the small-pox, which perhaps she had at the same time as her royal mistress, in 1694, aided in inspiring three poets (see "On my Lady *Hide* having the Small-pox, Soon after the recovery of Mrs. *Mohun*," in Gildon's *A New Miscellany of Original Poems*, pp. 325–326; "To Mrs. Mohun, on her Recovery," by Charles Hopkins, in Nichols's *Select Collection of Poems*, ii, 209; "On Madam Mohun and Mr. Congreve's Sickness," in *Poems on State Affairs*, ii, 261). Miss Mohun died in July, 1710, being then a maid of honor to Queen Anne (Luttrell, *op. cit.*, vi, 610). Since Thackeray makes Beatrix Esmond a maid of honor to Queen Anne, one wonders on what terms she and Miss Mohun were.

[1] *MS. Diary of the Earl of Anglesey*, Brit. Mus. Add. MS. 18730, fol. 20b. The date of the birth of the fourth Lord Mohun has hitherto been incorrectly given. In his *History of Dunster*, Lyte says Lord Mohun was born in 1674 (p. 490),

Durham on April 23, his grandfather, Lord Anglesey, and George Viscount Halifax acting as godfathers.

although he quotes a letter of Lady Nottingham (*Hatton Correspondence*, Camden Society, i, 187), under date of December 13, 1692: "That wretched creature my Lord Mohun, who is not sixteen years old until April next. . . ." Lyte fixed 1674 as the date of Lord Mohun's birth, because (1) he was married in 1691, and (2) he was summoned to Parliament in October, 1695. But another grandson of Lord Anglesey was married at seven years of age (*Hist. MSS. Comm. Reports*, xiii, pt. vi, 275, *MS. Diary of the Earl of Anglesey*); and Lord Mohun actually did not take his seat in the House of Lords until July 4, 1698 (*Journals of the House of Lords*, xvi, 338). Seccombe, in the *D. N. B.*, xxxviii, 105, gave 1675 for Lord Mohun's birth-year, as did G. E. C. in his *Complete Peerage*, v, 323. These are apparently H. L. Stephen's authority for putting Mohun's birth in 1675 and giving his age as "about two" at his father's death (*op. cit.*, ii, 59, n. 1), as well as for T. C. and W. Snow (*Esmond*, p. 489). Among Mohun's contemporaries there was as much uncertainty concerning the date of his birth as there is among modern authorities. According to *A True and Impartial Account of the Animosity, Quarrel and Duel, between the late Duke of Hamilton and the Lord Mohun* (London, 1712), Mohun was under forty at his death and less than twenty when tried in 1692 (p. 22). More specific is *An Elegy on the Death of Charles Lord Mohun, who was Slain by Duke Hamilton on November the 15th, 1712, in the 38th Year of his Age.* Another pamphlet, *The Whole Lives, Characters, Actions, and Fall of D. Hamilton and L. Mohun* (London and Newcastle, 1712), says he was born at Molton-Hindmarsh in Gloucestershire in 1662! This paper is generally filled with errors, of which some seem deliberate misstatements. "A Catalogue of the Barons of England" in "A Catalogue of the Nobility . . ." prefixed to *A Chronicle of the Kings of England . . .* by Sir Richard Baker (8th ed., London, 1684) has the statement that when the third Lord

The godmothers were his grandfather's sister, Mrs. Philippa Mohun, and Mrs. Tressam, Lord Anglesey's sister.[1]

At the time of the birth of his son, Lord Mohun was on what proved to be his deathbed. On November 17, 1676, he had served as second to his friend Lord Cavendish, later fourth Earl and first Duke of Devonshire, in the latter's duel with John Power.[2] In their first encounter, Cavendish and

Mohun died, his son, "the now Baron," was in his first year. The compiler of this catalogue and Lady Nottingham appear to have been the only persons hitherto recorded as giving at all correctly Lord Mohun's birth-year.

[1] *Ms. Diary of the Earl of Anglesey*, Brit. Mus. Add. MS. 18730, fol. 21.

[2] Lord Cavendish's opponent probably was John Power, son of Pierce Power, a cousin of Lord Anglesey's son-in-law, Lord Power, later first Earl of Tyrone. Burke, *Landed Gentry of Ireland*, ed. of 1912, p. 573. This John Power was an officer in the French service. Cf. Lady Chaworth's letter of November 23, 1676, to Lord Roos, *Hist. MSS. Comm. Reports*, xii, pt. 5, 32, *MSS. of the Duke of Rutland*. It is not improbable that Lord Cavendish's efforts in 1675 toward securing an address from Parliament to the King, praying that he recall his subjects from the military service of Louis XIV (Grove, *Lives of . . . the Dukes of Devonshire*, pp. 38–40), had as much to do with the quarrel between Cavendish and Power as the dispute at the ball at Whitehall of which Lady Chaworth writes (*loc. cit.*). In his biography of the Duke, Grove makes no mention of Lord Cavendish's duel with Power; and J. A. Hamilton says that Lord Cavendish "fought and dangerously wounded Lord Mohun" (*D. N. B.*, ix, 372, art., "Cavendish, William, first Duke of Devonshire").

WILLIAM, FIRST DUKE OF DEVONSHIRE

LORD MOHUN ENTERS

Mohun had disarmed their adversaries. As the four were returning from the scene of the meeting, Lord Cavendish walking with Power's second, an Irishman named "Brummingham," [1] and Lord Mohun with Power, another quarrel broke out, and in the exchange of thrusts which followed, Power ran Mohun through the stomach.[2] Lord Mohun died, as the result of the injury, on September 29, 1677,

[1] This was, no doubt, the Honorable Edward Birmingham, son of Francis twelfth Lord Athenry, in the Irish peerage. He succeeded as thirteenth Baron Athenry on April 12, 1677 (when Lord Mohun's heir was one day old). It is said that he was one of twenty-two children (Lodge, *Peerage of Ireland*, iii, 47). Mohun's opponent was Lord Lieutenant of Mayo in 1689, and held a captaincy in the Earl of Clanricarde's Regiment of Foot. Outlawed in 1691, he was pardoned in 1700, and died in 1709 (G. E. C., *Complete Peerage*, rev. by Gibbs, i, 296). Lord Athenry, as a Catholic and an Irishman, would have been from those circumstances probably quite eager to fight two Protestant Whigs like Mohun and Cavendish.

[2] Letter of Dr. W. Denton to Sir R. Verney, November 20, 1676, *Hist. MSS. Comm. Reports*, vii, 494, *MSS. of Sir Harry Verney*. Dr. Denton's account of the duel explains the apparent discrepancies between other reports of it. Lady Chaworth, in a letter to Lord Roos on November 23, says that Lord Cavendish quarrelled with Power (*Hist. MSS. Comm. Reports*, xii, pt. 5, 32, *MSS. of the Duke of Rutland*); Sir Philip Perceval, writing on December 15 to Sir Robert Southwell, gives "one Brummigan" as Lord Mohun's opponent (*Hist. MSS. Comm. Reports, MSS. of the Earl of Egmont*, i, 52), and Lord Anglesey names Power as Mohun's slayer (*Diary*, fol. 29), as does a newsletter of November 20, 1676 (*Hist. MSS. Comm. Reports*, xii, pt. 7, 130, *MSS. of S. H. Le Fleming*).

and was buried in St. Martin's in the Fields.[1] He had chivalrously and truthfully declared that he had not been hurt in Lord Cavendish's quarrel, attempting thus to secure his friend from molestation.[2]

Of the early life of the fourth Lord Mohun we know little;[3] presumably he was cared for by his termagant[4] of a mother, who was married a second time, her husband being William Coward, sergeant-at-law, and for many years a member of Parliament for Wells.[5] This match took place probably after

[1] Lord Anglesey, *op. cit.*; letter of John Verney to Sir R. Verney, October 8, 1677 (*Hist. MSS. Comm. Reports*, vii, 470, *MSS. of Sir Harry Verney*); but see G. E. C., *Complete Peerage*, v, 323, who gives St. Giles's in the Fields as the place of Lord Mohun's interment, and October 7, 1677, as the date.

[2] Letter of C. Hatton to Lord Hatton, December 30, 1676, *Hatton Correspondence*, i, 142–143.

[3] A few references of no importance occur in Brit. Mus., Add. MS. 18730, the *Diary of the Earl of Anglesey*, already quoted.

[4] An amusing account of Lady Mohun's battle in March, 1678 (N. S.), with Anne Love, "a Shop-keeper in *The Newe Exchange*," occurs in a letter of Lady Chaworth to Lord Roos, of April 11, 1678 (*Hist. MSS. Comm. Reports*, xii, pt. 5, 49, *MSS. of the Duke of Rutland*). Lady Mohun took the quarrel before the House of Lords (*Journals of the House of Lords*, xiii, 194, 195; *Hist. MSS. Comm. Reports*, ix, pt. 2, 110, *House of Lords Calendar*). Abundant testimony as to Lady Mohun's temper is to be found in the *Diary* of her father, Lord Anglesey (*Hist. MSS. Comm. Reports*, xiii, pt. 5, 261–277, *MSS. of Lieut. Gen. L. Annesley*; and Brit. Mus. Add. MS. 18730).

[5] It is said that before marrying Lady Mohun, Coward paid her debts of fifteen hundred pounds (Lyte, *op. cit.*,

1684.[1] In 1679 the House of Lords passed a bill to enable the trustees of Lord Mohun's estates to sell timber and to make other arrangements for paying the debts (amounting to sixteen thousand pounds) of the second and third lords, as well as for raising a marriage portion for the infant daughter of the

p. 488). William Coward was a member for Wells in the third, fourth, and fifth Parliaments of Charles II, the third, fourth, fifth, and sixth of William III, and was reëlected to the first Parliament of Queen Anne (Cobbett, *Parliamentary History*, vols. iv, v, vi, *passim*). He died either before taking his seat on October 20, 1702, or, at any rate, during the session, as in *The History of the Reign of Queen Anne, Digested into Annals*, Year the Third, he is described in a list of the members of the House of Commons, as deceased (p. 276). The William Coward who sat for Wells in the second Parliament of Great Britain (Cobbett, *op. cit.*) was perhaps a relative and possibly the same William Coward who joined in a petition to the House of Lords, presented December 17, 1707, protesting against the inefficient convoying of merchant ships in which he and other City traders were interested (*Journals of the House of Lords*, xviii, 366, 381–382; see, for Coward's evidence on his examination before the Peers, *The History and Proceedings of the House of Lords*, ii, 195 ff.). It was this William Coward, probably, who died in 1716, and on account of whose death a writ for the election of a member for Wells was issued on June 16 of that year. The election took place on June 27 (Boyer, *The Political State of Great Britain*, xii [July–Dec., 1716], 291). It is said that Lady Mohun bore children to Sergeant Coward (G. E. C., *Complete Peerage*, v, 323), but I can learn nothing of them. Lady Mohun outlived her husband, having been buried at Lee, in Kent, March 2, 1714/5 (*Ibid.*).

[1] It is not mentioned in Lord Anglesey's *Diary*, which ends with that year.

third Lord.[1] Sir Charles Orby acted as the guardian of the fourth Lord during his minority.[2] Nothing is known of Lord Mohun's education, except that he did not do as others of his family before him [3] had done, and enter Exeter College, Oxford.

A catchpenny pamphlet, published in 1712, after

[1] *Journals of the House of Lords*, xiii, 499, 504, 529, 532; *Hist. MSS. Comm. Reports*, xi, pt. 2, 118-119, *House of Lords MSS.*

[2] *MSS. of the House of Lords*, N. s., ii, 519 ff. Sir Charles Orby, Bart., was the son of Sir Thomas Orby. He was commissioned major of the Queen's Troop of Horse Guards, May 1, 1676; lieutenant-colonel of Sir J. Talbot's Regiment of Dragoons, February 22, 1678; adjutant-general of Horse, August 2, 1685; lieutenant and lieutenant-colonel of the Third Troop of Life Guards, May 24, 1686; colonel of the Queen's Regiment of Foot, November 11, 1688. He was removed by the Prince of Orange in the following month. (Dalton, *English Army Lists*, i, 188, 206; ii, 2). On May 10, 1692, Sir Charles was among the Jacobites for whose arrest a proclamation was issued. Others were the Earls of Scarsdale, Newburgh, Middleton, and Dunmore, and Sir John Fenwick. With Lords Newburgh and Griffin, he surrendered himself on June 9 (Luttrell, *op. cit.*, ii, 448-449, 477). This arrest was in consequence of Young's pretended discovery of a plot in which the Bishop of Rochester was implicated (Macaulay, *History of England*, chap. 18). Sir Charles may have been the Jacobite lieutenant-colonel of horse quoted in a letter of August 17, 1694, to St. Germains, as criticizing the English Jacobites for indecision and lukewarmness (Macpherson, *Original Papers*, i, 490-491). Sir Charles Orby died in 1716. In some way he was related to the Mohuns.

[3] For example, John first Lord Mohun received his B.A. at Oxford in 1608, having been a member of Exeter College (Lyte, *op. cit.*, p. 485; see also *Ibid.*, p. 484).

LORD MOHUN ENTERS

Mohun's death,[1] has a passage on his early life and rearing, which is worth quoting:

Lord Mohun having very Honourable Parents, endued with the Ornaments of Piety and Virtue, no Care was wanting in them to give this their only Son all the Advantages of Education suitable to his Birth and Quality; but his roving Genius took no Delight in Learning, for he spent his Time in Raking, Dancing, Fencing and Musick, and unhappily gave himself up to all manner of Vices that the Country and Town afforded.

For after the Death of his Father, being turned of 21 Years, he took Possession of his Estate, excepting that part of it which was left his Mother for a Jointure, which was about 3000 *l. per annum.* He then took to keeping company with the greatest Rakes of Quality, and went about Town, breaking of Windows, beating of Constables and Watchmen, &c.

Yet notwithstanding his lewd way of Living, he Married a Sister of the Earl of *Macclesfield*, but his Lordship still following a Rakish Life, there arose a Disgust between his Lordship and his Lady, which occasioned a Separation, and his Lordship never lived with his Lady any more.

In this time of Separation, his Lordship was a great frequenter of the Play-House, where he fell in Love with one Mrs. *B——dle*.[2]

---

[1] *The Whole Lives, Characters, Actions, and Fall of D. Hamilton and L. Mohun.* Printed by J. White, London and Newcastle, 1712.

[2] Mohun seems not to have been in love with Mrs. Bracegirdle, but on December 9, 1692, he and Captain Hill, the former then fifteen, the latter, sixteen years of age, did dine

A NOBLE RAKE

Much the same sort of story of Mohun's youth is given by a later writer,[1] from whom, as well as from the author of the account quoted above, Thackeray probably drew:

He came to the title during his minority, and, in consequence of the second marriage of his mother, we are told that his education was much neglected, and that he was at a very early age, left to follow his own inclinations without restraint. He profited by this license to such an extent, that before he was twenty years old, he had plunged into every species of vice and debauchery; and contracted intimacies with the vilest profligates of the day, with whom he constantly identified himself, in all their drunken brawls and midnight atrocities.

From a combination of these two passages, no doubt, is derived Colonel Westbury's character of Lord Mohun:

. . . if my Lord Mohun were a commoner, I would say, 't was a pity he was not hanged.[2] He was familiar with dice and women at a time other boys are at school being birched; he was as wicked as the oldest rake, years ere he had done growing; and handled a sword and a foil, and a bloody one too, before he ever used a

---

with Mrs. Elizabeth Sandys of the playhouse. *Tryal of . . . Lord Mohun . . . for the Murder of William Mountford.*

[1] *Memoirs of . . . the Kit-Cat Club*, pp. 120 ff.

[2] Cf. Hearne, writing November 17, 1712, after Mohun's death: "This Ld. Mohun should have been hang'd some Years agoe for Murder, which he had committed divers times." *Remarks and Collections* (ed. by C. E. Doble for the Oxford Historical Society), iii, 483.

razor. . . . He will come to a bad end, will that young lord; and no end is bad enough for him.[1]

Although the authors of these works have certainly erred in many particulars of fact, some of which occur in the passages quoted above,[2] yet, in want of absolute evidence to the contrary, it seems that one may accept the accounts given in them of Mohun's youth as at least certainly not improbable and, indeed, very likely to be close to the truth in their general outlines. John Evelyn's terse characterization of Mohun at fifteen as "exceeding dissolute,"[3] cannot be bettered.

There is some mention of Lord Mohun in the reports made to the French King by Eusébe Renaudot, Louis XIV's secret agent among the English Jacobites. Renaudot asserts that Lord Mohun is one of the noblemen of Somerset and Devon who can be relied upon by the dethroned James II.[4] It is possible that the Frenchman's informant counted upon

[1] *Esmond*, bk. II, chap. 2.

[2] It is implied in the first extract that Mohun was of age when he succeeded his father. As has been seen, he was, in fact, under six months old. He did not marry a sister of any Earl of Macclesfield, but the granddaughter of the first earl and a niece of the second and third.

The second passage certainly suggests that Mohun began his notorious career at a later age than he actually did.

[3] *Diary*, ed. by Bray, ii, 385, under February 4, 1692/3.

[4] Haile, *Queen Mary of Modena*, p. 281, quoting the *Renaudot MSS.* in the Bibliothèque Nationale.

the influence of Sir Charles Orby with his ward.[1] Certainly the young Lord Mohun did not lean long toward the party of the banished King.

The circumstances of Lord Mohun's early life cease to be conjectural and begin to become a matter of historical record when, at the age of fourteen, he was first married, his wife being Charlotte Manwaring, daughter of James Manwaring, and granddaughter of Charles first Earl of Macclesfield. The wedding took place in the summer of 1691.[2]

This marriage appears to have been even more unhappy than that of the bridegroom's parents; and complications resulting from it led, over twenty years later, to Mohun's own death. It seems likely, from the youth of the contracting parties, as well as from other circumstances, such as the marriage of Lady Charlotte Manwaring, mother of the bride, to Sir Thomas Orby, son to Mohun's guardian,[3] that the match was one of convenience only.[4]

---

[1] Since the commission as colonel of the Queen's Regiment of Foot, given on November 11, 1688, by James II, had been revoked by William III, it is reasonable to suppose that Sir Charles was even then well known as a Jacobite. See *supra*, p. 12, n. 2.

[2] Luttrell, *A Brief Relation of State Affairs*, ii, 274.

[3] Burke, *Extinct and Dormant Baronetcies*, ed. 1838, p. 393, art., "Orby of Croyland."

[4] Mrs. Manley says of the marriage: "He [Lord Mohun] had married her [Charlotte Manwaring] against his then Interest, without a fortune or the hopes of any." *New Atalan-*

LORD MOHUN ENTERS

According to the pamphleteer quoted earlier,[1] the blame for Lord Mohun's separation from his first wife, which occurred after a few years, lay with the husband. Another story, however, is related by Mrs. Manley.

[Mohun] carried her [Lady Mohun] down to his fine Villa, where he show'd an excessive Regard and Fondness of her. When his Affairs recall'd him, he resign'd her to the Care of his Uncle; whom he conjur'd to make it his Business, to serve and divert her in his Absence. The Traytor perform'd the last Part with no ill Sucess; he corrupted her Principles, though her Education and Temper had not made it a very difficult Work. In a Word, he supply'd by Night the Absence of his Nephew, being really fallen in Love with his Niece's Charms, which he pursu'd the Conquest of without any Remorse. But having once taught her what it was to make a breach in her Duty, she would enjoy the Benefit of it, without confining her self to him alone. In effect, she coquetted with all the Country, so greedy of Flattery and Adoration, that she fell as low as the Vilest to procure it, even from those that dishonour'd her. At the Baron's Return he quickly saw (being a Man clear-sighted, full of penetration and Understanding) the libertine Airs she had assum'd: She was yet very dear to him; he could not have a Suspicion of her Vertue, without mortal Pangs to his Repose. But not to put her on her Guard, he forebore to complain, yet so dexter-

---

tis, p. 298. In view of Mohun's tender age, this would tend to indicate that the union was arranged by the guardians of the children.

[1] See *supra*, p. 13.

ously and successfully pursu'd her, that he had the Mortification to surprize her in his Uncle's Bed, after which he never saw her more. She fell to the Many and the Unworthy, and made herself so scandalous, that an Uncle of hers [1] (justly incensed) died, and left her Lord a hundred and forty thousand Crowns, for no other Merit, as to him, but using her as she deserved. Conscious of her Crimes, she has not dared to sue him for a Pension. But this Stratagem, as some pretend, has been found out by her needy Lover of the Divan, to have it given out, that she was cast away in a Storm, coasting the Island from one Port to another; upon which she has chang'd her Name, and remains conceal'd, not doubting but the Baron would marry so soon as he was assured of the News; which he could not very well be, because all the Wretches in that little Vessel, where the Baroness pretended to be embark'd, were cast away. 'T is a moot Point if she be really dead or living; if the latter, 't is scarce known to any but her Lover. But however, the Baron dares not trust the Report, for fear she should be alive, and finding him married, have Power to sue him as the prior Wife, and at least secure to herself a Consideration, besides the Obloquy that would rest upon his second Lady and her Children, if he should have any by her.[2]

Mrs. Manley's account of Lord Mohun's marital troubles should, I think, be regarded with some doubt. It appears likely that the guilty uncle (if guilty he was) was James Mohun of Polmangan,

[1] Charles second Earl of Macclesfield, who died November 5, 1701.
[2] Mrs. Manley, *New Atalantis*, pp. 298 ff.

LORD MOHUN ENTERS

only brother of the third Lord.[1] A Captain James Mohun, on April 15, 1698, was bound for a thousand pounds, as one of Lord Mohun's sureties, when the latter on that date was released from the Tower on bail.[2] Lord Mohun's uncle died in 1699 or 1700.[3] We may surely believe that Lord Mohun would not have called upon his wife's lover to act as his bondsman. We have, then, four alternatives: the James Mohun who was one of Lord Mohun's sureties in 1698 was not his uncle; the discovery of Lady Mohun's guilt occurred after 1698, although the intrigue had been carried on previously; the seduction took place between 1698 and the death of James Mohun a year or two later; Mrs. Manley invented or perverted the incident. Of these four possibilities, the last, although like the others undemon-

---

[1] Lyte names the children of Warwick second Lord Mohun (*op. cit.*, pp. 487–488). It seems improbable that the alleged seducer should have been one of Mohun's maternal uncles, of whom those surviving were the first Lord Altham and the Very Reverend Richard Annesley, Dean of Exeter, and perhaps their younger brothers, Arthur and Charles (Burke, *Dormant . . . and Extinct Peerages*, pp. 6–7). The betrayer appears to have been living at or near Boconnoc. There is no evidence of much intimacy, however, between Mohuns and Annesleys, even though one of Lord Mohun's bondsmen in 1697, when he was first arrested for the murder of Captain William Hill, was his cousin, Lord Anglesey (*infra*, p. 55). Hence it is more probable that the alleged seducer was a Mohun than an Annesley.

[2] *Infra*, p. 59.   [3] Lyte, *loc. cit.*

A NOBLE RAKE

strable, offers the most attractive solution of the problem.

It seems that Lady Mohun really was drowned, for no question of bigamy ever was raised in regard to Mohun's second marriage, which took place probably in March, 1710.[1] Lady Mohun's death is placed in the year 1705 or 1706, by a modern Cornish historian, who reports that it was in a passage to Ireland with "one of her gallants" that she was lost.[2] The daughter, Elizabeth, born to Lady Mohun, was never recognized by Lord Mohun as legitimate, and in his will, in which he left her a thousand pounds, he describes her as his pretended daughter.[3]

---

[1] See *infra*, p. 135.

[2] Gilbert, *Parochial History of Cornwall*, i, 67.

[3] *Last Will and Testament*, in *Hist. MSS. Comm. Reports*, xv, pt. 2, 346, *MSS. of J. Eliot Hodgkin*. The document is dated March 23, 1710/1. The Honorable Elizabeth Mohun was born after 1692, since she was a minor in 1713 (N. S.) (*Hist. MSS. Comm. Reports*, *loc. cit*). On June 8, 1717, she was married to the Honorable Arthur St. Leger, son of the first Viscount Doneraile in the Kingdom of Ireland. She gave birth to a son, Arthur Mohun St. Leger, later third Viscount Doneraile, on August 7, 1718, and died in December, of the same year (Burke, *Peerage and Baronetage*, 80th ed., 1921, art., "Doneraile"; Letter of Fanny Oglethorpe to the Duke of Mar, December 11, 1718, in *Hist. MSS. Comm. Reports*, *Stuart MSS. of the King of Great Britain*, vii, 621). It will be noted that Elizabeth Mohun was left one thousand pounds by her putative father, instead of one hundred pounds as pre-

vious biographers have asserted. Probably the second name of her son was a protest against Lord Mohun's assertion of her illegitimacy. Burke's self-contradictory assertion that the last Lord Mohun left no issue is, of course, an error (*Dormant . . . and Extinct Peerages*, ed. 1883, p. 370).

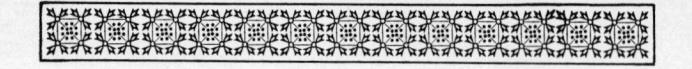

II

A CAREER BEGINS

IT is not, however, with the events of Lord Mohun's married life that we are concerned here. Soon after his somewhat precocious entrance into wedlock though, he makes his first appearance in the rôle of duellist, so closely associated with his name that Professor Seccombe [1] gives it as Mohun's occupation.

The first of the many notorious affairs in which Mohun was engaged as principal or accessory occurred on December 7, 1692. While the two were in drink, Mohun had quarrelled with Lord Kennedy,[2] son of John seventh Earl of Cassilis, and challenges were exchanged. King William, learning

---

[1] *Dictionary of National Biography*, xxxviii, 105.

[2] John Master of Cassilis, called Lord Kennedy, was only son to the Earl of Cassilis by his first wife, Susan, daughter of James first Duke of Hamilton. He was born about 1672. He was married by special license June 18, 1697, to Elizabeth, daughter of Charles Hutchinson of Outhorpe, Notts. Lord Kennedy died in his father's lifetime in 1700 (G. E. C., *Complete Peerage*, rev. by V. Gibbs, iii, 77–78). Curiously Mohun's last duel was with another grandson of the first Duke of Hamilton.

A CAREER BEGINS

of the quarrel, sought to prevent a meeting by confining the two lords to their lodgings, and the Earl of Nottingham used his good offices in promoting a reconciliation between them. This, however, did not last long; for within a few days, Mohun and Kennedy fought, both, it is said, being wounded.[1]

Evidently, however, Lord Mohun's wound was not serious, for only two days later he was concerned in a much more serious affair, to which several references are made in *Esmond*. Among Lord Mohun's friends was a certain youthful officer, the sixteen-year-old Richard Hill, captain of the grenadier company in Colonel Thomas Erle's Regiment of Foot.[2] Hill had contracted a violent passion for the famous actress Anne Bracegirdle,[3] and, desiring to

[1] Luttrell, *A Brief Relation of State Affairs*, ii, 628–629, 631, 636; *Hatton Correspondence*, i, 187. The quarrel appears to have taken place about a week before the duel. Seccombe affirms that Mohun escaped from his arrest with the aid of the Earl of Warwick, and states further that both Mohun and Kennedy were disarmed (*op. cit.*). H. L. Stephen repeats this story (*State Trials Political and Social*, ii, 59, n. 1).

[2] Dalton, "The Murder of Mountfort, the Actor," *Notes and Queries*, ser. VIII, x, 1 — 2; and Idem, *Army Lists*, iii, 270. Hill was commissioned in Viscount Lisburne's, afterwards Colonel Coote's, Regiment of Foot in 1688, at twelve years of age. On March 21, 1692 (N. S.), he exchanged with Captain Vincent Googene for the latter's grenadier company in Erle's Foot. In spite of his extreme youth, Hill seems to have seen service in Ireland and France with his regiment.

[3] Mrs. Bracegirdle is said to have been a daughter of Jus-

marry her, paid his addresses to her. Not unnaturally, as she was considerably older than Hill, she repulsed his attentions quite firmly. His ill-success in his suit Hill attributed, not to his own possible lack of attractiveness, but to the influence [1] of

tinian Bracegirdle of Northamptonshire, and to have been brought up to the stage by the Bettertons. Born about 1663, she began acting, perhaps in 1680, at Dorset Gardens. Later she removed to the Theatre Royal, and in 1695 seceded to Lincoln's Inn Fields with Betterton. In 1707, being then at the Haymarket, she renounced the stage in a fit of pique at Mrs. Oldfield's successful rivalry. She died in September, 1748, at her house in Howard Street, and was buried in the cloisters of Westminster Abbey. Her beauty and vivacious charm made her extremely popular during her stage career. She was courted, among others, by Congreve and Rowe, to the former of whom, it was rumored, she was secretly married. See *D. N. B.*, vi, 141–142, art., "Bracegirdle, Anne," by J. Knight; Cibber, *Apology*, pp. 102–104; Genest, *Stage*, ii, 375 ff.; and cf. the following note.

[1] Most writers have considered the character of Mrs. Bracegirdle to have been without a blemish; as, for example, Cibber, *op. cit.*, pp. 102–104; Aston, as quoted by Genest, *op. cit.*, ii, 377; Mrs. Manley, *New Atalantis*, i, 232; *D. N. B.*, vi, 141–142, art., "Bracegirdle, Anne," by J. Knight. Macaulay admits her technical chastity, but refers it to frigidity (*History of England*, iv, 313). Genest's opinion was the same (*loc. cit.*). Lord Birkenhead, with astonishing naïveté, bases his belief in the legitimacy of the relations between Mountford and Mrs. Bracegirdle upon the fact that Mountford "was a married man living with his wife, who knew" the other actress (*Famous Trials of History*, p. 79). Indeed, the two women belonged to the same company. On the other hand, Tom Brown accuses Mountford of intimacy with the actress (*Letters from the Living to the Dead*, "Bully Dawson to Bully

MRS. ANNE BRACEGIRDLE

A CAREER BEGINS 25

the popular actor-dramatist, William Mountford,[1] whom he believed to have libelled him to Mrs.

W——"; "From worthy Mrs. Behn the Poetess to the Famous Virgin Actress"; and "The Virgin's Answer to Mrs. Behn"; in Brown's *Works*, ii, 186–187, 250–254, 254–257, respectively). Brown, however, as is seen from his "The Ladies Lamentation for their Adonis," was prejudiced against Mountford because of the latter's Whiggishness (*Works*, iv, 314–316). Charles Gildon's views as to Mrs. Bracegirdle's morals are like those of Brown; see his *Comparison between the Two Stages*, quoted by Genest, *op. cit.*, ii, 377. Professor Nicoll places her with Nell Gwyn, Moll Davis, and Mrs. Barry, as unchaste (*History of Restoration Drama*, p. 72). It should be said that in all probability scandalous rumor concerning the relations of Mountford and Mrs. Bracegirdle had come to Hill's ears, and had helped to increase his hatred of the player.

[1] William Mountford was born about 1659, the son of a Captain Mountford of Shropshire. He joined the Duke's Company in 1673, as an actor of juvenile parts. His first great success was in 1685 as Sir Courtly Nice in Crowne's comedy of that name. The next year he was married to the comic actress Susannah Perceval. Through his fine appearance, melodious voice, and histrionic ability, he acquired high reputation as an actor, especially of romantic parts, but was excellent in any he essayed. He was a favorite of Queen Mary; hence, perhaps, her disgust at Mohun's acquittal, for which see the quotation from her diary, given by Edwin and Marion S. Grew in *The Court of William III*, p. 238. Mountford was concerned in the production of six plays, of one of which he was apparently sole author. This is the comedy of *Greenwich Park*. See *D. N. B.*, xxxix, 211–213, art., "Mountford, William," by J. Knight; Cibber, *Apology*, pp. 78–80, 95, 123; T. Cibber *et al.*, *Lives of the Poets*, iii, 43 ff.; *Biographia Dramatica*, i, 531 ff.; Tom Brown, *Works*, iv, 314–316.

Bracegirdle, and upon whom he swore a bloody vengeance.[1]

Hill resolved also upon more vigorous measures for winning the actress's affections. Accordingly, on the night of December 9, 1692, having provided a coach and six, and being escorted by several soldiers of his regiment, in company with Lord Mohun, Hill lay in wait for her near her lodgings. His intention was to carry her away by force to Totteridge, where, during the week that he planned holding her a prisoner, he designed, presumably by fair means or foul, to secure her assent to their marriage.[2]

The "two brats," [3] Mohun and Hill, had met at the playhouse at six that evening. Evidently anticipating trouble, Hill had borrowed a case of pistols.[4]

---

[1] *Tryal of . . . Lord Mohun before the House of Peers . . . for the Murder of William Mountford;* Pub. by Command of the House of Peers. Printed by Edw. Jones, London, 1693. Testimony of John Hudson, George Powell, Mrs. Knight, and Mrs. Elizabeth Sandys (or Sands).

[2] *Ibid.*, testimony of William Dixon, coachman, Thomas Lake, footboy to Captain Hill, and of Mrs. Bracegirdle. Lake gave evidence that his master had provided nightclothes for the lady. See also Mrs. Dorothy Browne's testimony.

[3] As Tom Brown calls them in his "The Ladies Lamentation for their Adonis," the scurrilous "Elegy on the death of Mr. Mountford the Player," which has already been cited (*supra*, p. 24, n. 1).

[4] *Tryal of . . . Lord Mohun;* testimony of Mrs. Sandys; Mrs. Browne testified that Lord Mohun told her that at the time of their attempt at kidnaping Mrs. Bracegirdle they had six or seven charged pistols in the coach.

A CAREER BEGINS

At the theatre they had quarrelled with Rogers, the boxkeeper, over the price of admission, and had threatened the shareholders of the house with mutilation, if they were checked. Possibly because of a desire at disguise, perhaps only because of a boyish freak, the two had exchanged coats several times during the evening, and later Hill was wearing Lord Mohun's coat.[1]

The young sparks stationed themselves with their coach and soldiers in the street through which Mrs. Bracegirdle must pass on her way to her lodgings from the house of Gawen Page, where she had supped. When the actress at last appeared, she was accompanied by her mother, Mrs. Martha Bracegirdle, her brother,[2] and Page. Taking no account of her escort, Hill seized Mrs. Bracegirdle, and, assisted by his soldiers, attempted to force her into the coach. But her struggles and cries, and those of her mother, made the abduction no easy matter. Page also intervened, and was struck at by Hill with his sword. The commotion soon aroused the neighborhood to such an extent that Hill was obliged to forego his design and to allow Mrs. Bracegirdle to continue on her way. During the struggle, Lord

[1] *Tryal of . . . Lord Mohun*, testimony of John Rogers.
[2] *Ibid.*, speech of the Attorney General, Sir John Somers, in opening the case. No one else mentions Hamlet Bracegirdle; although summoned, he did not appear as a witness.

Mohun seems, prudently enough, to have remained in the coach, and to have taken no active part in the attempt at abduction.[1] If he had received a wound in his encounter with Lord Kennedy, only two days earlier, it may be that the part of an onlooker had been forced upon him. Later in the evening Mohun averred that he had protected Mrs. Bracegirdle, "for the Rabble would have torn her to pieces," and that they could have carried her away if they had desired, since they had six or seven loaded pistols in the coach. His only part, he said, had been to serve his friend.[2]

The abduction having failed, Hill's soldiers vanished, as did, apparently, the coach. Hill himself insisted, however, on accompanying Mrs. Bracegirdle to her lodgings, where he desired several times to be allowed to enter and endeavor to make his peace with her.[3] This she refused, whereupon Hill and Mohun began patrolling the street before her door, sending messages to her begging for admission, and threatening Mountford.[4] She would not, however, see Hill, who continued, with his companion, to walk before her lodgings from one end of

[1] *Tryal of . . . Lord Mohun*, testimony of Mrs. Anne Bracegirdle.
[2] *Ibid.*, testimony of Mrs. Browne, Mrs. Bracegirdle's landlady.
[3] *Ibid.*, testimony of Ann Knevitt.
[4] *Ibid.*, testimony of Mrs. Mary Page and Mrs. Browne.

A CAREER BEGINS

Howard Street to the other. It is said that Sir John Shorter, Sir Robert Walpole's father-in-law, and Lord Mayor of London in 1687, was going down Norfolk Street to his house that night, when Mohun, mistaking him for Mountford, came up to him and embraced him, saying: "Dear Mountford." Discovering his error, Mohun then permitted Shorter to go on. The latter had hardly reached his house before Mountford actually arrived.[1]

In the meantime, being apprehensive of trouble when Mountford, who lived near by, should appear on his way home, Mrs. Page, and then Mrs. Browne, set out for the actor's house to endeavor to have a warning sent him.[2] Having informed Mrs. Mountford[3] of her husband's danger, Mrs. Browne started

---

[1] *Walpoliana*, ii, 97; quoted by J. B. C. in a letter to *Notes and Queries*, Ser. I, ii, 516, on "The Assassination of Mountford in Norfolk Street, Strand." Both by J. B. C. and by the author of *Walpoliana*, this action of Mohun is interpreted in the blackest fashion, but somewhat unwarrantably, since Mohun's motives on the night of Mountford's murder have never been absolutely established. In the anecdote are certain errors of fact which do not add to its credibility. Mountford was attacked in Howard Street, not Norfolk Street, and he was not assailed by assassins hired by Mohun, as the anecdotist would have one believe.

[2] *Tryal of . . . Lord Mohun*, testimony of Mrs. Page and Mrs. Browne.

[3] Susannah Perceval was born about 1667, the daughter of Thomas Perceval, a minor actor at the Duke's Theatre. She went on the stage early, appearing in 1681 at the Theatre

back for Mrs. Bracegirdle's lodgings. On the way she met Mountford, whom she attempted to apprise of the risk of assassination which he was incurring. But for some reason he would not listen to her and went on.[1]

While Mrs. Page and Mrs. Browne had been about these errands, the watch had come up; and, seeing two men walking in the street with their swords drawn, the constable, John Davenport, had inquired into their purpose in so doing. The boys responded that one of them had a sweetheart in a house near by, and that they would leave when they had finished drinking her health in a bottle of wine. Mohun offered the constable his sword, saying he was a peer; he explained Hill's drawn weapon by asserting that the captain had lost his scabbard in Drury Lane.[2] As apparently Davenport suspected

Royal in Durfey's *Sir Barnaby Whig*. In July, 1686, she was married to William Mountford, the actor. After Mountford's death she was again married, another actor, John Verbruggen, being her second husband. In 1703, she died in childbirth. She was survived by her husband, two daughters by Mountford, and at least one child by Verbruggen. Mrs. Perceval-Mountford-Verbruggen was considered the best comic actress of her day; Cibber praises especially her Melantha in *Marriage à la Mode* (*Apology*, pp. 100-102). See *D. N. B.*, lviii, 215-217, art., "Verbruggen, Mrs. Susanna," by J. Knight, and cf. *infra*, pp. 45-46.

[1] *Tryal of . . . Lord Mohun*, Mrs. Browne's evidence.

[2] *Ibid.*, testimony of John Davenport, constable, William Merry, Thomas Fennell, and James Bassett, watchmen.

A CAREER BEGINS

the truth of these stories, he set about making inquiries concerning them at the White Horse Tavern in the neighborhood.[1] While he was so engaged, Mountford appeared in Howard Street, but did not turn up to his house in Norfolk Street,[2] coming on, instead, to the two youths.[3]

From the testimony of the various eyewitnesses, as well as from the statements made before his death by the unfortunate Mountford,[4] the facts as to the events which followed, seem to be these. On arriving where Hill and Mohun were, Mountford exchanged friendly salutations with Mohun. Mohun appears then to have made some remark concerning Hill's hopes regarding Mrs. Bracegirdle, and Mountford's supposed influence over the actress. To this Mountford replied: "My Lord, has my wife disobliged your Lordship? If she has, she shall ask your

[1] *Tryal of . . . Lord Mohun.*

[2] It is perhaps worth noting that Sir Roger de Coverley seems to have lodged, while in town, in Norfolk Street, and it was by turning up from Fleet Street into Norfolk Street that he escaped the Mohocks. See *Spectator*, No. 335, March 25, 1712.

[3] *Tryal of . . . Lord Mohun*, testimony of Edward Warrington.

[4] *Ibid.*, testimony of George Powell, Gawen Page, John Bancroft, surgeon, and William Hunt, in which Mountford's ante-mortem statements are repeated. The quarrel and assault upon Mountford are described by Mrs. Browne, Mrs. Brewer, Thomas Lake, Elizabeth Walker, and Anne Jones.

pardon; but as for Mrs. Bracegirdle, she is no concern of mine; and I hope your Lordship will not vindicate such an ill man as Mr. Hill in such a matter as this." Hill, who had bidden Lord Mohun hold his tongue, now struck Mountford, cried to him to draw, and ran him through before he could defend himself. Notwithstanding his wound, Mountford appears to have drawn his sword, and to have made a pass or two at Hill, breaking his blade in so doing. Murder was cried, and Hill turned and fled.[1] Mountford had strength enough to reach his own home unaided, where he fell on the floor in his blood.[2] The watch came up from their researches at the White Horse, and placed Lord Mohun under arrest, but not until one of Mrs. Bracegirdle's friends had pointed him out.[3]

From the date of the affair to the present it has been said that Mountford's death was the result

[1] *Tryal of . . . Lord Mohun*; thus Mountford's statements on his deathbed and the testimony of Mrs. Browne and Mrs. Brewer. Thomas Lake, Elizabeth Walker, and Anne Jones testified that Mountford drew and exchanged several passes with Hill, breaking his sword in so doing; according to them the fatal thrust was given after Mountford's weapon was out. It should be remembered that, of the last three, Lake was Hill's servant, who had testified differently upon the inquest, and Elizabeth Walker, who was Mrs. Bracegirdle's, had admitted a grudge against "the players."

[2] *Ibid.*, testimony of Gawen Page.

[3] *Ibid.*, testimony of Mrs. Page.

The Indian Queen

MRS. ANNE BRACEGIRDLE AS THE INDIAN QUEEN

A CAREER BEGINS

of a peculiarly dastardly plot between Hill and Mohun: that while Mohun, by prearrangement, diverted Mountford's attention, Hill ran him through before the actor could draw his sword.[1] It has even been asserted that Mohun embraced Mountford or held him while Hill stabbed him.[2] In no account by an eyewitness is it said that Lord Mohun embraced Mountford or kissed him. On the other hand, it appears certain that Hill struck Mountford, as he and Lord Mohun conversed, and that the stabbing followed very soon. As to the existence of a definite agreement between the two boys whereby one was to divert their victim's attention, while the other attacked him, no proof is adducible.[3] In fact, only under exceptional circumstances could the making of such an arrangement be established. That, however, two debauched, drunken boys might have evolved such a scheme is, it must be confessed, by no means impossible.

Yet another and not unnatural explanation of the apparent treachery of Mohun and Hill may at least be suggested. Hill had for some time been meditat-

---

[1] So Thackeray himself, *Esmond*, bk. II, chap. 2; but cf. *Ibid.*, bk. II, chap. 5.

[2] Luttrell, *A Brief Relation of State Affairs*, ii, 637.

[3] The anecdote related by Sir John Shorter would seem to point toward the existence of such a plot (*supra*, p. 29). See also the life of Mountford in the *Biographia Dramatica*, i, 533.

ing vengeance on Mountford on account of the latter's supposed interference with the young soldier's courtship of Mrs. Bracegirdle. The intended abduction of the actress had completely failed, serving only to increase her distaste for Hill. Exasperated to the point of seeking to carry out his threats, Hill and his companion had lingered in the street, awaiting Mountford's return to his house, or Mrs. Bracegirdle's weakening in her resolve not to see her suitor. Mountford appeared, and approached the persons whom he saw in the street. As he and Mohun spoke together, Hill, infuriated by his jealousy, — perhaps, too, aroused by his potations, and nervous from the strain, — struck Mountford, and without full realization of the action, pushed at him immediately with his drawn sword, before the actor could unsheathe his own weapon.[1] Such an explanation of the affair is only conjecture, and, in any case, does not excuse Hill for his precipitancy, but it may account for the circumstances of Mountford's killing, while avoid-

[1] The Earl of Birkenhead, in his *Famous Trials of History*, concluding what is, on the whole, a quite accurate account of the affair, says: "It is highly probable that there was no design against Mountford, that the meeting was by chance and that Hill acted without premeditation. It was an affair of seconds . . ." (p. 88). Possibly Hill did not expect to see Mountford that night, but it seems likely, nevertheless, that he proposed attacking the actor at sight.

A CAREER BEGINS 35

ing the stigmatizing of Captain Hill and Lord Mohun for a prearranged act of the basest treachery.

The circumstances of Mountford's death have often been incorrectly related. Luttrell reports that Mohun, Hill, and others dogged the actor from the playhouse to his lodgings, where they killed him because he had prevented their abduction of Mrs. Bracegirdle.[1] The same story was told by Robert Harley, with the addition that a Mr. Knight was with Mohun and Hill, and that Mountford received three wounds.[2] Tindal says that Mountford was killed as he returned home from seeing Mrs. Bracegirdle to her lodgings.[3] The anonymous biographer whose "Life" of Mountford is prefixed to Tonson's edition of the actor's plays, says that the subject of his biography was killed about 1696, by a wound in the back with a sword. His "misfortune" was concerted by Hill and Mohun.[4] The author of the account of the murder in Cibber's *Lives of the Poets* [5]

[1] *A Brief Relation of State Affairs*, ii, 637.
[2] In a letter to Sir Edward Harley, dated December 10, 1692, in *Hist. MSS. Comm. Reports*, pt. 2, xiv, *MSS. of the Duke of Portland*, iii, 509. Cf. also Francis Gwyn's letter of over a year later to Robert Harley, as quoted, *infra*, where it seems Mohun was held responsible for Mountford's death.
[3] *The Continuation of Mr. Rapin's History of England*, ii, 71–72.
[4] *Six Plays, written by Mr. Mountford*, i, ix, x.
[5] III, 43 ff.

gives the incidents with considerable accuracy, but seems to impute to Mohun and Hill a deliberate plot to slay Mountford. We are told in the sketch of Mohun's career, in *Memoirs of the Celebrated Persons Forming the Kit-Cat Club*,[1] that Mountford was attacked while on his way to the house of Mrs. Bracegirdle, whom Hill was about to marry. The affair is placed subsequent to 1698. Macaulay embellishes somewhat his story of the murder. He says that Hill and Mohun, after failing to carry off the actress "went away vowing vengeance," and swaggered about the streets near Mountford's dwelling. When the player arrived, "a short altercation took place between him and Mohun," during which Hill stabbed him. Macaulay also appears ignorant of the youth of the boys.[2] J. E. Thorold Rogers repeats the statement that Mountford was slain in defending Mrs. Bracegirdle from her abductors.[3]

With some writers, Hill has dropped completely out of the affair. Thus Dr. Humfrey Prideaux, Dean of Norwich, in a letter dated December 11, 1692, says that Lord Mohun fought with a player "yesterday," and killed him. The modern annotator adds: "Montford [*sic*] the player was, in reality,

---
[1] Pages 120–121. [2] *History of England*, iv, 313–314.
[3] *Collection of the Protests of the House of Lords*, i, 108.

A CAREER BEGINS

murdered in cold blood by Lord Mohun."[1] In his relation of an anecdote already referred to,[2] the author of *Walpoliana* appears to believe Mohun the assailant of Mountford.[3] Thackeray himself says that Lord Mohun had fought over Mrs. Bracegirdle.[4] Previously he had at least suggested that the actor's murder was the result of a plot to which Mohun was a party.[5]

Most amazing are the following present-day instances of this error. Mary F. Sandars informs us, in *Princess and Queen of England: Mary II*,[6] that in consequence of a love affair Lord Mohun had murdered Mountford. H. B. Irving, in his *Judge Jeffreys*,[7] refers to "Mountford, the handsome actor, who was afterwards murdered by Lord Mohun." Marion S. Grew goes into particulars in *William Bentinck and William III*. According to this sadly inaccurate account, Mohun's advances had been rejected by Mrs. Bracegirdle. Believing Mountford to be his successful rival, Mohun, with the aid of a friend, had set upon the player in the

[1] Letter addressed to Richard Coffin, *Hist. MSS. Comm. Reports*, v, 583, *MSS. of J. R. Pine-Coffin*.
[2] *Supra*, p. 29.
[3] *Walpoliana*, ii, 97.
[4] *Esmond*, bk. II, chap. 5.
[5] *Ibid.*, bk. I, chap. 14.
[6] Page 344.
[7] Page 319.

street and had stabbed him to death.[1] Mr. A. S. Turberville, in his *The House of Lords in the Reign of William III*, gives a fairly correct account of the affray, although he says that upon Mountford's appearance Mohun engaged him in an "altercation" in the course of which Hill stabbed the actor.[2] The strange mistakes of Mr. Turberville in regard to the events of Mohun's subsequent career will be noted later.[3] Mr. "Lewis Melville's" errors in his account of the Hill-Mountford affair are most curious. In his *Some Aspects of Thackeray* [4] he asserts that Mohun was concerned with the Earl of Warwick in Mountford's death, and that the two peers were tried for the murder before the House of Lords, who acquitted them.

T. C. and W. Snow, in the notes to their edition of *Esmond*,[5] first state that "it was on her [Mrs.

---

[1] Pages 210, 211. In *The Court of William III*, Edwin and Marion S. Grew give, however, a considerably less inaccurate account of the affray, allotting Hill his proper part, although over-emphasizing that of Lord Mohun — as in the reference to his "brutal murder" of the actor. (*The Court of William III* appeared in 1910; *William Bentinck and William III*, in 1924. Dr. W. F. Koenig of the Library of Congress informs me that Marion S. Grew and Marion E. Grew are one and the same person; this fact makes the discrepancies between her two narratives all the more remarkable.)

[2] Page 42. Mr. Turberville here is borrowing from Macaulay.

[3] *Infra*, p. 63. [4] Pages 205–207. [5] Oxford, 1915.

A CAREER BEGINS

Bracegirdle's] account that Lord Mohun was concerned in the murder of Mountford."[1] In fact, it was rather on his friend Hill's account that Mohun was present: Mohun himself seems not to have been in love with the actress. Next, they assert that Mountford "was killed by Lord Mohun"![2] Mr. Montague Summers, in the "Introduction" to his *Shakespeare Adaptations*,[3] refers to Mountford's "dastardly assassination by Lord Mohun," and goes on to say that the actor was stabbed by Mohun, "a fellow of the vilest character."

Certainly such glaring errors in fact go to show the need for a careful study of Mohun's career, based upon the records that exist, and motivated neither by the desire to blacken his character unduly nor by the wish to extenuate his many faults, but to present as accurate and impartial a narrative of the events of his life as is possible.

For the time being, the murder seems to have sobered the fifteen-year-old man about town. When one of the watch took Mohun by the sleeve, he "shook and quak'd and trembled as if you would tear it [Mohun's sleeve] to pieces," making no resistance or any effort to escape.[4] But by the time of his arrival at the Roundhouse, where he spent the

[1] Page 494.   [2] Page 520.   [3] Page xc, n.
[4] *Tryal of . . . Lord Mohun*, testimony of James Bassett, watchman.

rest of the night, he had regained his courage. Learning then from the constable that Hill had escaped, he exclaimed: "God Damme, I am glad he is not Taken, but I am sorry he has no more money about him; I wish he had some of mine; and, I do not care a Farthing if I am Hang'd for him."[1]

Mountford survived his wound until 12.30 in the afternoon of December 10. The sword of Captain Hill had gone "in and out by his Back-bone behind his left side," causing a fatal wound.[2] As has been said, Mountford was able, however, not only to draw his sword upon Hill, but to regain his house before falling, and later to make repeated statements regarding Hill's attack upon him.

[1] *Tryal of . . . Lord Mohun*, testimony of John Davenport.

[2] *Ibid.*, testimony of John Bancroft, surgeon. John Bancroft, who attended Mountford and whose testimony on Lord Mohun's trial has already been cited (*supra*, p. 31, n. 4), was himself a dramatist, being the author of *Sertorius* (pr. 1679) and of *Henry II* (pr. 1693), the latter of which is one of the *Six Plays* published as Mountford's by Tonson in 1720. The "Epistle Dedicatory" to Sir Thomas Cooke is signed by Mountford. It is said that, in reality, Bancroft also wrote the play of *Edward III* (pr. 1691), which was published as Mountford's and likewise was included among his collected works. The dedication of *Edward III* to Henry Viscount Sydney is signed by the actor, but tradition asserts that Bancroft made Mountford a present of the play. Bancroft died in 1696, and was buried in St. Paul's, Covent Garden (*Biographia Dramatica*, i, pt. 1, 19; ii, 291; Birrell and Garnett's Catalogue No. 11 [Restoration Literature], item 18).

A CAREER BEGINS

Mountford, who was, at the time of his death, one of the most popular of English actors, was buried on December 13, at St. Clement Danes, where, it was estimated, a thousand persons were present. An anthem was sung by some of the choristers from Whitehall, and the royal organist played.[1]

On Saturday, December 10, Mohun was taken before the justices at Hicks Hall, who admitted him to bail in the sum of two thousand pounds, the sureties being Lady Mohun's uncle, Lord Gerard, and Charles Montague. The coroner's inquest returning a finding of murder against both Mohun and Hill, a warrant was issued for the former by Lord Chief Justice Holt.[2] Mohun's often-demonstrated ability for keeping out of the grasp of the law until he was prepared to stand trial had developed early, however, and he seems to have evaded arrest for almost a month.[3] Finally, on January 11, 1692/3, he petitioned the House of Lords, proposing to give himself up, asking for a speedy trial,[4]

[1] Luttrell, *op. cit.*, ii, 641.   [2] *Ibid.*, ii, 638.

[3] From Luttrell, *loc. cit.*, as well as from ii, 641, one would suppose that Mohun's rearrest followed immediately the issuance of the Lord Chief Justice's warrant. That this is not the case appears from the language of Mohun's petition in which he says that to avoid a chargeable imprisonment he withdrew himself. *Hist. MSS. Comm. Reports*, xiv, pt. 6, 294 ff., *House of Lords MSS.*

[4] According to Macaulay, Lady Mohun, the young nobleman's mother, "threw herself at William's feet, but in vain.

and desiring that, in the meantime, he be admitted to bail.[1]

The Lords agreed that a convenient time be fixed for Mohun's trial and that, until its occurrence, he should be imprisoned in the Tower.[2] On the thirteenth of January, Mohun was arrested in the antechamber of the House of Lords, while he was awaiting an answer to his petition,[3] and was put temporarily in the custody of the Usher of the Black Rod, Sir Thomas Duppa. The next day Mohun was committed to the Tower,[4] and his sureties discharged.[5] The trial was set for January 31, in Westminster Hall.[6]

After much time spent in consideration of the arrangements for the trial and in their preparation, the Lords took their places in Westminster Hall at about noon of the appointed day.[7] The King was among the spectators, but went away about three

'It was a cruel act,' said the King: 'I shall leave it to the law'" (*History of England*, iv, 314).

[1] *Hist. MSS. Comm. Reports*, xiv, pt. 6, 294 ff., *House of Lords MSS*.

[2] *Ibid.*

[3] Luttrell, *op. cit.*, iii, 11.

[4] *Hist. MSS. Comm. Reports*, xiv, pt. 6, 294 ff., *House of Lords MSS.*; *Journals of the House of Lords*, xv, 182, 184.

[5] Brit. Mus., Add. MS. 38855.

[6] *Journals of the House of Lords*, xv, 184.

[7] *Tryal of . . . Lord Mohun.*

A CAREER BEGINS

o'clock.[1] The Marquis of Caermarthen, who had been appointed Lord High Steward for the occasion, presided.[2] The Crown was represented by the Attorney General, Sir John Somers, the Solicitor General, Sir Thomas Trevor, and Sergeant Tomson. For Lord Mohun appeared Sir Thomas Powis, Mr. Price, and Mr. John Hawles.[3]

The trial was opened by the Lord High Steward, who showed a considerable amount of tenderness for the young prisoner, calling attention to his rank and youth, and suggesting that, if convicted, he might expect leniency, if any ground for it existed.[4] The case then was opened, and the taking of testimony begun. The first day was occupied with the hearing of witnesses [5] and the summing up of the

---

[1] Luttrell, *op. cit.*, iii, 26; Evelyn, *op. cit.*, ii, 335. William III, according to Evelyn, was satisfied that Mohun "was culpable."

[2] *Journals of the House of Lords*, xv, 207.

[3] *Ibid.*, xv, 195. Mr. Wallop, instead of Mr. Price, was one of the counsel originally proposed for Lord Mohun (*Hist. MSS. Comm. Reports*, xiv, pt. 6, 295, n., *House of Lords MSS.*). Sir Thomas Powis, or Powys, later acted as one of the counsel for Lord Mohun in his mother's suit against him (*House of Lords MSS.*, N. S., ii, 519 ff.).

[4] *Tryal of . . . Lord Mohun.*

[5] Lord Birkenhead professes himself struck by the "skill and discrimination" displayed by Lord Mohun in the cross-examination of the witnesses, and finds therein a demonstration that Mohun was a "man" of native ability who might have gone far if he had chosen (*op. cit.*, p. 84). Mohun spent

evidence. On February 1, the House debated the case and put a number of questions to the judges, whose presence had been ordered. The Lords did not sit on the next day, as it was Candlemas. The third of February was taken up with further debate and questioning the Judges. Finally, on the fourth, the vote was taken. Of eighty-three peers present, sixty-nine found Lord Mohun not guilty, and fourteen pronounced him guilty.[1] Among the

about fourteen years in active attendance upon the House of Lords, without achieving any position. The fact is, of course, that the questions which aroused Lord Birkenhead's admiration were framed for the fifteen-year-old prisoner by his counsel, Sir Thomas Powis, Mr. Price, and Mr. Hawles. Later in the same work Lord Birkenhead says: "To question witnesses is an art which demands both practice and natural ability" (p. 146). There is no reason for thinking that Mohun as a mere boy was a practiced cross-examiner, or that he ever had any special ability in that field.

[1] The result of the trial was no surprise. In a letter to Lord Hatton, dated January 31, 1692/3, Charles Hatton says the opinion was that Mohun would be acquitted (*Hatton Correspondence*, ii, 189); Robert Harley, writing to Sir Edward Harley on February 4, says: "This day, the town having clamoured at the delay, gave judgment of not guilty" (*Hist. MSS. Comm. Reports*, xiv, pt. 2, *MSS. of the Duke of Portland*, iii, 513); Luttrell noted in his diary on January 31: "believ'd he will be acquitted" (*op. cit.*, iii, 26). There was, however, some criticism of the outcome. Robert Harley, in the letter above quoted, says: "They have taken a news writer into custody for saying the evidence was strong enough to hang a commoner"; and Lyte reports wits of the day as saying that there was nothing fair about the trial except the ladies of fashion in the gallery (*History of Dunster*, p. 491).

A CAREER BEGINS

former were the six dukes present, the officers of state, the Lord High Steward, the Marquis of Halifax (Mohun's godfather), the Earls of Marlborough, Macclesfield (Lady Mohun's grandfather), Sunderland, Mulgrave, Dorset, Devonshire (as whose second the third Lord Mohun had received his death wound), and Lord Godolphin. The Earls of Portland, Rochester, Nottingham, and Kingston were among those voting guilty. The vote being taken, the Marquis of Caermarthen announced its outcome, pronounced Mohun acquitted, and breaking his white staff, declared the High Court dissolved.[1]

But, although Mohun was found guiltless of Mountford's murder by the House of Peers, Mrs.

Queen Mary is reported as having considered the outcome of the trial a proof of the universal corruption of English life (quoted from her *Memoirs*, p. 59, by Foxcroft, *Life and Letters of . . . [the] First Marquis of Halifax*, ii, 166–167, n. 5). Yet, as Foxcroft says, ". . . a doubt arises in our mind on reading the evidence whether a modern jury would have convicted Mohun, a boy not sixteen" (*Ibid.*). Macaulay has no doubts as to the injustice of the verdict, and says, "No person . . . can doubt that the crime of murder was fully brought home to the prisoner." Such, he adds, was the opinion of the King. The historian quotes one peer as excusing his vote by saying, "After all the fellow [Mountford] was but a player; and players are rogues" (*History of England*, iv, 314). On the other hand, Lord Birkenhead — to whose account of the trial reference has already been made — does not hesitate to say that on the face of the evidence, "the acquittal was right" (*op. cit.*, p. 88).

[1] *Tryal of . . . Lord Mohun.*

Mountford, widow of Hill's victim, did not cease in the attempt to secure some sort of punishment for Mohun. Soon after his acquittal, Mrs. Mountford began an appeal of the case in the Court of King's Bench.[1] This had not as yet come up, when, on September 10, 1693, her father, Thomas Perceval, was arrested for clipping coin.[2] Perceval was tried at the Old Bailey on October 12, and found guilty. He was sentenced to death on October 17, but before the date of his execution — October 23 — had arrived, he was reprieved.[3] Mrs. Mountford had petitioned the Queen for his pardon, and had seemingly secured it, it is said, on the condition that she withdraw her appeal against Mohun.[4] She presumably did so, since we hear no more of the appeal, and since there is no evidence that the sentence against her father was ever carried out.[5]

Hill was never brought to justice, but seems to

[1] *Journals of the House of Lords*, xv, 247, 273; *Hist. MSS. Comm. Reports*, xiv, pt. 6, 294 ff., *House of Lords MSS*.

[2] Not long after this, it may be remarked, Mohun was reported as being very ill at Bath. Luttrell, *op. cit.*, iii, 197, under date of October 3, 1693.

[3] *Ibid.*, iii, 183, 205, 207, 212.   [4] *Ibid.*, iii, 207.

[5] Perhaps Perceval was among the criminals who on December 11, 1693, pleaded the King's and Queen's pardon at the Old Bailey. Luttrell, *op. cit.*, iii, 238. According to Summers, however, who gives an account of Perceval's career in the "Introduction" to his *Shakespeare Adaptations*, the convicted man "got as far as Portsmouth on his way to transportation, but died and was buried there" (p. xc).

A CAREER BEGINS

have fled into most effectual concealment when he ran down Surrey Street from the scene of Mountford's assassination. On December 29, 1692, John Simmonds received his company in Erle's Foot.[1] On January 19, 1692/3, he was reported captured in the Isle of Wight, and on February 7 as taken in Scotland; both stories were unfounded, however, and it is not until about 1703 that we hear of him again. Hill, who had gone in 1697 with Colonel John Gibson as a volunteer to Newfoundland, prayed Queen Anne for a pardon for his murder of Mountford, attaching to his petition certificates as to his good conduct from Colonel Gibson and the then Lieutenant General Erle. The Duke of Somerset interested himself in Hill's case; and as Captain Richard Hill is named in a list of officers recommended by the Duke of Ormonde for commissions in 1706, it is to be supposed that the pardon was granted.[2]

---

[1] Dalton, *Army Lists*, iii, 270.

[2] Dalton, "The Murder of Mountfort, the Actor." *Notes and Queries*, ser. VIII, x, 1–2. It might be noted that an extraordinary perversion of the story of Mountford, Hill, and Anne Bracegirdle occurs in *The Bracegirdle*, a novel by Mr. Burris Jenkins (Philadelphia, 1922). In it, Hill, who serves as villain, is represented as abducting the actress, and carrying her to France to his chateau, where the hero, who eventually marries her, rescues her, and of course kills Hill. This expedition is supposed to take place during the Anglo-French war of 1689–97, of which not a word is said!

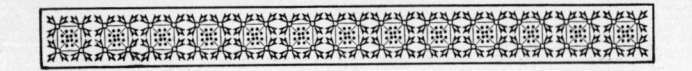

III

A YOUNG MAN ABOUT TOWN AND ELSEWHERE

THACKERAY has endowed Mohun with an amount of military experience which historical fact cannot justify. In reality, Lord Mohun's actual army service was not great, as I shall show. He was commissioned captain in the newly raised regiment of horse of his wife's uncle, the second Earl of Macclesfield, — who was a major general, — on February 16, 1693/4.[1] The first service that Lord Mohun is known to have seen[2] was with Lord Macclesfield's regiment in the unsuccessful attack of Admiral Lord Berkeley and General Talmash on Brest, June 7–8, 1694.[3] Like Lord Cutts, Lord Mohun volunteered to accompany the Marquis of

---

[1] Dalton, *Army Lists*, iii, 354.

[2] Luttrell says (*A Brief Relation of State Affairs*, iii, 283), under date of March 13, 1693/4, that the Earl of Warwick and Lord Mohun were to go as volunteers to Flanders with the Earl of Macclesfield, who himself was to accompany the King. Mohun's standing, however, was that of a regularly commissioned officer.

[3] Dalton, *op. cit.*, iii, 354, n. 5; *Ibid.*, iii, 334; Tindal, *The Continuation of Mr. Rapin's History of England*, iii, 254.

THOMAS, FIRST DUKE OF LEEDS

Caermarthen (son of the Lord High Steward of Mohun's trial of the previous year, who was now Duke of Leeds) on his hazardous and successful *reconnaissance* of the harbor of Brest on June 7.[1] It is not unlikely that Mohun was a member of one of the landing parties beaten off the next day by the French.

After the Brest fiasco, we know nothing definite of Mohun's military exploits,[2] except that he is said to have served in Flanders with his regiment.[3] He appears not to have distinguished himself, or to have been enough attracted toward the army to seek promotion, for he was still a captain, when, in 1702, he raised his own regiment of foot.[4]

There can scarcely be any foundation in fact for Thackeray's crediting Mohun with having served under the "Prince of Baden" on the Danube, and having "witnessed the rescue of Vienna from the Turk." No account of Mohun's life, contemporary

[1] Macaulay, *History of England*, chap. 20.

[2] He was back in England by October 7, 1694 (Luttrell, *op. cit.*, iii, 381), possibly returning with the Earl of Warwick. See a letter dated October 9, 1694, of Robert Harley to Sir E. Harley, in *Hist. MSS. Comm. Reports*, xiv, pt. 2, *MSS. of the Duke of Portland*, iii, 558.

[3] Dalton, *op. cit.*, iii, 354, n. 5.

[4] Lord Mohun's commission as colonel of a regiment of foot was dated February 12, 1702 (N. S.). After service in Ireland and Spain, the regiment was disbanded in 1713. See Dalton, *op. cit.*, iv, 281.

or otherwise, mentions any such service. In the next place, Louis Margrave of Baden commanded the Imperial armies against the Turks from 1689 to 1693, when he was sent to the Rhine front of the Empire to operate against the French.[1] It is, to say the least, improbable that Lord Mohun, between the ages of twelve and sixteen, should have served in the Imperial forces. Further, in July or August, 1691, Lord Mohun was in England, for he was married in one or the other month.[2] It was just at this time — August 19, 1691, — that the Margrave won his greatest victory over the Turks, at Szalankemen, and thereby may be said to have rescued Vienna for the time being from the menace of the Ottomans.[3] One can hardly think that the bridegroom of fourteen hurried from the altar to the Middle European battlefield. The virtual conclusion of the Imperial-Turkish wars and final freeing of Vienna from Turkish threats came with the crushing of the Turkish army at Zenta on Sep-

[1] Lodge, in *Cambridge Modern History*, v, 368–369.

[2] Luttrell, *op. cit.*, ii, 274 (entry for August [10?], 1691).

[3] Mailáth, *Geschichte des Oestreich. Kaiserstaates*, iv, 235–243. T. C. and W. Snow, in the notes to their edition of *Esmond* (p. 489), assert that Thackeray refers to the Turkish siege of Vienna in 1683; but this is unlikely and unnecessary. Mohun is first introduced as a distinctly young man, which he would not have been, had he served on the Continent sixteen years before; and Vienna was in peril from the Turks at least twice after 1683.

A YOUNG MAN ABOUT TOWN 51

tember 11, 1697, by the Imperialists, under Prince Eugene of Savoy.[1] Mohun could not have fought in this battle, since on September 14, only three days later, he killed Captain William Hill of the Foot Guards at the Rummer Tavern in Charing Cross.[2]

The truth would seem to be that Thackeray has invented the greater part of the military adventures with which he credits his Lord Mohun. They certainly do not seem to be drawn from the life of the historical Mohun.

But although Mohun's army life was by no means remarkable, he managed to keep himself in the public eye by his exploits in London. On Sunday, October 7, 1694, for some unexplained reason, he attempted to kill a coachman in Pall Mall. Being prevented by Francis Scobell, Member of Parliament for St. Michael's, he cut Scobell over the head, and later challenged him.[3] A meeting, however, seems not to have occurred.

[1] Lodge, *Cambridge Mod. Hist.*, v, 368–369.
[2] See *infra*, pp. 53 ff.
[3] Luttrell, *op. cit.*, iii, 381. Francis Scobell of Mena-Gwyns, Cornwall, sat in the House of Commons nine times, between 1689 and 1714, for St. Michael's, Grampound, St. German's, Launceston, and St. Mawe's, respectively. Cobbett, *Parliamentary History*, v, vi, vii. He married Mary, the younger daughter of Sir Joseph Tredenham of Tregoran, and member for St. Mawe's, succeeding to the Tredenham properties at Sir Joseph's death, on April 24, 1708. *The History of the Reign of Queen Anne, Digested into Annals*, Year

A NOBLE RAKE

It was, perhaps, in the course of the winter of 1694/5, that Mohun's encounter with Dyer, the newsletter writer, took place. On December 21, 1694, Dyer's presumption in noticing the proceedings of the House of Commons in his letters was called to the attention of that body. He was brought in the next day by the sergeant at arms and reprimanded on his knees at the bar by the Speaker.[1] According to the available accounts, it was "some time" after this that the unfortunate publicist indiscreetly referred in a letter to Lord Mohun. The latter thereupon sought out Dyer at a coffee-house, showed him the offending sheet, and when its author had acknowledged his responsibility for it, cudgelled him until he swore never again to mention his assailant.[2]

---

the Sixth, p. 380. Possibly Scobell's politics, which, like those of his father-in-law, were opposed to the Whiggism of the Mohuns, increased Lord Mohun's animosity. Francis Gwyn, writing October 13, 1694, to Robert Harley, says: "I perceive the Lords will have more blood to answer for than Mr. Montford's by saving the Lord Mohun, for he is far from mending." *Hist. MSS. Comm. Reports*, xiv, pt. 2, *MSS. of the Duke of Portland*, iii, 558.

[1] Cobbett, *op. cit.*, v, cols. 862–863.

[2] *Ibid.*, n. See also Hunt, *The Fourth Estate*, i, 164–165; May, *Constitutional History of England*, ii, 107. Hunt refers to Kennett's *History of England* as a source, but there is no reference in the 1719 edition to Mohun's beating Dyer. It is interesting to note that, after Mohun's death, Dyer was reported as not crediting in his letters the report of General

A YOUNG MAN ABOUT TOWN

Mohun's next adventure occurred on the night of April 8, 1697, when, for some unknown cause, he and one "Captain Bingham"[1] fought in St. James's Park. They were parted by the sentinels, but not before Mohun was wounded in the hand.[2]

Mohun's next affair was more serious. On September 14, 1697,[3] while drinking with a party at the Rummer Tavern in Charing Cross,[4] Mohun

Maccartney's attacking the wounded Duke of Hamilton (*A Strict Enquiry into the Circumstances of a late Duel*, p. 16). This fact certainly speaks for the journalist's forgiving spirit.

[1] Luttrell, *op. cit.*, iv, 207.

[2] Dalton, in his *Army Lists*, gives no Captain Bingham who could have fought Mohun in 1697. Perhaps Luttrell has erred in giving the name, and Captain Richard Bankham was Mohun's opponent. Bankham was commissioned ensign in the Earl of Bath's Regiment of Foot on February 21, 1689; lieutenant in Sir R. Atkin's Regiment of Foot, April 23, 1694; adjutant, January 29, 1696; on half-pay in 1697, when the regiment was reduced. Dalton, *op. cit.*, iii, 51; iv, 155.

[3] The occasion was doubtless the celebration of the signing of the Treaty of Ryswick. The news of the conclusion of the peace negotiations on the eleventh of September was made public on the fourteenth, and was attended by a general jubilation. See Macaulay, *op. cit.*, chap. 22.

[4] An undated letter of Richard Steele to his wife was written from the Rummer Tavern, Covent Garden (No. *303, *Epistolary Correspondence*, ed. by J. Nichols, i, 354). This was probably the tavern in which Hill was stabbed. Samuel Prior, uncle of the poet-diplomat, was one time proprietor of the Rummer, and it was there possibly that Matthew was an apprentice (Seccombe, "Lesser Verse Writers," *Cambridge History of English Literature*, ix, 164). Other Rummer taverns were to be found at about this time in Soper Lane,

A NOBLE RAKE

quarrelled with Captain William Hill, late of the Coldstream Guards,[1] and stabbed him. Hill survived his wound,[2] until the afternoon of the next day.[3] Mohun, who had promptly gone into hiding,[4] was charged with manslaughter in the verdict of the coroner's jury, brought in September 16.[5] Mohun remained at liberty until October 22, when

Queen Street, in the City (Margaret Verney, *Memoirs of the Verney Family*, iv, 249, and note 1; see also *Tom Double, returned out of the Country: Or the true Picture of a Modern Whig, set out in a second Dialogue between Mr. Whiglove and Mr. Double, at the Rummer-Tavern in Queen-Street*, cited in *The History and Proceedings of the House of Lords*, ii, 39); and in Gray's Inn Passage (Tom Brown, "A Bantering Letter to a Vintner," *Works*, iv, 267).

[1] William Hill was commissioned ensign in the Coldstream Guards, May 1, 1690; he was wounded at Landen, July 19, 1692, and at Namur, July 1, 1695; he did not serve with the Coldstreams in the Brest expedition of 1694. Hill was promoted to lieutenant, to rank as captain, July 15, 1695; he had left the Guards by 1696. Dalton, *op. cit.*, iii, 138; iv, 68; MacKinnon, *Coldstream Guards*, i, 235, 244, 248.

[2] It was "in his belly near the navel," and was "one inch long and 12 inches deep," *Coroner's Inquisition*, KB 10, No. 9 Michaelmas Term, 9 William III.

[3] *The Post Man*, September 14–16, 1697.

[4] Luttrell, *op. cit.*, iv, 296; letter of W. Snowe to Robert Harley, on October 23, 1697, in *Hist. MSS. Comm. Reports*, xiv, pt. 2, *MSS. of the Duke of Portland*, iii, 592.

[5] *Coroner's Inquisition*, KB 10, No. 9 Michaelmas Term, 9 William III. Luttrell, writing on September 18, says that the verdict had been reached (*op. cit.*, iv, 280); *The Post Man*, September 21–23, dates the inquest on September 20; a newsletter in the Public Records Office places it on September 22 (*State Papers Dom., Wm. & Mary*, viii, no. 35).

A YOUNG MAN ABOUT TOWN

he was taken at the Earl of Warwick's house in Essex Street.[1] He was at once brought before Chief Justice Holt, who admitted him to bail. According to one account, his sureties were the Marquis of Halifax (Mohun's godfather), the Earl of Anglesey (his cousin),[2] and the Earl of Warwick.[3] Another source informs us that the bondsmen were Lord Warwick, the Earl of Macclesfield (Lady Mohun's uncle), Colonel Coote,[4] and Sir Robert Tyrrell,[5] each for three thousand pounds.[6] Mohun seems not to have remained at liberty long. On, or shortly

---

[1] Luttrell, *op. cit.*, iv, 296; letter of W. Snowe to Robert Harley, *supra*.

[2] James Annesley, third Earl of Anglesey, was nephew to Phillippa Lady Mohun, and hence first cousin to the fourth Lord Mohun.

[3] Luttrell, *loc. cit.*

[4] Whether this was Colonel Richard Coote, who succeeded to the command of Lord Lisburne's Regiment of Foot, on February 1, 1692 (N. S.), or Lieutenant Colonel Chidley Coote, commissioned in the Duke of Schomberg's Regiment of Foot, January 3, 1694, I do not know. See Dalton, *op. cit.*, iii, 270.

[5] Sir Robert Tyrrell was perhaps connected by marriage with the Mohuns. He may have been a relative of James Tyrrell, captain lieutenant in Lord Macclesfield's Regiment of Horse, in which Lord Mohun held a commission (Dalton, *op. cit.*, iii, 354). This James Tyrrell was no doubt the Captain Tyrrell who, with Mohun, accompanied Lord Macclesfield on his mission to Hanover, in 1701 (Toland, *An Account of the Courts of Prussia and Hanover*, p. 64). See *infra*, p. 110, n. 1.

[6] Snowe's letter to Harvey, *supra*.

before, November 9,[1] he was indicted for Hill's murder by the Grand Jury of Middlesex, and committed to the Marshalsea Prison.[2] He petitioned the House of Lords on December 13, to be removed to the Tower.[3] The Peers ordered that a writ of *certiorari* be issued,[4] and on December 20, Mohun was brought to the bar in the House, by the Marshal of the King's Bench, on a writ of *habeas corpus*, whereupon he was placed in the custody of the Usher of the Black Rod, Sir Fleetwood Shepherd.[5] On December 22 it was ordered that Lord Chief Justice Holt attend the House the next day with the coroner's findings upon Hill's death.[6] The Earl

[1] Luttrell, *op. cit.*, iv, 303, entry of November 9. Coroner Robert White delivered the finding of his jury into the Court of King's Bench, on October 24 (endorsement on *Coroner's Inquisition, supra*, p. 54, n. 5).

[2] Newsletter, unsigned, dated December 21, 1697, *State Papers, Dom., Wm. & Mary*, viii, no. 160. The writer says that Mohun's commitment occurred on the last day of the term.

[3] Luttrell, *op. cit.*, iv, 318. Although Luttrell says that the petition was granted on the day of its submission, the *Journals of the House of Lords* do not bear him out (xvi, 179), nor does other evidence.

[4] *Journals of the House of Lords*, xvi, 179.

[5] *Journals of the House of Lords*, xvi, 183. Cf. Luttrell, *op. cit.*, iv, 321; newsletter, unsigned, of December 21, 1697, in *State Papers Dom., Wm. & Mary*, viii, no. 160.

[6] *Journals of the House of Lords*, xvi, 184.

A YOUNG MAN ABOUT TOWN

of Rochester reported on December 23 for the committee [1] who had considered Mohun's case:

That their Lordships have been attended by Mr. *White*, the Coroner of *Middl'x*; who said, "He had returned the Inquistion into the Crown-office"; but he produced the Verdict of his Jury, which was for Manslaughter; and said, "That, since he took his Inquisition, a Bill hath been preferred in the King's Bench against the Lord *Mohun*, and the Grand Jury found *Billa vera*; the Bill was for Murder; it being the Coroner's Duty, notwithstanding the Verdict of Manslaughter, to prefer a Bill for Murder, he being fineable if he should not do so." He said further, "That he hath known, when a Bill hath been preferred for Murder, that the Grand Jury hath found *Billa vera*, Manslaughter; but the Judges have blamed them for so doing, and have caused a new Bill to be drawn." [2]

The House then postponed further consideration of the case and action upon it to January 4.[3] As the result of other postponements,[4] no action was taken until January 10. Mohun's petition to be sent to the Tower was then acted upon favorably; and he was transferred from the custody of Sir

[1] Appointed December 20. *Journals of the House of Lords*, xvi, 183.
[2] *Journals of the House of Lords*, xvi, 185.
[3] *Ibid.*; cf. Luttrell, *op. cit.*, iv, 322; an unsigned newsletter, dated December 24, 1697, State Papers Dom., *Wm. & Mary*, viii, no. 173.
[4] From January 4 to January 5, and then to the tenth (*Journals of the House of Lords*, xvi, 187, 188).

Fleetwood Shepherd to that of Lord Lucas, Governor of the Tower. In addition, the Peers resolved to proceed to Lord Mohun's trial in Westminster Hall.[1] This resolution appears to have been forgotten, for nothing further was done until Mohun presented a petition to the House on March 1, in which he asked for a speedy trial.[2] In the meantime, Mohun's behavior in the Tower had been such that, as Lord Lucas on February 14 reported to the Peers, he had been forced to keep his prisoner under close confinement.[3]

This petition was referred to the same committee that had considered the proceedings in December against Mohun. The Earl of Rochester reported for it that the members were of the opinion that the King should be desired to order that Westminster Hall be prepared for the trial. The Lords then passed an appropriate resolution.[4] The trial, how-

---

[1] *Journals of the House of Lords*, xvi, 191; *Jornalls of ye House of Lords From ye 7. to ye 14th of Jan. 98*, in *State Papers Dom., Wm. & Mary*, ix, no. 18; newsletter, unsigned, dated January 11, *State Papers Dom., Wm. & Mary*, ix, no. 22. Cf. Luttrell, *op. cit.*, iv, 329.

[2] *Journals of the House of Lords*, xvi, 222; *Jornalls of ye House of Lords. March 1, 2 &c.* in *State Papers Dom., Wm. & Mary*, ix, no. 161.

[3] *Journals of the House of Lords*, xvi, 211.

[4] *Journals of the House of Lords*, xvi, 225; newsletter addressed to Sir Joseph Williamson, dated March 4/14, 1697/8, *State Papers Dom., Wm. & Mary*, ix, no. 167. Luttrell errs,

A YOUNG MAN ABOUT TOWN 59

ever, proved to be no nearer than before, and no action of any kind was taken for the next six weeks.

Finally, on April 14, Lord Mohun presented a petition to the House, in which he alleged that his imprisonment had "much impaired" his health, and prayed to be admitted to bail. In support of his assertion of bad health he submitted the certificate of Sir Thomas Millington, M.D.[1] The petition was received and read; and the House ordered that Mohun present himself the next day to be bailed.[2]

On the fifteenth, Mohun was brought before the House, and was admitted to bail, upon his own recognizance, for two thousand pounds, and with the Earl of Warwick, Sir Charles Orby (who had been Mohun's guardian), Captain James Mohun,[3]

it seems, in reporting that on March 2, "the committee of privileges ordered that scaffolds be immediately built in Westminster hall" for the trial (*op. cit.*, iv, 351).

[1] Sir Thomas Millington, then first Physician to the Queen, died January 5, 1703/4, in his seventy-fourth year. At the time of his death he was president of the College of Physicians, *The History of the Reign of Queen Anne, Digested into Annals*, Year the Second, Appendix, p. 24. He had attended William III, on his deathbed. Brodrick, *Compleat History of the Late War*, p. xvi, n. *a*. Sir Thomas was appointed physician to the Queen in June, 1702. Luttrell, *op. cit.*, v, 184. Sir Samuel Garth, in *The Dispensary*, canto v, ll. 207ff., pays a tribute to Sir Thomas Millington, under the name of "Machaon."

[2] *Journals of the House of Lords*, xvi, 262.

[3] James Mohun was commissioned ensign in the Earl of Bath's Regiment of Foot in November, 1687; on October 9,

and Thomas Windham,[1] as sureties for a thousand pounds each.[2]

Again we hear no more of Mohun, or his trial, for several weeks. At last, on July 4, 1698, he appeared before the Peers, pleaded his pardon from the King for Hill's murder, which was allowed and his bail discharged.[3] The same day Mohun presented his

---

1688, he became captain lieutenant; he resigned his commission to James II on December 20, 1688. Dalton, *Army Lists*, ii, 140, 190. I do not know precisely what his relation to Lord Mohun was. He may have been an uncle.

[1] Thomas Windham was probably a cousin of Mohun, and a son of the Lady Frances Annesley, who married, first, John Windham of Felbridge Hall, Norfolk, and, secondly, John Lord Haversham. Like Mohun's mother, Lady Haversham was a daughter of the first Earl of Anglesey. *The History of the Reign of Queen Anne, Digested into Annals*, Year the Ninth, p. 425.

[2] *Journals of the House of Lords*, xvi, 263-264; newsletter, unsigned, dated April 15, 1698, *State Papers Dom., Wm. & Mary*, x, no. 77, wherein the sureties are given as "The Earle of Holland, Sr. Tho: Orby [the first Lady Mohun's stepfather], Sr. Sa.: Mohun and Mr. Tho: Windham." "Sr. Sa.: Mohun" was probably "Ct. Ja.: Mohun". See also Luttrell, *op. cit.*, iv, 368.

[3] *Journals of the House of Lords*, xvi, 341. The pardon, as translated from the Latin by Mrs. A. May Osler, runs thus:

"Whereas by a certain Inquisition taken for the King at the parish of St. Martin in the Fields, within the Liberty of the Dean and Chapter of Westminster Cathedral, in the city of Westminster, county Middlesex, on 16 September, 9 William III before Robert White, gent., coroner there, on the view of the body of William Hill there lying dead, it was found by the jurors that Charles Lord Mohun, late of the

writ of summons to Parliament (having come of age on April 11, during his imprisonment in the Tower); after which he took the oaths, subscribed the necessary declaration, and assumed his place on the barons' bench.[1] On the next day, July 5, Parliament was prorogued;[2] and it was dissolved July 7.[3]

At first glance, the history of this affair seems inexplicable. Indicted for murder, arrested, and imprisoned, Mohun was never brought to trial, but was freed on bail, and, not long after, pardoned. The truth would seem to be that politics lay at the bottom of Mohun's escape from trial.[4] In 1698,

said parish on the 14th September in the said year instigated by the devil with violence feloniously assaulted the said William Hill and with a rapier, worth 10*s.* made of iron and steel, with his right hand stabbed the said William Hill in the stomach in the navel, so that he made a mortal wound, one inch in length and twelve inches in depth, whereof the said William Hill languished until the 15th and then died and a true bill to this effect was found against the said Lord Mohun.

"Now be it known that the King, of his especial grace pardons the said Charles Lord Mohun for the said felony and murder and all therewith connected and all indictments and forfeitures concerning the same, as well as outlawries, suits, action, demands, &c. and that he shall not in future be arrested nor imprisoned on account of the said premises or any other thing connected therewith.

"2 July.   by writ of Privy Seal."
(*Patent Roll* 3399, no. 2).

[1] *Journals of the House of Lords*, xvi, 341.
[2] *Ibid.*, p. 344.   [3] *Ibid.*, p. 345.
[4] If, as I have suggested, the murder was committed during the rejoicings connected with the termination of the

William III had lost much of his earlier popularity. Unsupported by his Queen, so generally loved, who had been dead now about four years, William III had alienated many of his earlier adherents by his ungenial manners, his fondness for his Dutch favorites, and his aversion to England save as a source of men and wealth wherewith to oppose France.[1] Even a single vote in the House of Lords was worth some concession. Lord Mohun, of an old Whig family, a Puritan in politics though perhaps not in manners, who came of age in April, 1698, surely deserved some consideration in spite of his habits and reputation. What more likely, then, than that Mohun's friends represented to William that grace shown the young peer would secure him absolutely for the King's side? Perhaps a bargain was struck, perhaps not; at any rate Mohun's public life demonstrated him to be quite as steadfast and strong a partisan of the principles of William III as that monarch could have desired.[2]

Congress of Ryswick, the King was perhaps all the more willing to overlook such a patriotic indiscretion as Mohun's may have been. See *supra*, p. 53, n. 3.

[1] See Macaulay, *op. cit.*, chaps. xxi–xxiv, *passim*, for an account of William's quarrels with his Parliaments, from the dispute over his grant of Welch crown lands to Lord Portland, up to his threat in December, 1698, to abdicate on account of the army controversy.

[2] This explanation, which may account also for the disappearance of the depositions taken in the inquest on Hill,

A YOUNG MAN ABOUT TOWN

In regard to Captain Hill's death, there have arisen, since, some remarkable stories. For instance, Mr. A. S. Turberville, in his *The House of Lords in the Reign of William III*,[1] follows a moderately accurate account of Mohun's part in the murder of Mountford with this curious passage:

> Five years later he [Mohun] was placed in precisely similar circumstances. This time in connection with the death of that very Captain Hill with whom he had been associated in his former escapade. Hill perished in a tavern brawl, in which Mohun was engaged. The coroner's verdict was one of manslaughter, and so once more Mohun escaped scot-free.

There is no necessity of pointing out the confusion of the two Captain Hills or the other inaccuracies of statement or implication in Mr. Turberville's remarks.

The next adventure of Lord Mohun was not long in following his pardon for the murder of William Hill; but as Thackeray has employed that event in *Esmond*, I shall return now to my analysis of the novel and take up the affair later.[2]

---

when suggested to the officials of the Public Records Office, was judged by them not improbable.

[1] *Oxford Historical and Literary Studies*, p. 42. "Issued under the direction of C. H. Firth and Walter Raleigh, professors of Modern History and English Literature in the University of Oxford."

[2] It ought, perhaps, to be said that during the period of his life which is being surveyed, Lord Mohun appeared as a

party in civil as well as in criminal proceedings at law. Upon the death of his grandmother, Katherine Lady Mohun, in April, 1692, Mohun and his attorney, one Reynold Couch, seized the property which had been her jointure. Phillippa Lady Mohun claimed the lands involved, which amounted to five hundred pounds a year, and sued her son for them. Losing her suit in the lower court, she appealed it to the House of Peers, which affirmed the decision on March 22, 1696/7. Lady Mohun and her second husband, Sergeant Coward, seem to have continued their efforts to secure the property, but without success. See for particulars, *Hist. MSS. Comm. Reports*, xiv, pt. 6, 366–367, *House of Lords MSS.; Ibid.*, N. S., ii, 519 ff., and *Journals of the House of Lords*, xvi, 111, 124, 131; Luttrell, *op. cit.*, iv, 199; *House of Lords MSS.*, N. S., iv, 304, and *Journals of the House of Lords*, xvi, 645.

Mohun himself seems to have been twice plaintiff (in 1698 and 1700) in actions in Chancery brought against Dame Theophila Harris, widow, and others, concerning estates in Bodmin, Okehampton, Budleigh, and elsewhere in Devon and Cornwall. See *Chancery Proceedings*, Bridges Div., Bundle 206, no. 10; Bundle 219, no. 42. Theophila Harris was a connection of the Lords Mohun through the marriage of Cordelia, daughter of the first Lord to John Harris of Hayne, County Devon. Another daughter of John Lord Mohun was named Theophila. See Burke, *Dormant . . . and Extinct Peerages*, p. 370, and Lyte, *op. cit.*, p. 487.

IV

LORD MOHUN VISITS CASTLEWOOD

VERY speedily upon his introduction at Castlewood Lord Mohun becomes a favorite there, for he adroitly fits his conversation to the tastes of the various members of the family. He talks music [1] and gallantry to Lady Castlewood; for Esmond he has stories of his life at Vienna, Paris, and the other famous cities of Europe which he had visited in peace and war; with Lord Castlewood he exchanges tales of London dissipation.

Here again Thackeray has embellished Mohun's unlovely past. If he ever visited Vienna, it was during his attendance upon the Earl of Macclesfield in his mission to Hanover in 1701, two years subsequent to his story-telling at Castlewood. There is no record of Lord Mohun's ever having been in Venice. He may have visited Paris, as did so many young Englishmen of fashion, after the

[1] See *supra*, p. 13, the extract from *The Whole Lives, Characters, Actions, and Fall of D. Hamilton and L. Mohun*. If a source is needed for Thackeray's ascription of musical knowledge to Lord Mohun, it may be found in this pamphlet.

Peace of Ryswyck in 1697.[1] Perhaps it was there that he sought refuge in 1698–99, following the death of Captain Coote, since immediately after that event his companion, the Earl of Warwick, proposed to seek safety there.[2] But up to the time when he begins to influence the fortunes of the Castlewoods, there is no evidence that Lord Mohun's Continental travels had been more extensive than the meagre amount demanded by his military service.

Lady Castlewood, who had at first disliked her husband's new friend, soon is won over to complete confidence in him by his professions of repentance for his evil courses and his ready acceptance of her proffered books of devotion. As a result, in part, of her change of opinion, when Esmond returns to Castlewood for the long vacation of 1700, he finds Mohun there and more an intimate than ever.[3] During that year Henry had heard from his university friends "but ugly reports" of his Lordship. In the spring Lord Castlewood and his new crony

[1] The treaty was signed September 11, 1697 (Macaulay, *History of England*, chap. 22). It is barely possible that Mohun was in France for some time between September 14, when he killed Captain William Hill, and October 22, when he was arrested for the deed (*supra*, pp. 53–54).

[2] Howell, *State Trials*, xiii, col. 1002, testimony of Colonel Whiteman [Wightman] on Lord Warwick's trial.

[3] *Esmond*, bk. I, chap. 13.

MOHUN VISITS CASTLEWOOD 67

had ridden to Cambridge from Newmarket, where they had been for the racing, and had paid Esmond a short visit. On his arrival at Castlewood, Henry learns that Lord Castlewood has taken to play again, although he had renounced gaming at his marriage, and has apparently lost large sums of money to Lord Mohun — a fact which worries Lady Castlewood very much. Notwithstanding Lord Castlewood's admiration for his guest, his jealousy is easily aroused so that a pert remark by Beatrix nearly brings about a duel.[1] This is averted, however, and for the time being matters go on smoothly.

Very subtly Mohun lays siege to Lady Castlewood, who resents Esmond's attempts at interference. At last Henry appeals to Mohun himself, one day, as the two are driving, and urges him to cease gaming with Lord Castlewood [2] and to give up his

[1] Esmond remarks, in regard to Lord Castlewood's irritated comments upon Mohun's character: "My Lord Mohun was separated from his wife, and had had many affairs of honour; of which women as usual had been the cause." In fact, of all Mohun's brawls only one, so far as is known, — that ending in the death of Mountford, — had a woman at the bottom; and then Mohun had not been a principal, but merely the aide of the chief figure.

[2] Mohun asserts to Esmond that he always has played fair with Lord Castlewood, and tells of how once he had set a "dice-cogging" Alsatian for his ears, which he had won and had preserved in alcohol at his lodgings in Bow Street.

pursuit of Lady Castlewood. The conversation is ended by the running away of Mohun's ponies, an accident which has much to do with shaping subsequent events. For Lord Castlewood, who is riding with his children, seeing that Mohun's carriage has been overturned and its two occupants thrown out and hurt, gallops off for aid; and on reaching Castlewood, he cries to his wife that "Harry"[1] is killed, whereupon she faints, thereby arousing her husband's jealous suspicions again. Too, on the scene of the accident, Lord Castlewood finds a letter addressed to Lady Castlewood, which has been lost from Mohun's pocket. With this he confronts his guest, and they arrange a meeting for the future. When he can travel, Mohun then leaves Castlewood,[2] with a suspiciously cold parting from Lord Castlewood. Both Esmond and Lady Castlewood fear that a duel impends; but as Lord Castlewood

There seems to be no ground for Thackeray's endowing Mohun with this ghastly trophy.

[1] It is evident here why Thackeray changed Lord Mohun's name from "Charles," that of the historical Mohun, to "Henry" or "Harry." Upon Lord Castlewood's belief that Lady Castlewood swooned on hearing of "Harry" Lord Mohun's supposed death, instead of that of Henry Esmond, as was the case, rests, to a considerable degree, the quarrel and duel between the two noblemen, with its tragic outcome, upon which depends, in turn, the later course of the novel.

[2] *Esmond*, bk. I, chap. 14.

MOHUN VISITS CASTLEWOOD

pretends to have letters telling of Lord Mohun's departure for Paris, they are made easier in mind.

Lord Castlewood then feigns indisposition, and proposes to go to London to consult his physician, Doctor Cheyne.[1] Accompanied by Esmond, he leaves Castlewood for London, on the morning of Monday, October 11, 1700.

Upon their arrival in London the next day, Castlewood and Esmond stop at the Trumpet Tavern in the Cockpit, Whitehall.[2] Esmond then

[1] Unfortunately for Lord Castlewood, Dr. George Cheyne seems not to have come to London from Edinburgh until early in 1702 (N. S.). He was elected a member of the Royal Society on March 18, 1701/2. As Dr. Cheyne's first book was not published until 1702, he certainly had not acquired much fame by that time. For other details of Dr. Cheyne's life, see Dr. J. F. Payne, in *D. N. B.*, x, 217–219, art., "Cheyne, Dr. George."

[2] The only Trumpet Tavern traceable is that which stood in Sheer Lane, and which is connected with the memories of Steele and Addison. Sheer Lane, which owed its name to its dividing the city from the shire, opened into Fleet Street, opposite the spot where Child's Bank now stands. It was the lane next west of Bell Court. The clock tower of the High Courts of Justice now covers it. See Aitken, *Life of Steele*, i, 97; Besant, *London in the Eighteenth Century*, p. 322. Besant, in this work, as well as in his *London in the Time of the Stuarts*, reprints old maps of London on which Sheer Lane is shown. In the lane was the first meeting-place of the Kit-Cat Club, of which Mohun was a member. The Trumpet Tavern is frequently mentioned in the *Tatler*. There Isaac Bickerstaff's club met (*Tatler*, no. 133, February 11, 1709/10), and there Isaac, who lived in Sheer Lane, spent much

learns that Lord Mohun has not remained in Paris,[1] but has come back at Lord Castlewood's invitation, and that his patron has settled his debt to Mohun of sixteen hundred pounds. Although Lord Castlewood laughs at him, Esmond is now sure that a duel is on foot, and will not be induced to leave his patron. Lord Castlewood at last admits the quarrel and explains its grounds. In spite of Esmond's attempts to get a reconciliation under way, Castlewood is determined to fight. Henry insists upon acting as a second. They hope so to arrange the quarrel that the challenge may be given without mention

of his time (*Tatler*, no. 89, November 3, 1708). An advertisement in the *Tatler*, no. 201, July 22, 1710, is dated from the Trumpet. In all, thirty-eight *Tatlers* are dated from Sheer Lane. The association of the locality with Steele and the *Tatler* is illustrated by Mrs. Manley in the "Dedication" of her *Memoirs of Europe toward the Close of the Eighth Century*, addressed to Isaac Bickerstaff, whom, she says, she has attempted to find in Sheer Lane. The author of *A Letter to the Reverend Dr. Henry Sacheverell* likewise links Steele and the same locality; for the piece, which is signed "Isaac Bickerstaff," is dated "Sheer-lane, January the 19th, 1709/10" (Aitken, *Life of Steele*, i, 275, n. 1). Unquestionably Thackeray derived the name of Lord Castlewood's tavern from the *Tatler*, but moved the house further west to a more aristocratic neighborhood. "Cymon Wyldoats'" letter in the counterfeit *Spectator* paper, which Esmond concocted for Beatrix's benefit, is dated from "The Trumpet Coffee-House, Whitehall." *Esmond*, bk. III, chap. 3.

[1] This journey of Lord Mohun to Paris is probably not historical; see *supra*, pp. 65–66.

MOHUN VISITS CASTLEWOOD 71

of Lady Castlewood.[1] Colonel Westbury,[2] whom Castlewood has already secured as a second, now arrives at the tavern.

As had been arranged, the three then go in a carriage to the Duke's Playhouse, or "the theatre in Duke Street," where they see Wycherley's *Love in a Wood*.[3] Among the spectators are Lord Mohun, the Earl of Warwick,[4] and one Captain Macart-

[1] In spite of their precautions, the true cause of the quarrel was suspected; cf. Captain Westbury's speech to Esmond, and the Dowager Viscountess's letter to him, both in bk. II, chap. 2.

[2] Colonel Westbury, who appears in *Esmond*, bk. I, chap. 6, as Trooper Richard Steele's commanding officer, is probably an invention of Thackeray. The name of Westbury does not occur in Dalton's *Army Lists*.

[3] The meeting-place of the two parties is considered later, at pp. 99ff.

[4] Edward Rich, sixth Earl of Warwick and Holland, was born in 1673, and took his seat in the House of Lords, November 20, 1694. *Journals of the House of Lords*, xv, 433. He was commissioned captain in the Queen's Regiment of Horse on February 15, 1694 (N. S.), and certainly served abroad in that year. Luttrell, *op. cit.*, iii, 281; letter of Robert Harley to Sir E. Harley, October 9, 1694, in *Hist. MSS. Comm. Reports*, xiv, pt. 2, *MSS. of the Duke of Portland*, iii, 558. The Earl died July 30, 1701, leaving a widow and a son of about four years of age. Luttrell, *op. cit.*, v, 71. Lord Warwick inherited the political principles of his family, although he took little interest in the proceedings of the House of Lords. Tom Brown mentions him as a constant attendant in Hell upon the sermons of Tony Lee, the actor, who had become a Presbyterian parson. *Letters from the Dead to the Living*, in *Works*, ii, 7. Chancellor has confused the sixth and

ney.[1] Between the acts the six converse; Lord Mohun makes a rude remark to Mrs. Bracegirdle the actress, to which she replies by inquiring if he and his friends have come to stab any one as they had Mountford.[2] "My Lord's dark face grew darker at this taunt, and wore a fatal mischievous look,"[3] Esmond notes.

seventh Earls, and tells us that, on his deathbed, Addison sent for the sixth Earl "so that he might see how a Christian could die." It truly must have been "an awful scene" (as Chancellor calls it), since Addison had married the widow of the same sixth Earl, who had died eighteen years earlier. See *The London of Thackeray*, p. 37, n. It was the seventh Earl whom Rowe addressed in his verses "To Lord Warwick on His Birth-Day." Rowe was also the author of lines "Occasioned by His First Visit to Lady Warwick at Holland-House" and "Stanzas to Lady Warwick, on Mr. Addison's Going to Ireland."

[1] The career of George Maccartney, who figures in the Mohun-Castlewood duel of *Esmond*, as well as in the Mohun-Hamilton duel of the novel, and of history, is treated in Appendix B, p. 257. It should be noted here that Esmond gives him a wrong title, as he was commissioned lieutenant colonel in the Scots Foot Guards, on May 30, 1697. Dalton, *op. cit.*, iv, 174.

[2] See *supra*, pp. 23-35, where an account of Captain Richard Hill's murder of the actor William Mountford, in Lord Mohun's presence, is given.

[3] Though why it should is not clear, for, judging from what follows, Mohun is honestly anxious to avoid a duel with Lord Castlewood, if it can be done with honor. One must suppose either that Thackeray has forgotten consistency in order to deck out his villain as properly villainous, or else that we have here an example of one of those prophetic circumstances which, after an event has occurred, certain people recall, as having foreshadowed its happening.

MOHUN VISITS CASTLEWOOD

After the play, the six go, at Castlewood's suggestion, to Locket's tavern, the Grayhound, in Charing Cross,[1] to sup.[2] The party obtain a private

[1] Locket's tavern, the Grayhound, was one of the most fashionable London establishments of its kind in the later seventeenth and earlier eighteenth centuries. It stood at Charing Cross, where once was Drummond's Bank. Besant, *London in the Time of the Stuarts*, p. 292. The tavern is, as Summers says, frequently mentioned by Restoration and Augustan writers. *Shakespeare Adaptations*, p. 269, note to such a reference in Duffet's *The Mock-Tempest*, ii, 2. Swift, for example, names Locket's in *A Tale of a Tub* (sect. 2), as the place where Peter, Martin, and Jack, as men about town, ate. The Grayhound seems familiarly to have been called the "Dog." See Howell, *State Trials*, xiii, col. 972, testimony of James Crattle on Lord Warwick's trial for murder; and Tom Brown, *Letters from the Living to the Dead*, in his *Works*, ii, 189. Chancellor's idea that the sign as given in *Esmond* is fictitious, is, of course, wrong. *The London of Thackeray*, p. 33.

[2] The Rose Tavern, which had been considered as the scene for the quarrel, probably was suggested to Thackeray by his study of the Mohun-Hamilton duel, since it was there that the then General Maccartney and the Duke of Hamilton discussed the meeting of the two peers on the day before its occurrence, viz., on November 14, 1712. The Rose, which stood in Brydges Street, Covent Garden, was frequented by theatrical people, and was not of the best repute. Lady Castlewood mentions it to Esmond (bk. I, chap. 12, and see also bk. II, chap. 5). It was at the Rose that Hildebrand Horden, the promising young actor, was killed by Colonel Burgess in 1699. Cibber, *Apology*, p. 173; *Biographia Dramatica*, i, 366; Genest, *Stage*, ii, 144. A reference to the Rose is to be found in the *Tatler*, no. 2, April 14, 1709. It was there that Steele ordered a "Thirty Pound Dinner" for the claque he had provided for the first night of Addison's *Cato*.

room, where they order wine and cards. Esmond endeavors to forestall Castlewood in quarrelling with Mohun, but is not permitted to do so.[1] After a little play, Castlewood begins the quarrel. A challenge is given and accepted. The time and place are settled as at once in Leicester Fields. Chairs being ordered, the six set off, having made a pretense, when they had gone down into the bar, of being bound for Lord Mohun's house in Bow Street,[2] to drink a bottle in celebration of their reconciliation, before going to bed. The chairs are halted opposite the Standard Tavern in Leicester Square. The duelists enter the square, while their chairmen

Dennis's *The Character and Conduct of Sir John Edgar*, etc., quoted by Nicoll, *Eighteenth Century Drama, 1700–1750*, p. 18. Earlier references to the Rose occur in Shadwell's *The Scourers* (quoted by T. C. and W. Snow, *Esmond*, p. 490), and in Swift's *A Tale of a Tub* (sect. 2). "Melville" appears to have confused the Rose with Will's coffeehouse, the resort of men of letters. *Some Aspects of Thackeray*, p. 193.

[1] Thackeray perhaps errs in making Macartney, in his conversation with Esmond reveal himself, as the typical witty Teague of literature. Actually Maccartney was born in Belfast of Scotch parentage.

[2] There seems to be no foundation for Mohun's being assigned a residence in Bow Street. He lived somewhere farther west, in Westminster, in 1698. Howell, *op. cit.*, xiii, cols. 958, 1045, evidence on the trials of Lords Warwick and Mohun for Captain Richard Coote's murder. According to T. C. and W. Snow (*op. cit.*, p. 493), Bow Street "was inhabited by the more Bohemian and adventurous classes, especially actors."

MOHUN VISITS CASTLEWOOD

smoke, and watch the gate to give warning of anyone's approach. As had been decided, Esmond and Macartney, Westbury and Warwick engage. After a couple of minutes' fighting, being warned of some misadventure by the cry of the chairmen, Esmond drops his sword and turns, Macartney wounding him in the hand as he does so. Lord Castlewood is down, and Lord Mohun is over him. The former says he is a dead man. Mohun responds that he hopes not, adding that he would have apologized, had he been given the chance.

Castlewood then faints; Esmond and Westbury have the chairmen come into the field and take up their friend's body. Lord Castlewood is borne to "one Mr. Aimes, a surgeon, in Long Acre, who kept a bath, and there the house was wakened up, and the victim of this quarrel carried in."[1] Castlewood is put to bed, and his wound is dressed by the surgeon, as is Esmond's own hurt. Lord Castlewood, after confessing to Esmond his knowledge of Henry's legitimacy, dies. Esmond then goes to the Gatehouse, where he gives himself up.

[1] *Esmond*, bk. I, chap. 14.

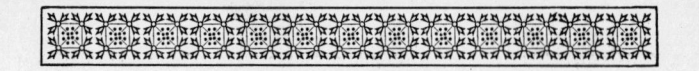

V

A DUEL IN LEICESTER FIELDS

AS Mudge and Sears observe in their *Thackeray Dictionary*,[1] the duel of the historical Lord Mohun which serves the author of *Henry Esmond* as a source for the meeting of Lord Castlewood and the Lord Mohun of the novel was the affair in the early morning of Sunday, October 30, 1698, in which Captain Richard Coote was killed. The resemblance between the two incidents is, however, not so great as is indicated by the writers cited. That such is the case may be seen from the outline of the events of the actual duel, as given below.

On the night of Saturday, October 29, 1698, Edward Earl of Warwick, with a party of friends,

---

[1] London, 1910, art., "Mohun, Lord [*sic*] Henry, or Harry." In his *State Trials Political and Social*, H. L. Stephen, at the conclusion of his account of Lord Warwick's trial for Captain Coote's murder, notes that Thackeray had employed the duel in *Esmond*, and gives some excerpts from the novel. He attempts no comparison of the actual affair and that reported in the novel, save to remark "that there seems to be some faint relationship between Captain Macartney, Lord Mohun's second ... and the Lord [*sic*] Macartney who afterwards assisted him in his final meeting with the Duke of Hamilton" (ii, 130).

EDWARD, SIXTH EARL OF WARWICK

DUEL IN LEICESTER FIELDS 77

consisting of his cronies, Lord Mohun[1] and Captain Richard Coote,[2] together with Mr. Richard

[1] See *The Whole Life and History of my Lord Moon, and the Earl of Warwick: With their Comical Frolicks that they Play'd*. London. Printed by J. Johnson in Fleet Street. 1711. In this collection of ribald stories, the two peers are represented as bosom friends. Luttrell mentions them as setting out together for military service on the Continent in 1694 (*A Brief Relation of State Affairs*, iii, 282); and according to the same authority Lord Mohun was arrested at Warwick's house after the death of William Hill (iv, 296); Lord Warwick possibly was then a surety for Mohun. In spite of the fact that "Warwick" occurs as a given name among the Mohuns, there would appear to have been no connection between them and the family of the earls of Warwick. See Lyte, *History of Dunster*, p. 487, n., and cf. *ibid.*, pp. 494–495. The Warwick Mohun who, in April, 1673, was commissioned captain in Lord Vaughan's Regiment, and whom Dalton calls a son of the second Baron, must have belonged to another branch, as that peer had but two sons. See *Army Lists*, i, 144.

[2] On his trial before the House of Lords, on March 28, 1699, for the murder of Captain Coote, the Earl not only emphasized his intimacy with the dead man, but produced a number of witnesses who testified to the closeness of their friendship.

Luttrell (*op. cit.*, iv, 445), calls Captain Coote a son to Sir Richard Coote. I have, however, been unable to trace him. Although he was said to have purchased an ensign's commission in the Guards in the summer of 1698, Dalton does not notice him in his *Army Lists*. None of the Richard Cootes therein mentioned can be the one who figured in the event to be described, unless, indeed, Richard Coote, jun., commissioned ensign in Colonel Richard Coote's Regiment of Foot on February 2, 1698 (N. S.), be he. Dalton, *Army Lists*, iii, 270. In that case, the Richard Coote who was appointed ensign in the Earl of Huntingdon's Regiment of Foot on March 10,

French,[1] arrived at Locket's tavern, the Grayhound, in the Strand. This was perhaps about eight o'clock.[2] They were later joined by Captain Edmund Keeting[3] and Captain George Dockwra.[4] A messenger

1702, would not be the same person (*op. cit.*) In all probability the unfortunate Captain Coote was an Irishman of the family represented in the Irish peerage by the Earls of Mountrath, the Earls of Bellamont, and the Lords Coote of Coloony. Richard was not an uncommon name among them. See Burke, *Dormant . . . and Extinct Peerages*, pp. 133–135.

[1] Luttrell calls him "Mr. French of the Temple," but later refers to him as "Captain" (*op. cit.*, iv, 445, 461). French is called "Captain" by the witnesses on Lords Warwick's and Mohun's trials (Howell, *State Trials*, xiii). Since Dalton does not give Richard French in his lists, it is reasonable, however, to suppose that he was a Templar, not a soldier.

[2] Howell, *op. cit.*, xiii, col. 957, testimony of Samuel Cawthorne on the Earl of Warwick's trial; cf. Captain Keeting's evidence. *Ibid.*, col. 998. It should be noted that in the accounts of the trials Cawthorne is called both "Joseph" and "Samuel." In the order of the House of Lords for his attendance as a witness his name is given as "Samuel" (*Journals of the House of Lords*, xvi, 417).

[3] Howell, *loc. cit.*, testimony of Captain Keeting. There is some discrepancy between the evidence of Keeting and Cawthorne, as to when Lord Mohun appeared at the Grayhound. The former alleged that he had not arrived at ten o'clock; the latter, that he came at about eight. It may well be that Lord Mohun was late in reaching the tavern; the point is, however, of no especial importance.

[4] George Dockwra was commissioned ensign in the First Foot Guards, July 15, 1695, to rank as captain. He became a lieutenant on May 15, 1704, but by 1709, had left the regiment. He served in the Vigo and Cadiz expedition of 1702.

DUEL IN LEICESTER FIELDS 79

was sent for Captain Roger James [1] of the Coldstream Guards, who was "almost fuddled," when he appeared about twelve o'clock.[2] Shortly after

(Dalton, *Army Lists*, iv, 66, n. 11, 67; v, 43, 44; Mackinnon, *Coldstream Guards*, i, 280). William Dockwra, who was perhaps George Dockwra's father, was among the proprietors of the Jersey colonies in America who surrendered their rights to the Queen, April 17, 1702 (*The History of the Reign of Queen Anne* . . . Year the First, p. 23). He was one of the respondents in the suit appealed from the Court of Chancery to the House of Lords on January 20, 1703/4, and was awarded thirty pounds costs when the appeal was lost (*Journals of the House of Lords*, xvii, 378, 421, 467). A Mr. Dockra, "the first Inventor of the *Penny-Post Office*," died at a great age in September, 1716. Boyer . . . *The Political State of Great Britain* . . . xii (July–Dec., 1716), 291.

[1] Roger James was commissioned lieutenant in the Coldstream Guards, April 23, 1697, to rank as captain. He served in Spain with the Guards, was wounded at Gibraltar, on February 1, 1704 (N. S.), again at Barcelona, and in 1706, was wounded and taken prisoner. He resigned in May, 1709, being disabled from his wounds. He then ranked as lieutenant colonel. Dalton, *op. cit.*, iv, 173; Mackinnon, i, 289.

[2] Howell, *op. cit.*, xiii, cols. 998, 1038, evidence of Captain Keeting on Lord Warwick's trial, and of Cawthorne on Lord Mohun's. Keeting testified that Captain James reached the tavern at about twelve o'clock; Cawthorne, the drawer, stated that James was sent for in the neighborhood of ten o'clock. Cawthorne also testified that, when James arrived, the scabbard of his sword was broken, and he broke the blade of his weapon by stamping on it. But, on the other hand, James almost certainly wounded the Earl of Warwick later in the night; and he arrived at the Bagnio, after the duel, with a sword but no scabbard. It was said, however, that Captain

Captain James's arrival, Captain Keeting,[1] being indisposed, paid his reckoning, and went home.[2]

There were then six in the party at Locket's — the Earl of Warwick, Lord Mohun, Captains Coote, Dockwra, and James, and Mr. French. The party drank together very amicably, it would seem, until between one and two o'clock in the morning. Then Coote directed certain "reflecting expressions" toward Mr. French, who resented them, and a quarrel broke out. French called for his reckoning and paid it. Then Lord Warwick proposed an adjournment to his lodgings, to drink and avoid more

---

Coote's sword was brought to the Bagnio, perhaps by Dockwra, who had his weapon in the sheath. James is alleged to have broken a sword on the floor at the Bagnio also. Warwick and French pretty certainly had their own weapons when he reached Mr. Amy's establishment (*Ibid.*, cols. 981-982, testimony of Henry Pomfret). Clearly there is a flaw in the evidence given.

[1] Edmund Keeting was commissioned captain in Colonel Henry Rowe's Regiment of Foot, April 23, 1694, and captain of the grenadier company in the Earl of Donegal's Regiment, June 28, 1701. He did not accompany his regiment to the West Indies in 1702. On November 19, 1706, he became major of Colonel Richard Coote's Regiment, where he was serving in 1717. Dalton, *George I's Army*, i, 176.

[2] Howell, *op. cit.*, col. 998, testimony of Captain Keeting on Lord Warwick's trial. In his résumé of the events at Locket's, Lord Birkenhead has only five revellers together, before Captain James's arrival, omitting Captain Keeting. He also has Captain Dockwra among the original party. The military titles are also confused (*Famous Trials of History*, p. 87).

DUEL IN LEICESTER FIELDS

serious trouble. Coaches were sent for, and, in the meantime, the party descended to the bar, where they had a glass of ale. Then Coote, who was sometimes quarrelsome, again angered French.[1] When Cawthorne, the drawer, returned from an unsuccessful quest for coaches, to say that he had obtained six chairs for the company, he found the guests at odds. Three — Lords Warwick and Mohun and Captain Coote — were on one side of the bar, and three — James, Dockwra, and French — were on the other. Swords were drawn, and Lord Mohun was bleeding from a wound in the hand received in parting the quarrellers.[2] Captain Coote remarked that he would laugh when he pleased and frown when he pleased. The two peers and Captain James strove to reconcile Coote and French, even threatening to send for a file of guardsmen to secure them.[3] Some time after, James told Cawthorne not to get the guards as the quarrel was over.[4] But in a moment

[1] Howell, *op. cit.*, cols. 996–997, statement of the Earl of Warwick on his trial.

[2] Mohun's hands were peculiarly vulnerable. In his duel with "Captain Bingham" in 1694, he was wounded in the hand. The surgeon who examined his body after his duel with the Duke of Hamilton, found "three Fingers of his Right Hand almost cut off." *The Case at Large of Duke Hamilton and the Lord Mohun.* Printed for E. Curll. London, 1712.

[3] Howell, *op. cit.*, col. 964, Cawthorne's testimony on Lord Warwick's trial.

[4] *Ibid.*

Coote and French got into chairs, with the intention of setting out for some place where they could settle their disagreement without interruption. Mohun prevented their departure, however, by asserting that he would kill any chairman who started away. The two then returned into the tavern,[1] Lord Mohun still exclaiming that there must be no trial of the matter at that time. He invited Coote to go with him to his lodgings at Westminster; and proposed as an alternative that he should accompany Coote to his; at any rate, there must be no duel.[2]

Mohun, — whose injured hand had been wrapped in a napkin by the drawer, — Warwick, and Coote then got into chairs, and set out. After their departure, Dockwra was heard to say to James and French: "We don't care a farthing for them; we will fight them at any time." They entered chairs, then, and followed the others.[3]

On reaching the end of St. Martin's Lane in the Strand, Coote ordered his chairmen to turn into it,

[1] Howell, *op. cit.*, cols. 980–981, evidence of Richard Edwards, chairman, on Lord Warwick's trial.

[2] *Ibid.*, col. 958, evidence of Cawthorne on Lord Warwick's trial; *Ibid.*, col. 1038, his testimony on Lord Mohun's trial; *Ibid.*, col. 1045, testimony of Robert Applegate, chairman, on Lord Mohun's trial.

[3] *Ibid.*, col. 966, Cawthorne's testimony on Lord Warwick's trial.

DUEL IN LEICESTER FIELDS   83

refusing, in spite of the entreaties of his companions, to go on to Westminster.[1] Lord Mohun, it is said, begged Coote, "as if it had been for an alms," that he would put off the business for that night. Coote responded, however, that he would make an end of it then. Accordingly he ordered his chairmen to follow the chairs which had just passed with French, James, and Dockwra, into Leicester Fields, and swore that unless they made haste to get there before "that other chair" (French's, doubtless), "he would run his sword into the breach of one of them." Mohun is said to have remarked then: "If you must go, I will go with you and see it." Thereupon the six chairmen went on through St. Martin's Lane to Leicester Fields, where they set down their passengers at the end of Green Street at the lower side of the square. From this point, after Mohun had paid the men, the three walked away in the darkness toward the Standard Tavern [2] at the opposite end of the square.[3]

[1] Coote, Lord Warwick, and Lord Mohun had halted for this argument at the back door of the Cross Keys tavern. Howell, *op. cit.*, xiii, cols. 967, 974, 976, 977, 978, testimony of Browne, Applegate, Peter Catro, and John Palmer on Lord Warwick's trial.

[2] Chancellor erroneously says that the Standard Tavern was probably of Thackeray's invention. *The London of Thackeray*, p. 33.

[3] Howell, *op. cit.*, xiii, cols. 1040, 1045, testimony of

In the meantime, the other three had been borne to the further side of the square and had been set down by the Standard Tavern, which stood near Leicester House.[1] The gentlemen had paid their men and had gone about their business; their bearers had promptly made for home.[2] The other chairmen had remained for a time at the opposite extremity of Leicester Square to light their pipes before setting off. Hardly had this been accomplished when there came a cry for "Chairs! chairs!" from the darkness toward the upper part of the square.[3]

Of the chairmen answering the hail, Thomas Browne, who, with William Crippes, had brought Captain Coote to the scene, went with his partner to the spot whence the cry had come. There they found several of the party from Locket's, who bade them lift their chairs over the railings — an order which, after demurring, they obeyed. Two gentle-

Thomas Browne and Robert Applegate, chairmen, on Lord Mohun's trial.

[1] Howell, *op. cit.*, cols. 978, 979, testimony of John Palmer and Jackson on Lord Warwick's trial; *Ibid.*, col. 1051, Jackson's evidence on Lord Mohun's trial.

[2] *Ibid.*, xiii, cols. 978, 979, 980, testimony of Palmer, Jackson, and Richard Edwards, at the Earl of Warwick's trial.

[3] Lord Birkenhead (*Famous Trials of History*, p. 87) asserts that these chairmen, "scenting further employment," had gone on their own initiative to the upper end of the square. This is not according to the testimony given on the trial.

DUEL IN LEICESTER FIELDS

men were holding up a third; according to the chairmen, these were Captains Dockwra and James with Coote.[1] The first two were crying out: "Dear Coote! dear Coote!" It proved impossible to place Coote in the chair, which, in the attempt, was finally broken.[2] It would seem that Coote expired while the endeavor to put him in the conveyance was being made.[3] The two gentlemen at last gave up their attempt to place the body in the chair and went away, leaving it with the chairmen. These —

[1] Not James and Dockwra with French, as Lord Birkenhead reports (*op. cit.*, p. 87). It was said by Browne, when testifying on Lord Mohun's trial, that he had heard that the two gentlemen supporting Coote were French and James; they were positively not Lords Warwick and Mohun. But, as French was himself seriously wounded, it seems more likely that Dockwra was assisting James in caring for the dying man than that French was James's companion. See Howell, *op. cit.*, xiii, cols. 1041–1042. French hailed a chair at the corner of the Fields, and reached the Bagnio first (see *infra*, pp. 87–88).

[2] Lord Warwick offered to pay any damage to the chair though it were a hundred pounds; nevertheless the chairmen had at the time of his trial received no compensation for their loss. Howell, *op. cit.*, cols. xiii, 968, 1041, 1043. Browne's evidence on Lords Warwick's and Mohun's trials.

[3] *Ibid.*, col. 968. Browne testified that, while the two gentlemen were supporting Coote, "he gave himself a spring from them" — probably a death agony. The chairmen thought Coote dead when they were trying to force him into the chair. Charles Hatton, writing to Lord Hatton, said that Coote ". . . before he could be carryed to a surgeoons, he dyed in ye chair." *Hatton Correspondence*, ii, 235.

86   A NOBLE RAKE

Browne and Crippes — spied the watch, to whom they reported the affair and its consequences, but the guardians of the peace refused to interfere, alleging the spot to be out of their ward. A surgeon was then called, who pronounced Coote to be dead.[1] The proper watch, appearing, took charge of the corpse and the chairmen. The body was carried to the Roundhouse in St. Martin's Lane, where it was identified in the morning by Stephen Turner, Captain Coote's man.[2]

Coote had received two wounds, each mortal:

> One on the breast near the collar bone, running downwards very deep, [of which] the orifice was about the length of half an inch, and about the depth of five inches; [the other] was on his left side too, near unto the short ribs, under the last rib; which was about the length of an inch, and of the depth of six inches, and it run through the diaphragma.

It was impossible to tell whether both wounds were made by the same sword or not.[3]

[1] Howell, *op. cit.*, xiii, col. 971, evidence of Crippes on Lord Warwick's trial.

[2] *Ibid.*, col. 994, testimony of Stephen Turner on Lord Warwick's trial. Lord Birkenhead's account of the events after the death of Coote is inaccurate in regard to the part taken by the watch (*op. cit.*, p. 87).

[3] Howell, *op. cit.*, xiii, col. 992, testimony of William Salmon, surgeon, at Lord Warwick's trial. From the questions asked Salmon on the trials of both Lord Warwick and Lord Mohun — especially on that of the former — there would

Robert Applegate and Peter Catro, who had carried Lord Mohun to Leicester Fields, also responded to the call for chairs. They refused to lift their conveyance over the railings into the square, when Lord Warwick ordered them to do so,[1] and then went to the corner of the Fields, where French hailed them. Saying he was a dead man, he ordered them to bear him quickly to the Bagnio in Long Acre. Either immediately upon entering the chair, or as they reached the end of Newport Street, French desired the men to open the chair and to pull off his clothes; but they refused, and kept on to Long Acre. When they reached the Bagnio, French was so weak that he fell on his knees after getting out of the chair.[2] Lord Warwick had secured the

appear to have been a thought on the Attorney General's part of proving that in the darkness and confusion Captain Coote was wounded, not only by an adversary, but by a friend as well. Sir John Hawles, the Solicitor General, summing up against Lord Warwick, indeed attempted to argue that he had engaged with Coote and had slain him. Howell, *op. cit.*, xiii, cols. 992–994, and see col. 1052.

[1] Evidently Applegate and Catro had appeared near the spot of the duel before Browne and Crippes, but being less accommodating than the latter, on seeing the circumstances had started away again.

[2] *Ibid.*, cols. 975, 977, testimony of Applegate and Catro on Lord Warwick's trial; *Ibid.*, cols. 1047, 1049, evidence of the same on Lord Mohun's trial. Their picking up French at the corner of the Fields after leaving the spot of the duel proves that their fare could not have been one of the two who were caring for Coote.

chair in which he had left Locket's, and, being wounded in the hand, had ordered himself, like French, to be carried to the Bagnio. Arriving immediately after French, he had the men arouse the house, and when he had borrowed a handkerchief from them to bind up his injured hand, he, with French, entered.[1]

The proprietor of the Bagnio, Henry Amy, a surgeon, being called up, — it was now about two o'clock in the morning, — dressed French's wound and the Earl's, which was near the first joint of his forefinger. Lord Warwick directed that if anyone came asking for him it should be said that he was not there; and he also gave instructions that French should be treated as his particular friend. In about half an hour after the arrival of Warwick and French, Captains James and Dockwra knocked at the door of the Bagnio. Upon learning their identity, Lord Warwick consented to their admittance.[2] A half an hour or so later, the Earl, James, and Dockwra left the Bagnio together, the first, as they were departing, again recommending French as his especial friend. French went away from the

[1] Howell, *op. cit.*, p. 87, cols. 975, 977, testimony of Applegate and Catro; cf. *Ibid.*, cols. 972, 973-974, evidence of James Crattle and John Gibson on the trial of Lord Warwick.

[2] *Ibid.*, cols. 987, 986, testimony of Henry Amy, and of his servant, Mrs. Goodall, on Lord Warwick's trial.

DUEL IN LEICESTER FIELDS 89

Bagnio at about one o'clock on the afternoon of Sunday, October 30.[1]

Early in the same morning, Lord Warwick with his two companions appeared at the Ship and Castle Tavern in Cornhill, where Captain Loftus Duckenfield [2] learned from them a few particulars of the duel. French, of course, had fought with Coote, and Lord Warwick with James, "as they believed." [3] They discussed going into the country,[4] and afterwards separating. Possibly the Earl of Warwick escaped to France to remain until it suited him to give himself up for trial.[5]

[1] Howell, *op. cit.*, p. 87, col. 983, testimony of Henry Pomfret, servant to Mr. Amy, on Lord Warwick's trial.

[2] Loftus Duckenfield was probably a son or grandson of Colonel William Duckenfield, and his wife Elenor, daughter of Sir Dudley Loftus, of Killyan, County Meath, and a relative of the Viscounts Lisburne. Lodge, *Peerage of Ireland*, vii, 246 ff. Loftus Duckenfield was first commissioned as captain in the late Lord Lisburne's Regiment of Foot, January 1, 1692 (N. S.). He became a captain in Sir R. Temple's Regiment, March 10, 1702; and was promoted major, October 25, 1704. Dalton, *Army Lists*, iii, 270; v, 107, 108.

[3] This clause is, perhaps, significant in view of the earlier-noticed inquiry, on Lord Warwick's trial, as to whether Captain Coote's two wounds came from the same sword or not, and the hypothesis that he and Lord Warwick had fought.

[4] Howell, *op. cit.*, xiii, col. 990, testimony of Captain Duckenfield on the Earl of Warwick's trial.

[5] *Ibid.*, col. 1002, testimony of Colonel Whiteman [Wightman] on Lord Warwick's trial.

French surrendered himself on or about November 25,[1] and, with Dockwra and James, who had also given themselves up,[2] was tried at the Old Bailey, on January 14, 1698/9. All three were found guilty of manslaughter.[3] French was pardoned by King William on June 28, 1699.[4] Probably neither James nor Dockwra suffered more inconvenience from his conviction than did French. We hear nothing more of the two soldiers until the War of the Spanish Succession.[5]

The reader will, no doubt, have been struck by a curious fact in the preceding account of the duel in the darkness of Leicester Square, and of the events following. By no one was Lord Mohun seen that night after he walked away in the obscurity from his chair. He was not mentioned as participating in the fighting; indeed, on his trial he asserted that, on account of his injured finger, he could not have acted as a second.[6] No one saw him about Coote's body after the duel. It is, perhaps, not improbable

[1] Luttrell, *op. cit.*, iv, 455; Luttrell adds: "It's thought the rest will doe the like."

[2] James and Dockwra must have surrendered at nearly the same time as French, since the trial of all three was set first, it would seem, for December 12, 1698, and was postponed. *Ibid.*, iv, 461.

[3] *Ibid.*, iv, 472.   [4] *Ibid.*, p. 532.

[5] See *supra*, p. 78, n. 4, p. 79, n. 1.

[6] Howell, *op. cit.*, xiii, col. 1055. Lord Mohun's speech in his own defence on his trial.

DUEL IN LEICESTER FIELDS

that, upon seeing Coote fall, being aware that he had no very savory reputation, and desiring to avoid, if possible, unpleasant complications for himself, Lord Mohun withdrew quietly from the scene, and made his way homeward. Upon his trial, Mohun sought to give the impression that he had gone from Leicester Square to his lodgings, apparently without witnessing the fighting.[1] Of this, however, one is a trifle incredulous.[2]

Certain it is, in any case, that Mohun, like the Earl of Warwick, hid himself from pursuit very effectually, and probably for the same reason, until there seemed an opportunity for a speedy trial, when the King was in England, and when Parliament was sitting.[3] Be that as it may, it was not until March 22, 1698/9, over three weeks after Lord Warwick had yielded himself,[4] that Lord

[1] Howell, *op. cit.*, cols. 1053–1055.

[2] Lord Birkenhead is similarly incredulous as to Mohun's not being present at the duel (*op. cit.*, p. 88); yet I cannot share his certainty that Mohun participated in the fray, with his wounded hand. Although Lord Birkenhead mentions the wound, he seems to overlook the fact that it was received when Mohun was parting the quarrellers at Locket's.

[3] Howell, *op. cit.*, xiii, col. 1002, evidence of Colonel Whiteman [Wightman] on Lord Warwick's trial.

[4] The Earl of Warwick surrendered himself on February 27, 1698/9. He was put that day in the custody of the Usher of the Black Rod, and, on the next, was sent to the Tower to await his trial. *Journals of the House of Lords*, xvi, 390.

92 A NOBLE RAKE

Mohun gave himself up.[1] One wonders whether, after all, it was Lord Mohun's skill in hiding himself or a lack of sharpness in the search for him that preserved him so long from arrest, since it appeared at his trial that several days after Captain Coote's death he had been at his lodgings and had there entertained a visitor.[2] Previously he had had surgical attention for his injured finger.

After some delay,[3] the trial of the Earl of Warwick[4] took place on March 28, 1699, before the House of Lords, sitting in Westminster Hall, as a High Court of Justice.[5] Lord Chancellor Somers presided as Lord High Steward.[6] For the Crown appeared the Attorney General, Sir Thomas Trevor, the Solicitor General, Sir John Hawles, and Serjeant Wright.[7] Lord Warwick's counsel was Sir

---

[1] *Journals of the House of Lords*, xvi, 411. On March 20, Mohun had petitioned the Peers to be tried on the indictment against him for Coote's death.

[2] Howell, *op. cit.*, xiii, col. 1053, testimony of an unnamed witness on Lord Mohun's trial.

[3] It took Sir Christopher Wren three weeks to prepare Westminster Hall for the trial. *Journals of the House of Lords*, xix, 60.

[4] The Peers had granted Lord Warwick's petition that he be tried separately, and not with Lord Mohun. *Hist. MSS. Comm. Reports, House of Lords MSS.*, N. s., iii, 360.

[5] *Journals of the House of Lords*, xvi, 422-425.

[6] *Ibid.*, pp. 422-423; *Hist. MSS. Comm. Reports, House of Lords MSS.*, N. s., iii, 360.

[7] Howell, *op. cit.*, xiii, cols. 939 ff.

JOHN, FIRST LORD SOMERS OF EVESHAM

DUEL IN LEICESTER FIELDS 93

Thomas Powis.[1] Among the spectators were the King, Princess Anne, Prince George, the Duke of Gloucester, and the French Ambassador.[2] The hearing continued until about ten o'clock at night. Lord Warwick was found not guilty of murder, but was convicted of manslaughter, the vote in both cases being unanimous. The Earl pleaded his clergy, under the statute of Edward VI, and was freed, with no more severe punishment than a gentle reprimand from Lord Somers.[3]

That Lord Warwick would be acquitted on the charge of murder must have been expected early in the proceedings. The case against him was weak: the effort by the Solicitor General, Sir John Hawles, to show that it was the Earl who had fought with Coote and killed him was foredoomed to failure. None of the witnesses for the Crown — the drawer at Locket's, the chairmen, and the household of the Bagnio — had seen the actual duel. The evidence all tended to show that, after failing as a peacemaker, Warwick participated in the fighting as Coote's second. Moreover, since French, who had

[1] *Journals of the House of Lords*, xvi, 412. Curiously, Lord Somers, Trevor, Powis, and Hawles had all been concerned in Lord Mohun's trial of six years before. See *supra*, p. 43.

[2] Luttrell, *op. cit.*, iv, 499.

[3] *Hist. MSS. Comm. Reports*, *House of Lords MSS.*, N. S., iii, 361.

actually slain Coote, had been found guilty only of manslaughter, it could hardly be expected that an opposing second, who was a peer, would be convicted of murder.

Lord Warwick attempted to call French as a witness, but was not permitted to do so. He produced a number of officers who testified to the close friendship between himself and Coote. Among these were several who attained distinction in future years, such as Colonel Andrew Blisset [Bisset],[1] Colonel James Stanhope,[2] and Colonel Joseph Whiteman [Wightman].[3]

[1] Andrew Bisset was, in 1699, a captain in the Coldstream Guards, ranking as lieutenant colonel. He died in 1742, a lieutenant general, and was buried in Westminster Abbey. Dalton, *Army Lists*, ii, 159; iv, 173. Bisset was a friend of Steele, who in the last number of the *Tatler* says of him: "I hope major-general Davenport, brigadier Bisset, and my Lord Forbes, will accept of my thanks for their frequent good offices, in proposing their readiness to partake any danger that should befall me in so just an undertaking, as the endeavour to banish fraud and cosenage from the presence and conversation of gentlemen." No. 271, January 2, 1710/11.

[2] James Stanhope in 1699 was a captain in the First Foot Guards, ranking as lieutenant colonel. He won fame as commander-in-chief in Spain, 1708–10, and died, after conspicuous service as a statesman under George I, as Earl Stanhope of Mahon, in 1721. Dalton, *op. cit.*, iii, 381, n. 1.

[3] Joseph Wightman was also a captain in the First Foot Guards, ranking as lieutenant colonel, in 1699. He served as commander-in-chief in Scotland in 1712, and fought at

DUEL IN LEICESTER FIELDS

Another of Lord Warwick's witnesses who testified to the friendship between him and Coote was Ensign Henry Disney of the First Foot Guards, who, as "Duke" Disney, was for years a friend of Swift, Pope, and Gay.[1]

On the following day, March 29, Lord Mohun appeared before the House of Lords for his trial, his counsel being Mr. William Atwood.[2] His defence was that he had striven to accommodate matters between Coote and French, and had followed the others to Leicester Square only in the hope of making peace. He had not acted as a second, he said, because of the injury to his hand sustained earlier in the night, while attempting to part the quarrellers at Locket's, and suggested that he had gone to

Sheriffmuir in 1715. He is said to have died after 1745. *Ibid.*, iii, 137, n. 18.

[1] Henry Desaulnois, of a family of French Protestant refugees, who anglicized his name to Disney, was commissioned ensign in the First Foot Guards, March 1, 1694, and lieutenant, February 15, 1703. He served as aide de camp at Blenheim; some time before the battle he had received a captaincy in Prince George of Denmark's Regiment of Foot. He became captain and lieutenant colonel in the First Foot Guards, March 11, 1708; colonel of a regiment of foot, October 23, 1710, serving in 1711 on the expedition to Canada. He died December 25, 1731, and was buried in Westminster Abbey. Dalton, *Army Lists*, iii, 362; *The Blenheim Bounty Roll*, p. 6, n. 34. For references to him in Swift's circle, see Swift's *Correspondence*, ed. by Ball, ii, 235; iii, 145, 153, 283.

[2] *Journals of the House of Lords*, xvi, 418.

his lodgings directly from the point at which he had left his chair.[1]

As the prosecution could not disprove the points of Mohun's defence, it is not surprising that the Lords voted unanimously, eighty-seven answering to their names, to acquit him of the charges both of murder and manslaughter.[2] When the Lord High Steward had pronounced him free, Mohun addressed the Peers, thanking them for their verdict, and promising so to conduct himself thereafter as to avoid giving them "any trouble of this nature for the future."[3]

---

[1] Howell, *op. cit.*, xiii, cols, 1053–1055, Lord Mohun's defence of himself on his trial. This passage has been commented upon, *supra*, p. 91.

[2] Lord Birkenhead does not agree with the verdict of the Peers regarding Mohun's guilt, saying that "he went to a murderous fight voluntarily and took part in it." *Op. cit.*, p. 88. In view of Mohun's wound, received earlier in the night, and in view of the fact that no evidence implicated him in the fighting in Leicester Fields, it is difficult to see how the former Lord Chancellor arrived at this conclusion.

[3] Howell, *op. cit.*, xiii, col. 1060; Luttrell, *op. cit.*, iv, 500; *Journals of the House of Lords*, xvi, 427; *Hist. MSS. Comm. Reports, House of Lords MSS.*, N. s., iii, 360 ff. Lord Birkenhead comments on Mohun's having "learned a lesson and profited thereby" (*loc. cit.*), apparently forgetting the circumstances of Mohun's death.

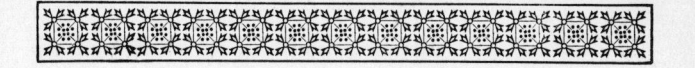

VI

THE DEATH OF LORD CASTLEWOOD

IT is quite clear from the preceding pages that for his account of Lord Castlewood's fatal duel with Lord Mohun, Thackeray followed the outlines of the affair in which Richard Coote lost his life. There can be no doubt either that Thackeray's knowledge of the historical duel came from the printed reports of the trials of Lords Warwick and Mohun for the murder of Captain Coote, that of the former probably being the chief source, as the fuller, and as giving details lacking in the more perfunctory presentation of the case against Lord Mohun. Some hints, too, came undoubtedly from material read by Thackeray [1] in preparation for his

---

[1] "Lewis Melville" says: "Diligent reading of eighteenth century memoirs was necessary for 'Esmond,' and Eyre Crowe, who from April 1851 was Thackeray's secretary and amanuensis, has related how the author, with him in attendance, spent much time in the British Museum Library, where in a room allotted to him for the purpose by Panizzi, he dictated the General Webb and Marlborough and Cadogan incidents. More of the book was written at the Athenæum

account of Mohun's last appearance in the novel — in his duel with the Duke of Hamilton.[1]

But it is only in their general outlines that Thackeray's Castlewood-Mohun duel and the actual Coote-French affair resemble each other. Neither in the circumstances of the duel in *Esmond*, nor in certain other particulars, has the novelist sought for, or attained, historical accuracy. To call attention to these discrepancies and to note how Thackeray turns fact into fiction, while preserving the aspect of verity, is the office of this chapter.[2]

Club, where one of the side rooms off the large library was placed at his disposal." *William Makepeace Thackeray; a Biography*, i, 336.

[1] A passage quoted from one of the pamphlets which Thackeray pretty surely had read occurs, *supra*, p. 13.

[2] It should be observed that the historians, biographers, and others who have mentioned it have not always given correctly the story of the Coote-French duel. Cobbett tells us that the fighting occurred in Lincoln's Inn Fields (*Parliamentary History*, v, col. 1197), having, no doubt, acquired this misinformation from *The History and Proceedings of the House of Lords*, ii, 1, n. C. Hatton, in his letter of November 1, 1694, to Lord Hatton, substitutes for Captain James, "one Tully," as a participant (*Hatton Correspondence*, ii, 235). The account of Mohun's life in a pamphlet several times quoted tells us that "upon a very slight occasion he [Mohun] Quarrel'd with one Captain Coot (a very Civil Gentleman) and his Lordship Stabb'd him throw the Back, as he was going into a Chair at *Chairing-Cross*, for which he Dy'd presently, of which his Lordship got clear" (*The Whole Lives, Characters, Actions, and Fall of D. Hamilton and Lord Mohun*). Chancellor informs the reader that "Mohun fought

DEATH OF LORD CASTLEWOOD

In the first place, the Coote-French quarrel was merely the culmination of a night of drinking — a common drunken falling-out, ending in a duel and wounds and death. On the other hand, the meeting of Lords Castlewood and Mohun had been expected for some time by the principals, who had both made preparations for it. They had so arranged their public quarrel that there should be no suspicion of its real cause. That Thackeray's duel took place on the night of Tuesday, October 12, 1700, and its original in the morning of Sunday, October 30, 1698, is a matter of no significance. The change of date doubtless resulted from Thackeray's desire to make the interval between Esmond's release from prison and his setting out on the Cadiz expedition as short as possible.

The meeting of the principals and their friends in *Esmond* at the Duke's Theatre, or "the theatre in

---

with Captain Coote and killed him" (*The London of Thackeray*, p. 30). Thus, one may expect that another Mohun legend, like that making him Mountford's slayer, is in the process of formation, and very shortly the man who sought to prevent a murder will be generally named as the murderer. Less serious is the error of T. C. and W. Snow, who mention the fact that Warwick and Mohun had been concerned in the Coote-French duel, but say that both were acquitted on their trials (*Esmond*, p. 494). These editors do not, however, notice that Thackeray utilized the historical duel in his novel.

Duke Street," as it is called once, is unhistorical.[1] In 1700, Mrs. Bracegirdle had been for five years with the players at the theatre in Little Lincoln's Inn Fields.[2] She is not known to have played in Wycherley's comedy of *Love in a Wood*.[3] There is, further, no "breeches part" in that play. It appears also that *Love in a Wood* had not been presented for years before 1700, and was not revived until many years later.[4] The notion of a meeting at the playhouse was derived by Thackeray probably from one of three possible sources. Lord

[1] For one thing, the theatre built by the Duke's Company, in 1671, stood in Salisbury Court, Fleet Street. From its situation on ground once belonging to the garden of the Earl of Dorset, it was generally called the Theatre in Dorset Garden. After 1682, when the King's and Duke's companies united and moved to the Theatre Royal in Drury Lane, the Duke's Theatre was used only occasionally when elaborate spectacles were offered. Lowe, *Thomas Betterton*, pp. 111, 127. At the time of Dryden's funeral, prize fighters were performing at the Duke's Theatre. Ned Ward, *The London Spy*, pt. xviii, p. 428. For other mention of this playhouse and its surroundings, see *Ibid.*, pt. vii, p. 154–155, pt. xviii, p. 432.

[2] This stood in Portugal Street opposite the end of Carey Street, where the museum of the Royal College of Surgeons is now situated. Lowe, *op. cit.*, pp. 148–149.

[3] See Genest's incomplete list of Mrs. Bracegirdle's parts, in *Stage*, ii, 379–380.

[4] *Love in a Wood* was revived at Drury Lane, August 15, 1718, being advertised as not acted for thirty years. *Ibid.*, ii, 622. Cf. Melville, *Some Aspects of Thackeray*, pp. 187–188; *Life of Thackeray*, i, 339–340.

DEATH OF LORD CASTLEWOOD 101

Mohun and Richard Hill, as we have seen,[1] were at the playhouse in Drury Lane on the night of Mountford's murder. Mohun and General Maccartney went to the play together on the night of November 14, 1712 — that preceding the morning of Mohun's last duel.[2] In one of the many pamphlets called forth by the deaths of the Duke of Hamilton and Lord Mohun, it is stated (wrongly) that the two met at the theatre on the night before their duel, "and there they say the Challenge was given."[3]

Of the participants in the historical duel only Mohun and Warwick are taken into the novel; and, of course, in fact, these two were merely Coote's seconds, Mohun probably not engaging at all. Maccartney was not concerned in any way with Coote's death.[4] We find in the novel, roughly speaking, Lord Castlewood playing Coote's part;

[1] *Supra*, pp. 26–27.

[2] *Tryal of John Hamilton*, London, 1712, testimony of Rice Williams, Lord Mohun's footman.

[3] *The Lives and Characters of James Duke Hamilton and Brandon . . . And Charles Lord Mohun. . . .* London: Printed by J. Read near Fleetstreet.

[4] General Maccartney, who figured in the Mohun-Hamilton duel as Mohun's second and as such is again mentioned in *Esmond*, is substituted for one of the figures in the Coote-French affair in the interest, doubtless, of economy of characters, as well as to assist in establishing the point, hinted at, but not asserted, that he was a kind of henchman of Lord Mohun.

Captain Westbury, Mohun's; Esmond, Warwick's; Lord Mohun, French's; Lord Warwick, Dockwra's; and Macartney, James's. And in this changing about there are certain twists in the parts filled by the various characters so that the shifts of identity are by no means simple.

The mock quarrel in *Esmond* arises over cards; the genuine quarrel between Coote and French started over some offensive jest, or "reflection," of the former. Castlewood insults Mohun before the servants of the tavern; Coote began his quarrel with French when only their four companions were present. In both the novel and in the actual occurrence, the parties leave Locket's in chairs. In the former, however, their pretended destination is Lord Mohun's house in Bow Street; their purpose, to drink there to their reconciliation. Actually, Lord Warwick's invitation to his friends to go to his house to drink was unheeded by the quarrelsome among them, and Lord Mohun's similar desires were also unattended by a favorable reception. The duelists of history pretty clearly were bound for Leicester Fields to fight, and not for Lord Mohun's lodgings in Westminster.[1] No doubt Lord Castlewood's re-

[1] If this had not been the cause, the two groups would hardly have found their respective ways to a convenient fighting ground, there to meet by accident in the darkness.

DEATH OF LORD CASTLEWOOD 103

mark to the barwoman [1] at the Grayhound, as the party left, that the dispute was made up, comes from Captain James's words to Cawthorne, the drawer, regarding the settlement of the quarrel between Coote and French.[2]

Both in fact and in fiction the duelists halt their chairs in Leicester Square.[3] In *Esmond*, however, the chairmen light their pipes and watch the fighting, at the same time guarding the gates to the square. Actually, as we have seen, the chairs were dismissed and three were borne off home; the remaining three were halted near the end of the square opposite the duelists, while the chairmen were lighting their pipes. This operation seems so to have delayed their departure that the men heard the calls for them after Mr. French and Captain Coote had been wounded. In truth, after having reluctantly hoisted their chairs [4] over the rails into the

---

[1] There is no mention, in the accounts of Lord Warwick's or Lord Mohun's trial, of a barmaid at Locket's. She would seem to be an addition by the novelist.

[2] *Supra*, p. 81.

[3] French, Dockwra, and James were set down at the Standard; Lords Warwick and Mohun and Coote left their chairs at the entrance into Green Street, opposite the tavern. Howell, *op. cit.*, xiii, cols. 967 ff., and 1039 ff., the evidence given by the several chairmen on Lords Warwick's and Mohun's trials.

[4] It will be remembered that the first pair of chairmen to reach the spot of the Coote-French duel refused to lift their

square, Browne and Crippes were unable to get the body of Captain Coote into their vehicle, and were forced to leave it on the ground until they had summoned a surgeon and — presumably — the watch. In the novel, on the other hand, Lord Castlewood is borne away without difficulty to the Bagnio. Coote, it should be noted, died on the field without surgical attention, whereas Lord Castlewood survives perhaps five or six hours.[1]

Thackeray's unfortunate peer is taken to the Bagnio in Long Acre, kept by "one Mr. Aimes, a surgeon,"[2] and it is there that he expires. It will be recalled that Lord Warwick and Mr. French, both of whom were wounded, were carried to the Bagnio, where the proprietor, Mr. Amy, a surgeon, dressed their hurts. There they were joined later by Captains James and Dockwra. It might be noted that Mr. Amy was one of the surgeons called to attend the Duke of Hamilton after his duel with Lord Mohun in 1712;[3] he was among the witnesses at the trial of Colonel John Hamilton, the Duke's second.[4] It was at the Bagnio, too, that General

---

conveyance over the rails into the square, and started away (*supra*, p. 87).

[1] The duel occurred at midnight, according to Esmond. Lord Castlewood seems to have died at about six in the morning. *Esmond*, bk. I, chap. 14.

[2] *Ibid.* [3] *Tryal of John Hamilton.* [4] *Ibid.*

DEATH OF LORD CASTLEWOOD

Maccartney and Lord Mohun spent the night before the latter's meeting with the Duke.[1] Esmond later mentions Mr. Amy as attending Queen Anne in her fatal illness.[2]

Lord Mohun escapes unhurt in the novel, although Mr. French was wounded in the historical duel, and although the real Lord Mohun was hurt in the hand before the party had left Locket's. Lord Warwick was wounded by his opponent, Colonel Westbury, according to Thackeray. Actually, Lord Warwick was hurt in the right hand. From this circumstance, no doubt, arose Henry Esmond's wounded right hand. Though in the novel only Lord Castlewood and Esmond go to the Bagnio, in truth all the participants in the original duel, save only Lord Mohun and the unfortunate Captain Coote, eventually arrived there.

The reply of Lord Castlewood to Lord Mohun's question to him after the former's fall, "I believe I'm a dead man," can be paralleled by French's like remark to the chairmen who carried him from Leicester Fields to Long Acre.[3] Lord Mohun's generally pacific attitude during the scenes in *Esmond*

---

[1] *Tryal of John Hamilton*, testimony of Richard Cook, servant at the Bagnio.

[2] *Esmond*, bk. III, chap. ii.

[3] Howell, *op. cit.*, xiii, col. 1047, testimony of Robert Applegate on Lord Mohun's trial.

(for Lord Castlewood virtually drives him into fighting) and his regrets after Castlewood has fallen owe something to the vigorous but ineffectual efforts made by him in fact to prevent the quarrel between Coote and French from having serious consequences. There is, of course, a difference between the real situation, where Lord Mohun was friend of all the party, and attempted to act as such, and that in the novel, where, as the villainous would-be seducer of his friend's wife, he is cast as a principal in the quarrel.

After Lord Castlewood's death, Esmond goes to the Gatehouse [1] and gives himself up. In truth, it seems to have been nearly a month before any of the participants in the original affair surrendered. After he has recovered from the effects of the hemorrhage which has resulted from his agitation at Lady Castlewood's visit to him, Esmond is told by the prison-keeper's wife of Lord Castlewood's funeral.[2] She informs him, too, of Lords Mohun and Warwick[3] being in hiding, and of Lady Castlewood's

---

[1] T. C. and W. Snow suggest that, inasmuch as Esmond does not mention his removal from the Gatehouse in Westminster to Newgate, where he certainly later is confined, Newgate, instead of the Gatehouse, was meant here by Thackeray (*op. cit.*, p. 496). There seems to be no very sound reason, however, for this theory.

[2] *Esmond*, bk. II, chap. 1.

[3] Warwick, she says, is ready to take his trial.

DEATH OF LORD CASTLEWOOD

visit with her two children to the King at Kensington, to demand justice upon the slayer of her husband.

The two lords are brought to trial. According to Esmond, Lord Warwick on being tried by the House of Lords, Lord Somers presiding, is found not guilty. On the other hand, Lord Mohun, when tried, is found guilty of manslaughter, but, on pleading his clergy, is released. Here Thackeray, in accordance with the demands of his plot, has given Lord Warwick the fortune of Lord Mohun, and has transferred to Lord Mohun the result of the Earl's trial.

Esmond, Westbury, and Macartney, in the novel, are tried at Newgate, are found guilty of manslaughter, — like French, Dockwra, and James, — plead their clergy, and are sentenced to a year's imprisonment, or during the King's pleasure. As was not the case with French, at any rate, Esmond and his companions seem to have lain their year in prison. Part of Esmond's time is spent in hearing the details of Lady Castlewood's pursuit of vengeance.[1] Her vigor in prosecuting her revenge

---

[1] Captain Richard Steele "of Lucas's Fusileers and secretary to my Lord Cutts," serves Esmond as ambassador to Lady Castlewood. Steele was not, however, commissioned captain in Lord Lucas's Regiment of Foot until March 10, 1702. Previously he had been ensign to Lord Cutts's own company of the Coldstream Guards. See Dalton, *Army Lists*, iv, 173 n.; v, 100. Steele became secretary to Lord Cutts in

upon Lord Mohun may have some connection with the pertinacity with which Mrs. Mountford sought to have him punished for his part in the death of her husband.[1]

1696, and perhaps acted in this capacity until Lord Cutts went to Ireland as Commander-in-chief in the earlier part of 1705. By July of that year Steele and Cutts had fallen out over money affairs (Aitken, *Life of Steele*, i, 134 ff.), and do not appear to have made matters up before the general's death in 1707. Steele was not appointed gentleman usher to Prince George of Denmark until August, 1706 (Luttrell, *A Brief Relation of State Affairs*, vi, 17, under August 15, 1706; Aitken, *op. cit.*, i, 150). This position was vacated at the Prince's death, October 28, 1708 (Aitken, *op. cit.*, i, 225). Steele's first visit to the Lady Castlewood on Esmond's behalf, Thackeray indicates as subsequent to the publication of *The Christian Hero*, April 15 to 17, 1701 (Aitken, *op. cit.*, i, 67). Indeed, on the night of the duel (October 12, 1700) Captain Westbury is represented as telling Esmond of Steele's commission in the Guards and of his having written *The Christian Hero*. It is known to Lady Castlewood that Steele is bringing out a "new" comedy. His earliest play, *The Funeral*, was first acted after October 9, 1701, and his next, *The Lying Lover*, was produced on December 2, 1702 (Aitken, *op. cit.*, i, 72, 91). Pretty certainly Thackeray's chronology would put Steele's visit to Lady Castlewood earlier than April, 1701. Steele's reminiscence of beating a drum "at the coffin" of his own father (*Esmond*, bk. II, chap. 2) is derived from the *Tatler*, No. 181, June 6, 1710. T. C. and W. Snow call attention to the fact that Steele, although introduced by Thackeray at Castlewood in 1691 as a trooper, really did not enter the army before 1694 (*op. cit.*, p. 560). They also note that Steele did not become a member of Prince George's household until 1706 (*Ibid.*), but overlook Thackeray's other deviations from history, and, as well, date *The Lying Lover* in 1704 (*Ibid.*, p. 519).

[1] *Supra*, pp. 45–46.

SIR RICHARD STEELE, KNT.

DEATH OF LORD CASTLEWOOD 109

Esmond is finally released, and, after a period of waiting, is commissioned ensign in Quin's Fusileers.[1] His entrance into the army dates from about February 15, 1701/2,[2] for his commission was "scarce three weeks old," when William III died, on March 8. In August, 1702, when Esmond has joined his regiment at Portsmouth, he learns that Lord Mohun is absent from England in attendance upon his wife's uncle and his colonel, the Earl of Macclesfield, who has gone as ambassador to the Elector of Hanover, with the insignia of the Garter and the new Queen's compliments to her heiress, the Electress Dowager Sophia.

Here Thackeray has placed the mission of Lord Macclesfield exactly a year after it really occurred.[3]

[1] This regiment must have been invented by Thackeray, since there is no mention of it in Dalton's *Army Lists*. Cf. T. C. and W. Snow, *op. cit.*, p. 502.

[2] Lord Mohun was commissioned colonel of the regiment of foot which he had raised, on February 12, 1702 (N. S.). Dalton, *Army Lists*, iv, 10. The imminent war with France was responsible for an expansion in the English military establishment at this time.

[3] In this part of *Esmond*, Thackeray's chronology is unusually confused. For example, while Henry is ill at the Gatehouse and before his trial, he receives a letter from the Dowager Viscountess in which a reference occurs to the Pretender, who just had been "proclaimed at St. Germains, King of Great Britain [*sic*], France, and Ireland" (bk. III, chap. 2). Lord Castlewood died October 13, 1700; certainly the commoners engaged in the affair were tried very shortly;

In fact, the Earl set out in July, 1701, for Hanover, attended by the Viscount Say and Sele, Lord Mohun, and Lord Tunbridge, son and heir to the Earl of Rochford, Sir Andrew Fountain, Captain Tyrrel,[1] the Reverend Doctor Sandys (Lord Maccles-

in any case Esmond obviously was not ill between ten and eleven months. The fact is that James II, the deposed King of England, died at St. Germains September 6, 1701 (O. S.), and immediately his son was proclaimed King of England at the gates of that palace. *D. N. B.*, xxix, 197, art., "James II," *Ibid.*, lxi, 320, art., "William III," both by Sir A. W. Ward; Haile, *Mary of Modena*, pp. 353-354; Brodrick, *Compleat History of the Late War*, p. xiv. This discrepancy is also noted by T. C. and W. Snow, *op. cit.*, p. 501. And the United Kingdom was not born until 1707.

[1] James Tyrrel, or Tyrrell, was a son of James Tyrrell, the historian, and probably a relative of the Sir Robert Tyrrell who was a bondsman of Lord Mohun in 1697 (*supra*, p. 55). James Tyrrel the younger was commissioned captain lieutenant in Lord Macclesfield's Regiment of Horse on February 16, 1694. He served in General Cadogan's Regiment of Horse during a part of the War of the Spanish Succession, and was brevetted major on January 1, 1707 (according to Dalton, *George I's Army*, i, 121, n., lieutenant colonel). He was appointed colonel of a regiment of foot in succession to Sir Roger Bradshaigh, on April 21, 1709. In 1713 he retired on half-pay, but in 1715 he returned to the service as colonel of a regiment of dragoons which he had raised. He continued in the army until his death in August, 1742, when he ranked as lieutenant general. In 1714 Tyrrel was appointed Groom of the Bedchamber to George I, and from 1722 to 1742 he was member of Parliament for Boroughbridge. See Dalton, *Army Lists*, iii, 354, n.; v, 232; vi, 248; Idem, *George I's Army*, i, 121, n.; ii, 336, 384, 429; *D. N. B.*, xix (ed. of 1909), 1369, art., "Tyrrell, James," by E. Irving Carlyle.

field's chaplain), King, the Herald, John Toland, and between thirty and forty other gentlemen. Of the whole party, about half, including Mohun and Toland, had come with the Earl from England; the others, including no doubt Lord Tunbridge, the son of a Dutch favorite of the King, had been picked up in the Netherlands as the party passed through.

The ambassador and his suite were met on the Hanoverian frontier by officials deputed by the Elector, and were escorted to the city of Hanover, where the Earl, with as many of his companions as could be accommodated, was lodged in one of the largest houses therein. The other Englishmen were placed in neighboring residences and maintained at the Elector's expense. Lord Macclesfield kept open house at Hanover for all the Englishmen passing through the city, as well as for those who had come with him. Orders had been given by the Elector that no Englishman should be charged for food or drink by any of his subjects, unless payment were offered. The guests were served tea and coffee every morning in their bed-chambers by the Elector's own servants. All manner of wines were as common as beer. No wonder that it was said, "It was a continu'd Feasting." [1]

[1] Toland, *An Account of the Courts of Prussia and Hanover* (ed. of 1714), p. 60.

The visitors were entertained with music, balls, and plays. They ate in turn at the Elector's table, and were the objects of much attention from the ministers of state. Coaches and chairs were at the disposal of all who desired them for excursions.

But some time was given to business. The Earl presented the Electress Dowager and the Elector with a copy of the Act of Succession, by which the English throne was secured to them and their heirs after the King and the Princess Anne. The Garter insignia were presented by King, the Herald, to the Elector, and Toland contributed his mite, which Luttrell describes as "a treatise lately wrote in relation to the succession, intituled, Anglia Libera, or the Limitation and Succession of the Crown of England explained and asserted." [1]

The Elector's not unnatural elation at the prospect of his promotion from a small German principality to a major kingdom did not exhaust itself with mere feasting and entertainment. He made a number of fine presents to the ambassador and his suite, including various oil portraits of the Electoral family for the enthusiastic Toland.[2]

On his return from Hanover, Lord Macclesfield went by way of Loo, where he reported to William III

[1] *A Brief Relation of State Affairs*, v, 67.
[2] Toland, *op. cit.*, pp. 60–65.

DEATH OF LORD CASTLEWOOD

upon his reception in Hanover, the account giving the King much satisfaction. Lord Mohun arrived in London on October 29,[1] probably at the same time as Lord Macclesfield, who, on October 30 or 31, seems to have given the lords justices an account of his mission.[2] The Earl survived his return only a few days, dying of a fever on November 5.[3]

---

[1] Luttrell, *op. cit.*, v, 105.   [2] *Ibid.*
[3] *Ibid.*, v, 106. Charles, second Earl of Macclesfield, was born at Paris about 1659, the son of the then Lord Gerard of Brandon, and his wife, Jeanne de Civelle. He was naturalized in 1676–77, by act of Parliament. At fourteen he was mobbed for attacking the porter of Bedlam Hospital, who had insulted him. At nineteen he boxed a page's ears in St. James's Park with such vigor as to break the boy's neck. He was concerned in the presentment by the Middlesex Grand Jury of James Duke of York as a Popish recusant. He was implicated in the Rye House Plot in 1683, but was acquitted. In 1685 he was rearrested in connection with Monmouth's rebellion, was again accused of complicity in the Rye House Plot, was tried for treason, and found guilty, but was reprieved, pardoned, and his attainder was reversed. Lord Brandon, as he then was, sat for Lancashire in Parliament, in 1679, 1680–81, and 1688–89–94. He succeeded his father as Earl of Macclesfield, January 7, 1693/4.

In June, 1683, Lord Brandon married Anne, daughter of Sir Richard Mason, but they separated in March, 1684/5, and never again lived together. After the countess had given birth to a daughter in 1695 and a son in 1696, the Earl sued for a divorce in the Court of Arches in 1697, and in the House of Lords later in that year.

It will be seen that Macclesfield, as a brawler, a fierce Whig, and an unhappily married man, was well suited to sympathize with his nephew by marriage. See *D. N. B.*, vii,

A NOBLE RAKE

Lord Mohun seems to have conducted himself with propriety while on this mission. Toland says:

> My Lord Viscount SEA and Seal, my Lord MOHUN, and my Lord TUNBRIDGE, were treated as became their Quality, and with particular Kindness and Confidence, as Persons that were sincerely devoted to the Family: and because when my Lord MOHUN was very young, and not capable to distinguish his Company, he had the misfortune to commit some Excesses, I am glad to be able to tell you . . . of my own Knowledge, that none of the Company was more generally acceptable, that none liv'd with greater Sobriety, nor deliver'd himself on all Occasions with better Judgment or in politer Language; and he still continues to convince the World of his Reformation, as he is like to prove an Ornament to the Upper-house of Parliament.[1]

Of the company in general, Toland says:

> . . . if any of 'em (as I know of none) did misbehave himself, it cou'd not well be otherwise among so many young People; and I defy the like number, unless they shou'd be pick'd on purpose, to carry themselves more decently.[2]

1096–1097, art., "Gerard, Charles, second Earl of Macclesfield," by J. M. Rigg; G. E. C., *Complete Peerage*, v, 192; Margaret Verney, *Memoirs of the Verney Family*, iv, 230–231; *Journals of the House of Lords*, xvi, *passim*.

[1] Toland, *An Account of the Courts of Prussia and Hanover* (ed. of 1714), pp. 63–64.

[2] *Ibid.*, p. 61. Toland writes thus of manners in general at Hanover: "The Court . . . is extremely polite, and even in Germany it is accounted the best both for Civility and Decorum. The Vice of Drinking (for which that Nation is so

DEATH OF LORD CASTLEWOOD

Years later it was said of Lord Mohun's conduct on Lord Macclesfield's mission that "He behaved himself so discreetly at the Court of *Hannover*, where he accompanied the late Earl of *Macclesfield* . . . that he left an excellent character behind him with that most Serene Elector, and the Princess *Sophia*, his Mother."[1] In any case, on March 13, 1702/3, Lord Mohun acted as proxy for the Elector at his installation as a Knight of the Garter.[2]

Thackeray has taken other liberties with fact in giving the status of his "comrades" in the "late misfortune." "Captain" Macartney, according to Esmond, was at Portsmouth also with his regiment of Fusiliers, bound for Spain under the Duke of Ormonde. In fact, however, Maccartney's commission as first lieutenant colonel of the Scots Foot Guards was renewed August 25, 1702.[3] Maccartney served with no regiment of fusiliers until 1716, when

much branded) is so far from reigning here, that tho no body is abridg'd of his pleasure in this respect, yet I never knew greater Sobriety, nor a more exact Government in a privat Family" (p. 53).

[1] *A True and Impartial Account of the Animosity, Quarrel and Duel, between the late Duke of Hamilton and the Lord Mohun* (London, Printed and Sold by A. Baldwin, 1712), p. 28. Note that this is the Whig *True and Impartial Account;* the Tory pamphlet with much the same title was printed by John Morphew.

[2] Luttrell, *op. cit.*, v, 276–277.

[3] Dalton, *Army Lists*, v, 219.

he was commissioned colonel of the Royal Scots Fusiliers.[1] He arrived in Spain only in 1706, with the rank of brigadier general, after three campaigns under Marlborough on the northern allied front, as colonel of a regiment of foot.[2]

As to the Earl of Warwick's whereabouts at the time of Esmond's sojourn at Portsmouth, one wonders whether Thackeray is indulging in a sly jest. For Lord Warwick who, Esmond says, had "returned home," had actually died a year earlier — on July 30, 1701![3]

[1] See *infra*, p. 257, Appendix B, Lieutenant General George Maccartney.

[2] Dalton, *op. cit.*, iii, 45, n. 13; v, 17, 224. Cf. *supra*, p. 72, n. 1.

[3] Luttrell, *op. cit,*, v, 76; cf. *supra*, p. 71, n. 4.

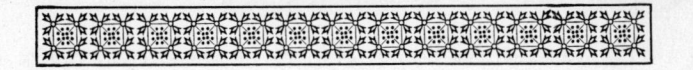

VII

COLONEL AND BRIGADIER

AFTER Esmond's embarkation on the Vigo expedition [1] in that apocryphal corps, Quin's Fusileers, and Lord Mohun's setting out with Lord Macclesfield on the latter's mission to Hanover,[2] we have only passing references to Mohun, or to his affairs, for many pages.[3] On Esmond's return from the Spanish campaign, certain of his friends propose to introduce him to Anne Bracegirdle, "about whom Harry's old adversary Mohun had drawn swords, a few years before my Lord and he fell out," [4] and for a short time Henry thinks himself in love with her.[5]

[1] In bk. II, chap. 3, Esmond joins his regiment at Portsmouth and leaves England in the month of August; but in chap. 5, the fleet and troopships sail on July 1, from Spithead, and, after delays at Portsmouth and Plymouth, are off Cape Finisterre on July 31. Actually the fleet sailed on July 12–13 (cf. T. C. and W. Snow, *Esmond*, p. 504).

[2] See *supra*, pp. 110–113, as to the actual date of Lord Macclesfield's embassy.

[3] Such as little Lord Castlewood's threats (bk. II, chap. 3), and the two following allusions to persons with whom Mohun had been concerned in one manner or another.

[4] See *supra*, pp. 23 ff., for an account of this event.

[5] *Esmond*, bk. II, chap. 5.

When, in the spring of 1706,[1] Frank, the young Lord Castlewood, comes to join his regiment on the Continent and meets Esmond at Bois-le-duc, he brings a "budget of news from home: ... how he had got the better of Mr. St. John, both over the bottle and with Mrs. Mountford, of the Haymarket Theatre (a veteran charmer of fifty, with whom the young scapegrace chose to fancy himself in love)."[2] Here Thackeray curiously and completely disregards historical accuracy. If Susannah Perceval was nineteen at the time of her marriage to William Mountford in 1686,[3] she could not have been fifty in 1706. But the fact is that she was not living in 1706, having died three years earlier in childbirth, while the Drury Lane Company, to which she belonged, was performing at Bath in the summer of 1703.[4] Early in 1694, probably, Mrs. Mountford had married John Verbruggen, a member of Betterton's company at Drury Lane.[5] She never played at the

[1] Although in their "Chronology," T. C. and W. Snow give correctly 1706 as the year of young Lord Castlewood's joining the army, yet in their note to p. 261, they give 1704 as the year of Castlewood's affair with Mrs. Mountford (*op. cit.*, p. 520). They note her death in 1703.

[2] *Esmond*, bk. II, chap. 11.

[3] J. Knight in *D. N. B.*, lviii, 215–217, art., "Verbruggen, Mrs. Susanna."

[4] *Ibid.*; see also Cibber, *Apology* (London, 1826), p. 174; Genest, *Stage*, ii, 277.

[5] Knight, *D. N. B.*, *loc. cit.*

COLONEL AND BRIGADIER 119

theatre in the Haymarket, which was opened on April 9, 1705, over a year subsequent to her death.[1]

It is not until after the capture of Lille by the Allies in 1708 [2] that Lord Mohun in person reënters Esmond's narrative. Mohun, Lord Castlewood, and Esmond meet in Lille at the officers' mess of Handyside's Regiment. The career of the first is thus brought down to date by Esmond:

[1] Genest, *op. cit.*, ii, 329. It is possible that Thackeray had confused mother and daughter. Mrs. Susannah Mountford, daughter of the actor and his wife, was on the stage by 1704, as she had a benefit at Lincoln's Inn Fields, June 26, of that year. Genest, *op. cit.*, ii, 310. Later she retired temporarily, as mistress of Lord Dursley, heir to the Earl of Berkeley. Mrs. Manley, *New Atalantis*, i, 22. This was, no doubt, between 1708 and 1712, when she appears not to have acted. Later, she lived with the actor Barton Booth, but broke with him in 1718 to follow a Mr. Minshull, who seems to have treated her badly. She eventually lost her mind and retired from the stage (Genest, *op. cit.*, ii, 658 ff.). The career of the daughter certainly would justify Thackeray's ascription of intrigues with her to Lord Castlewood and Henry St. John; but she, too, seems never to have acted at the Haymarket. Possibly Susannah Mountford's one-time protector was the Peter Minshull (or Minshall) who, with his sisters, was engaged in litigation with Lord Mohun in 1711 and 1712, and in 1713 and 1715, after the latter's death, with Lady Mohun (cf. *infra*, pp. 199–200).

[2] The siege of Lille began August 13, 1708. The city was surrendered November 23, and the citadel on December 11, of that year. See Maycock, *Marlborough's Campaigns*, pp. 115, 117, 127, 128, 130; and cf. Brodrick, *Compleat History of the Present War*, p. 270.

My Lord Mohun, who had a troop in Lord Macclesfield's regiment of the Horse Guards, rode this campaign with the Duke. He had sunk by this time to the very worst reputation; he had had another fatal duel in Spain; he had married and forsaken his wife; he was a gambler, a profligate, a debauchee. He joined just before Oudenarde; and, as Esmond feared, as soon as Frank Castlewood heard of his arrival, Frank was for seeking him out, and killing him. The wound my Lord had got at Oudenarde prevented their meeting, but that was nearly healed, and Mr. Esmond trembled daily lest any chance should bring his boy and this known assassin together. They met at the mess-table of Handyside's regiment at Lille; the officer commanding not knowing of the feud between the two noblemen.

Esmond had not seen the hateful handsome face of Mohun for nine years, since they had met on that fatal night in Leicester Field. It was degraded with crime and passion now; it wore the anxious look of a man who has three deaths, and who knows how many hidden shames, and lusts, and crimes on his conscience. He bowed with a sickly low bow, and slunk away when our host presented us round to one another. Frank Castlewood had not known him till then, so changed was he. He knew the boy well enough.[1]

In this passage Thackeray has, as usual, taken liberties with historical fact, but has preserved enough of the truth and has adhered closely enough to possibility to make his account of Lord Mohun's adventures at least plausible. As has been seen,[2] Lord Mohun had held a commission in the regiment

---

[1] *Esmond*, bk. II, chap. 15.   [2] See *supra*, p. 48.

COLONEL AND BRIGADIER

of his first baroness's uncle, the second Earl of Macclesfield. But Charles Earl of Macclesfield commanded, not a regiment of Horse Guards, but of ordinary cavalry,[1] and upon his death in 1701, the command had been given to Thomas Lord Windsor.[2] In 1702 Mohun had raised a regiment of foot of which, on February 12 of that year, he was appointed colonel.[3] This regiment was first stationed in Ireland, where it remained from its arrival in 1702 [4] to its departure thence for Spain in 1706.[5]

[1] Dalton, *Army Lists*, iii, 334, 354, etc. The first Lord Macclesfield, Charlotte Lady Mohun's grandfather, had commanded the guards of Charles II in the latter's progress to Whitehall, May 29, 1660, and had been commander of the Life Guards from 1660 to 1668, when he sold his commission for twelve thousand pounds to the Duke of Monmouth. Lord Macclesfield had also commanded the body-guard of the Prince of Orange in his advance from Torbay to London in 1688. *D. N. B.*, xxi, 215–216, art., "Gerard, Charles, first Earl of Macclesfield," by J. M. Rigg. That Thackeray quite deliberately gave Mohun a military rating which was not his is proved by the following entry in his MS. *Notebook for Henry Esmond* (now in the possession of the New York Public Library): "Lord Mohuns troop of horse in the E of Macclesfields regiment" (p. 5). T. C. and W. Snow find this mention of "Macclesfield's Regiment" inexplicable (*op. cit.*, p. 527). It may be accounted for, I believe, by the details noted above.

[2] Dalton, *op. cit.*, v, 232.   [3] *Ibid.*, iv, 10, 281.

[4] Luttrell says under date of August 4, 1702, that Mohun's Regiment was among those ordered to Ireland (*A Brief Relation of State Affairs*, v, 201). Dalton informs us that the regiment was sent to Ireland in 1704 (*Army Lists*, v, 265, n.). This, would appear to be an error, since Lord Mohun was reported in 1703 as proposing to join his regiment there.

[5] Dalton, *loc. cit.*

During the Irish service of his regiment, Mohun appears to have busied himself chiefly with such questions of promotion or cashiering as arose.[1] It may be that he visited Ireland in the summer of

[1] Letter of Lord Mohun to the Duke of Ormonde, December 3, 1704, asking that Captain Solomon Rapin (brother of the historian) be made major (*Hist. MSS. Comm. Reports*, N. S., *MSS. of the Marquess of Ormonde*, viii, 122); letter of the Same to the Same, December 14, 1704, asking that provision be made for the captain lieutenant (*Ibid.*, viii, 125); letter of the Same to the Same, from London, January 11, 1704/5, mentioning Captain Griffin May's "unfortunate accident" (perhaps a duel?) and the Duke's resolution to break him (May commanded the grenadier company), and requesting promotion again for his captain lieutenant, as well as for "Mr. Tucks" (Captain Thomas Tuck, Captain Edward Juckes, or Ensign George Juckes?), Ensign John Grosvenor, and Ensign Thomas Poole, respectively (*Ibid.*, viii, 132–133); letter of the Same to the Same, from London, January 31, 1704/5, thanking the Duke for his promotion of the captain lieutenant (*Ibid.*, viii, 137); letter of the Same to the Same, from London, March 6, 1704/5, again interceding for Captain May (*Ibid.*, viii, 143); letter of the Same to the Same, from London, April 24, 1705, pleading for the restoration of May's commission or the giving him the company of Captain Phillip Gery who had recently died (*Ibid.*, viii, 151). The dates of certain of the letters which are summarized above are slightly different in the lists of the documents in the Marquess of Ormonde's collection, as given in *Hist. MSS. Comm. Reports*, vii, pt. 2, 808–809. The Captain May mentioned above was perhaps the same Mr. May whom Swift charged the Earl of Wharton with recommending to the Duke of Ormonde as "a very honest gentleman," only to describe him on his withdrawal from the Duke's presence as "the greatest rogue in Christendom" ("A Short Character of Thomas Earl of Wharton," Swift's *Works*, ed. by Roscoe, i, 354).

1703.[1] The regiment seems to have been, on the whole, quite bad. In January, 1704/5, the Duke of Ormonde, Commander-in-Chief in Ireland, inspected Mohun's regiment, and, as a result of its bad condition, refused to send it to serve on the fleet, saying he "could not answer the sending them where there was like to be action." [2] At this time, too, according to the Duke, the colonel and his field officers were on bad terms.[3]

A number of its officers had served in the Earl of Denbigh's Dragoons, which was disbanded in 1697.[4] Among the more demonstrably disreputable officers was William Cecil, one of Mohun's ensigns, who had killed his landlady at Ryegate, because she would not accept a bad half-crown from him. Cecil had, consequently, been condemned to the gallows, but had been saved by a reprieve.[5] Captain Griffin May, whose reputation was perhaps generally unsavory,[6] appears, in 1704, to have been concerned in some scrape which resulted in his leaving the army.[7]

[1] Luttrell, *A Brief Relation of State Affairs*, v, 303.
[2] Letter of the Duke of Ormonde to the Lord Treasurer, dated February 5, 1704[/5], *Hist. MSS. Comm. Reports*, N. S., *MSS. of the Marquess of Ormonde*, vii, 777.
[3] *Ibid.*   [4] Dalton, *Army Lists*, iii, 360.
[5] *Ibid.*; cf. Luttrell, *op. cit.*, iii, 482, 505, 508. Cecil was commissioned Brevet Lieutenant Colonel in General Sybourg's Regiment of Foot, July 1, 1712 (Dalton, *loc. cit.*).
[6] See *supra*, p. 122, n. 1.
[7] Dalton, *Ibid.* May's name is not on Dalton's list of the

Captain Henry Harte, or Hartus,[1] died early in the year 1705/6, leaving the accounts of the regiment in great confusion; before, they had not been "in the best order in the world."[2] In the same year, Captain Charles Otway quarrelled with the agent for the regiment, and killed him.[3] In the late summer of 1707, an affair occurred at Yeovil between two of Mohun's officers which curiously parallels the colonel's own fate five years later. Lieutenant William Phillips and a Lieutenant "Shan"[4] fought, and both were killed.

Though it was said at one time that the regiment refused to embark for Spain,[5] yet it saw its active

commissioned officers of Lord Mohun's Regiment in 1706 (*Ibid.*, v, 265).

[1] Dalton spells the name "Hartus" in *Army Lists*, v, 265.

[2] Letter of Lord Cutts to the Duke of Ormonde, Dublin, February 9, 1705/6, *Hist. MSS. Comm. Reports*, N. s., *MSS. of the Marquess of Ormonde*, viii, 218, in which Lord Cutts speaks unfavorably of "Captain Harte"; the Same to the Same, Dublin, March 23, 1705/6, *Ibid.*, viii, 226.

[3] Petition of Charles Otway to Lord Cutts, to be dated before August, 1706. *Hist. MSS. Comm. Reports, MSS. of Mrs. Frankland-Russell-Astley*, p. 195.

[4] Luttrell, *op. cit.*, vi, 209, under date of September 4, 1707. No name resembling Shan is given by Dalton in his lists of the officers of Mohun's regiment, excepting that of Peter Chargneau, the surgeon; yet in 1706 David Levada was surgeon. *Army Lists*, v, 103–104, 265.

[5] In an intercepted letter in French, dated London, February 8, 1705/6. It is said further that Colonel Maccartney was given Lord Mohun's regiment, but that Mohun would

COLONEL AND BRIGADIER 125

service there. It was among the forces captured at Brihuega in December, 1710.[1] There evidently the regiment had been recruited, as Lord Galway had reported it as "reduced some time before the Battle of *Almanza*," in 1707.[2] There is no evidence that Mohun was ever with his men in Spain; on the contrary, existing indications seem to show that, in spite of his reported desire to go there,[3] he was never in that kingdom.[4] The regiment went abroad under the command of the lieutenant colonel, Isaac Petit.[5] When he was killed in 1706, at the siege of

receive another in Flanders, "where his Lordship is very eager to fight under the Duke of Marlborough." *Hist. MSS. Comm. Reports, MSS. of the Duke of Portland*, viii, 213.

[1] Dalton, *Army Lists*, v. 265, n.

[2] Together with Farrington's, Hamilton's, Brudenal's, Allen's, and Toby Caulfield's regiments. Lord Galway's returns of the establishment in Spain at the time of the battle of Almanza, *Journals of the House of Lords*, xix, 209.

[3] Letter of Lord Cutts to the Duke of Ormonde, Dublin, July 31, 1705. *Hist. MSS. Comm. Reports*, N. S., *MSS. of the Marquess of Ormonde*, viii, 169–170.

[4] No biographer, contemporary or otherwise, mentions any service in Spain by Lord Mohun. His name does not appear in any of the councils of war reported in Freind's *An Account of the Earl of Peterborough's Conduct in Spain* (second edition, London, 1707). At a council held at Alicant, September 6, 1706 (O. S.), Lieutenant-Colonel George Whitmore and Major Solomon Rapin of Mohun's regiment were present, but not their colonel. See Colonel A. Parnell's *War of the Succession in Spain* (London, 1905), p. 163, n. 1, where the author says, "Lord Mohun did not accompany his corps."

[5] Parnell, *op. cit.*, p. 193.

Alicant,[1] where he was in charge of the engineering operations, Colonel Petit was succeeded by Major George Whitmore.[2]

But Lord Mohun's absentee colonelcy did not mark the limits of his military preferment, for on December 25, 1705, he was commissioned brigadier general.[3] Earlier in that year he was said to have resigned his colonel's commission, out of pique at his failure at that time to be promoted as was Lord North and Grey, who, it was reported, was advanced to brigadier general for his services at Blenheim in 1704,[4] where he had lost his right hand.[5] In 1708, Mohun sold his colonelcy to Captain James Dormer[6] of the First Regiment of Foot Guards, for

[1] Dalton, *Army Lists*, iii, 381, n. 4.

[2] *Hist. MSS. Comm. Reports, MSS. of Mrs. Frankland-Russell-Astley*, p. 195, n., where Whitmore is said to have been commissioned major on March 6, 1706, and lieutenant colonel, August 5, 1706. He had seen his first service in the Earl of Denbigh's Dragoons (Dalton, *op. cit.*, iii, 360).

[3] Dalton, *op. cit.*, v, 17. Colonel George Maccartney received his brigadier's commission on the same day (*Ibid.*).

[4] Luttrell, *A Brief Relation of State Affairs*, v, 533, under date of March 24, 1704/5. On February 27, Luttrell had reported that Lord North and Grey had been promoted. *Ibid.*, v, 524. According to Dalton, however, Lord North and Grey did not become a brigadier general until June 1, 1706 (*Army Lists*, v, 17; *The Blenheim Bounty Roll*, p. 46, n. 1). Dalton is probably correct as to the date of Lord North and Grey's promotion.

[5] Dalton, *Blenheim Bounty Roll*, p. 46, n. 1.

[6] James Dormer was commissioned lieutenant, ranking as

COLONEL AND BRIGADIER

three thousand pounds;[1] Colonel Dormer's commission was dated May 1, 1708.[2] With the sale of his regiment, Mohun's soldiering, such as it was, appears to have ceased, and complete devotion to politics to have taken its place.

From the preceding sketch of Mohun's later military experience, one can see how Thackeray has made free with fact. From brigadier general and colonel of a regiment, Mohun is reduced to a captaincy in the Guards in the regiment of a man who had been dead seven years, and who in life had not commanded the Guards.[3] Evidently Lord Mohun

captain, in the First Foot Guards, May 1, 1702. He served at Blenheim, Ramillies, Saragossa, and Madrid, and was captured with his regiment at Brihuega. He died December 24, 1738, as a lieutenant general and colonel of the First Troop of Horse Grenadier Guards. Dalton, *Blenheim Bounty Roll*, p. 30, n. 8.

[1] Letter of E. Lewis to Robert Harley, dated May 20, 1708, *Hist. MSS. Comm. Reports, MSS. of the Duke of Portland*, iv, 490.

[2] Dalton, *Blenheim Bounty Roll*, p. 30, n. 8. In a letter from Brussels of May 16, 1708, the Duke of Marlborough, writing to the Duke of Somerset, promises to ask the Queen to agree to Lord Mohun's resigning his regiment to Colonel Dormer. *The Letters and Dispatches of John Churchill, Duke of Marlborough*, ed. by General Sir G. Murray, iv, 13. Perhaps it is to Lord Mohun's selling his regiment that his letter to the Duke of Marlborough refers (*Hist. MSS. Comm. Reports*, viii, 35, *MSS. of the Duke of Marlborough*).

[3] The first Earl of Macclesfield had commanded a Guards regiment. See *supra*, p. 121, n. 1.

could not have had "another fatal duel in Spain," if, as it seems, he had never been in that country. As to Mohun's marriage and his desertion of his wife, which Esmond mentions, the first had occurred seventeen years earlier, and as to the second, there is a reasonable doubt as to whether Lord Mohun's separation was not justifiable.[1] There is, however, no especial evidence as to the guilt of either. "Handyside's" Regiment, as Thackeray calls it, was serving in the West Indies in 1708.[2] It may be observed that Thackeray seemingly forgot the year of Lord Castlewood's death, since he subtracts 1700 from 1708 and gets nine years as a result. It was not until after his own decease, in 1712, that the historical Lord Mohun could have had literally so many as two deaths on his conscience.[3] Evidently Thackeray makes up his total from Mountford's, Lord Castlewood's, and the Spanish victim's deaths, ignoring the murder of

[1] See *supra*, pp. 17-18.
[2] Colonel Thomas Handasyde's Regiment of Foot was ordered to Jamaica in the first half of 1702, and served there until 1714, when the officers and staff returned to England to recruit, the privates remaining being organized as two independent companies. Cannon, *Historical Record of the Twenty-second, or the Cheshire Regiment of Foot*, pp. 5-6.
[3] Those of Captain William Hill (for which see *supra*, pp. 53 ff.), and of the Duke of Hamilton (see *infra*, pp. 218 ff.).

COLONEL AND BRIGADIER

Captain Hill,[1] for which Mohun was actually and unquestionably responsible.[2]

[1] *Supra*, pp. 53 ff.
[2] Perhaps Thackeray had merely recalled Swift's reference to Mohun as one "whose Hands had been already dy'd with three foul Murders." *Examiner*, November 13–20, 1712. See the *Post Boy*, November 18–20, 1712.

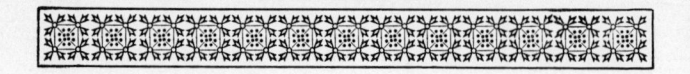

VIII

MAN OF *TON*

IN his account of the private life of Charles Lord Mohun from 1700 on, Thackeray again wanders from fact. As has been noticed in another place,[1] upon his acquittal for the murder of Captain Coote, Mohun vowed before the House of Lords so to conduct himself as to avoid giving the peers "any trouble" in the future.[2] Contemporary biographers agree in ascribing a considerable degree of reformation to Mohun after that time.[3] One among others may be quoted:

[1] *Supra*, p. 96.
[2] Howell, *State Trials*, xiii, col. 1060.
[3] See, for example, Mrs. Manley, *Secret Memoirs from . . . the New Atalantis*, ii, 290–291, 300; Toland, *An Account of the Courts of Prussia and Hanover* (ed. of 1714), pp. 63–64; Grove, *Lives of . . . the Dukes of Devonshire*, p. 249, n., where a "character" of Mohun before 1707 is given; *A full and true Account of a Desperate and Bloody Duel . . . between My Lord Moon and Duke Hamilton*, printed by Edw. Midwinter, London, 1712 (a penny pamphlet); *The whole Lives, Character, Actions, and Fall of D. Hamilton and L. Mohun*, London and Newcastle, 1712; *The Lives and Characters of James Duke Hamilton and Brandon . . . And Charles Lord Mohun . . .* London, printed by J. Read, 1712; *A Strict Enquiry into the*

MAN OF *TON* 131

And indeed, My Lord *Mohun*, after this last Misfortune [his trial for Captain Coote's death], did wonderfully reclaim; and what by his Reading; what by his Conversation with the Soundest and Ablest Statesmen, so well improved his Natural Parts, that he became a great Ornament to the Peerage, and a Strenuous Asserter of the Cause of Liberty and the late Revolution.[1] . . 'T is true, my Lord *Mohun*, like most Men in our cold Climate, still loved a merry Glass of Wine with his Friends. But in this he was the happy Reverse of some Men, who are said to owe all their bright Pa[rts] and fine Political Schemes to the Fumes of *Burgundy* and *Champaign*. For, on the contrary, My Lord *Mohun* was exemplarily temperate when he had any Business, either publick or private to attend. He behaved himself so discreetly at the Court of *Hanover*, whither he accompanied the late Earl of *Macclesfield*, whose Niece he had married, that he left an excellent Character behind him with that most Serene Elector, and the Princess *Sophia*, his Mother.[2]

In the not unflattering portrait of the reformed Lord Mohun which I have just quoted there is an element of truth as well as a certain amount of exaggeration. And it seems that, although he had

---

Circumstances of a Late Duel, With some Account of the Persons Concern'd on Both Sides, London, printed for J. Baker, 1713.

[1] In connection with this passage, my comments upon Mohun's politics, *supra*, pp. 61–62, should be read.

[2] *A True and Impartial Account of the Animosity, Quarrel and Duel, between the Late Duke of Hamilton and the Lord Mohun* (London, printed and sold by A. Baldwin, 1712), pp. 22–23.

abjured drunkenness and duels, Mohun was not unsusceptible to feminine charms. Mrs. Manley[1] thus reveals his intrigue with the Duchess of Shrewsbury:[2]

There's a certain Court Lady [the Duchess] and her two Daughters, one of them very handsome; they pass'd us so suddenly in the Parade last Night, and staid so small a time, that I knew not how to direct your Excellencies to their Observation; You might have also seen this Baron [Lord Mohun], for that his Coach always follows theirs as if by Instinct, ogling into it with all the application of large handsome Eyes: One would think it were a very unnecessary Question to ask who it was he ogled, the frightful Mother, or her beautiful Daughters? And yet it is at the former. If there is such a Thing as Incantation, as Magick to bewitch the Affections, *Ephelia* has certainly made use of it in regard to the Baron, to cause him to doat, with such super-

---

[1] For an identification of certain of the persons figuring in the passages quoted above, see the Key appended to the 1720 edition of Mrs. Manley's *Secret Memoirs from . . . the New Atalantis*. I follow the identifications of the Key with some misgivings and with the suspicion that there is a mystification in it. For I can nowhere discover that Adelaide Duchess of Shrewsbury had two daughters; on the other hand, Mrs. Griffith, whom Mohun married as his second wife, had; yet the reference to "Ephelia's" social charm agrees with what we know of the Duchess. Possibly Mrs. Manley here combined the Duchess and Mrs. Griffith under one name. Elsewhere I quote Mrs. Manley upon Mohun and Mrs. Griffith (*infra*, pp. 136 ff.).

[2] The career of Adelaide Duchess of Shrewsbury is sketched in Appendix A, *infra*, pp. 255–256.

natural Fervency, upon a Face hideous as hers. They tell you of her comick Wit, satyrical facetious Vein, with a peculiar Knack of entertaining Company, agreeably; that she sings well, is Coquet to the Height, and full of Amusement. But all her Attractions are foreign to a Woman of her Age! her squab Shape! The Aspect from her Face! would rather create Mortification. I ridicule no Body for being ugly! I beg your Divinities to believe it, nor for any Defects, that arise from Nature only, but in the Application of those Defects. What has such a Woman to pretend to Charms and Lovers, bless'd with the indearing Caresses of an honest Gentleman her Husband, whom she ungratefully repays, by her open Preference of the Baron? Not but his Charms deserve any Preference that were not criminal. Oh! the pretty remarkable Ways they have of making Assignations! The Lady is at Cards at some one House or other, the Baron has notice before-hand, and is sure to be there: Some Companies are malicious, they dare not whisper after so much ogling, so many wishing languishing Looks; that would be giving the Matter for gone; that would confirm all! but yet there must be Ways found out how to appoint a more fortunate Assignation than this is like to be. The Lady, vain of her Conquest (as very well she may, I defy her ever to enslave another, I do not mean of his Worth, but any Worth, tho' those were Happines's her Youth and Charms were well acquainted with (for she was not always so frightful as now) airy and debonair, takes a Billet from her Bosom, and gives it her dear Lord in Confidence to read, as some pretty satyrical Piece of Wit or Court Character that none of the Company are yet to see, she wou'd not have such a Thing publish'd from her Hand; she does not, for her part, love to be malicious; but her Baron is discreet, she is assured of him. Whilst she is thus running on with her senseless Apology, which is as easily seen thro' as *Ianthe's* Gawze *Turkish* Handkerchief, his Lordship with a grave Air, and now and then a seeming forced Smile, reads the Billet of Rendezvous; pretends by his Silence and Shrug of the Shoulder, to proclaim his Opinion, that 't is some notable dangerous Thing, wisely offers to put it into his Pocket, and falls to his Cards without speaking a Word of what it contains, or should contain. Here the Lady makes an Admiration! she won't be served so, she must have her Paper again; 't is of too great Consequence to leave in any one's Hands, even in his that she believes discreet, but no Body has seen it from her but the Princess and her shining Favourite.[1] It may in a little time be publick — with all her Heart — it shall never be so for her; she does not love to destroy Reputation. . . . Thus with a World of Intreaty the Billet is restored and replaced between those no small-beautiful Breasts of hers. The Assignation given; and the Lovers in a fair way of being so happy, as they can make one another.

But it is not always that they are thus straiten'd; such Difficulties are removed at *Barsina's*[2] House, where all Things are at their Devotion. The mutual Confidence that they have occasion for, creates mutual conveniency. . . .

I have Spleen and Indignation at seeing that handsome Baron, whose every Motion is agreeable, and whose fine Sense is so distinguishing lavish away those Perfections upon a Woman like *Ephelia*.[3]

---

[1] Probably Queen Anne and Mrs. Masham.
[2] Mrs. Manley does not identify *Barsina* in her Key.
[3] *The New Atalantis*, pp. 291–297.

By 1708, the first Baroness Mohun probably was dead. As has been said earlier,[1] Lady Mohun would appear to have been unfaithful to her husband, early in their wedded life, and a separation occurred, which was probably permanent.

Not deterred by his first experience, Lord Mohun remarried, his second wife being Elizabeth, daughter of Dr. Thomas Lawrence,[2] physician to Queen Anne, and widow of a "clerk comptroller of the Green Cloth," Colonel Edward Griffith or Griffin.[3]

---

[1] See *supra*, pp. 17 ff.

[2] Sir Thomas Lawrence, first physican to Queen Anne, and physician general to the army, was born perhaps about 1645. He was appointed physician to the garrison at Tangiers by Charles II, where he married the daughter of the Lieutenant Governor, by whom he had a large family. His six sons were all in the army or navy. Lady Mohun was his second daughter. He held employments under four successive monarchs from Charles II to Anne. *Gentleman's Magazine*, lvii, 191 (March, 1787). Lawrence was among the doctors attending William III in his last illness (Brodrick, *Compleat History*, p. xvi, n. *a*). His appointment as physician to Queen Anne was made in June, 1702 (Luttrell, *A Brief Relation of State Affairs*, v, 182); and at the death of Sir Thomas Millington in January, 1703/4, Dr. Lawrence succeeded him as first physician to the Queen. He was appointed in April of that year a commissioner of the sick and wounded (*Ibid.*, v, 413). He was among the physicians who treated Queen Anne in her fatal illness (Boyer, . . . *The Political State of Great Britain*, . . . viii, 627).

[3] Edward Griffith of Ballincar, County Sligo, entered the service of Prince George of Denmark. In the spring of 1691 he killed one Thompson in a duel. He was made equerry to

It is probably she whose relations with Lord Mohun are celebrated by Mrs. Manley as follows:

> Speaking of the merit of Wives, he [M. de St. Girrone] ask'd *Horatio* [the Earl of Peterborough] if he knew at *Constantinople*, such a one, naming a Lady who had found a method to double her Fortune by the Generosity of her Gallant, by which means her Husband became

---

the Prince in February, 1699/1700, and possibly had served the Princess Anne, as well as the Prince, as secretary. In April, 1702, he became a commissioner of the Board of Green Cloth. In the early part of 1704 (N. S.) he became a commissioner of the salt office, leaving then his post as equerry. At the time of the Prince's death in 1708, Griffith was comptroller of his household. Griffith served as a colonel in Lord Peterborough's Spanish expedition of 1707. He died of the dropsy, February 11, 1710/1. He was married twice, his first wife being a Miss Jennings, sister to Sarah Duchess of Marlborough. By his second wife he had two daughters, the elder of whom married William Stanhope, later Earl of Harrington, and the second of whom married Sir Robert Rich. See Burke, *Peerage and Baronetage*, p. 784, art., "Waldie-Griffith"; Luttrell, *op. cit.*, ii, 221, iv, 618, v, 164, 368, vi, 690; *The History of the Reign of Queen Anne* ... Year the Seventh, p. 247, and Year the Ninth, p. 336; G. E. C., *Complete Peerage*, v, 323; Lyte, *History of Dunster*, p. 494; Burke, *Dormant ... and Extinct Peerages*, p. 370; Collins, *Peerage of England*, iv, 288, v, 534, n.; Gilbert, *Parochial History of Cornwall*, i, 67. The name of Lady Mohun's first husband is found as both Griffith and Griffin. It occurs as "Griffin" in the Key to Mrs. Manley's *Memoirs of Europe*. It was not improbably Colonel Griffith who kept Steele, also a member of the Prince's household, for more than two hours away from his "Dear Prue" on the night of January 5, 1708 (letter of Steele, reprinted by Aitken, *Life of Steele*, i, 203).

infinitely fond of her, tho' he had ever been cool 'till then: at the same time continuing his Discourse, he enquir'd of his Lordship if he was not intimately acquainted with *Gratian* [Lord Mohun] of consular dignity? He has drank, my Lord, in favour of *Florella* [Mrs. Griffin], the Court Droll, out of *Circe* and Medea's Cup: for 't is certainly Infatuation that not leans but bows him that way, he's the first Man sure of sense, that doats in spight of Nature, or even in Contradiction to her. You know *Florella;* alas! can anything be so forbidding, not to say frightful? Yet he passes whole Days in kissing her toes, and playing with her Ears, a new method of Amour, and she brags of it. Will any body pretend to dispute of Taste after this? The honest Gentleman her Husband is the only one in the Empire that knows Them, and knows not their Intrigues; he is so jealous of his Honour, it wou'd certainly drive him to Extremity, therefore they forbear to tell him of it, tho' the Affair has been of a long standing. How much sincerity and Ignorance of what, 't is presum'd, we ought to know, can sometimes expose a Man? He was, a little before I left *Constantinople*, at a public Assembly, where the Consul show'd a very fine Diamond he had lately purchas'd: Every one gave their opinion of it, at length it came to his Turn; Why ay! says the poor Gentleman with a very ingenuous Air, 't is very fine but is it not great Vanity to lay out so much Money upon Right, when Counterfeit makes as good a Show? There's a *Bird* at home as glorious as the Sun, you wou'd swear she was stuck with Jewels, and all false. The whole Company had much to do to forbear laughing in his face, fortunately he was call'd away, and left 'em to do it among themselves, not forgetting to commend *Florella's* Address, who cou'd pass the real, substantial, resplendent Diamonds given her by *Gratian*, for false glittering Imaginaries, on the Credulity of her uxorious Husband.[1]

Whether the lady who figures in this sprightly story later became Lady Mohun, is not absolutely certain, yet it seems likely. The second marriage of Lord Mohun occurred probably in March, 1710/1.[2] So far as is known, the match was not an unhappy one. The second Lady Mohun was not an especially gifted woman, but appears to have been vivacious and of an easy temper.[3] After her husband's death

---

[1] *Memoirs of Europe*, pp. 270 ff.

[2] Lord Mohun's will was dated March 23, 1710 (*Hist. MSS. Comm. Reports*, xv, pt. 2, 346, *MSS. of J. Eliot Hodgkin*). It was drawn up after Mohun's second marriage. Mohun's extremely irregular attendance at the House of Lords during the latter part of the session of 1710/1 would be explained by his remarriage. See the *Journals of the House of Lords*, vol. xix. He was absent between March 22, 1710/1, and May 3, and after that date was present only once (May 22) before the prorogation of the House on June 12 (*Ibid.*). It should be noted, too, that in her *New Atalantis*, first published in 1709, Mrs. Manley represents Mohun as unwilling yet to remarry (pp. 299-300; and see *supra*, p. 18). Of course, Colonel Griffith was then living.

[3] For a bantering letter from the Earl of Peterborough to Lady Mohun, see Brit. Mus. MS. 22625 ff. 33 ff. Letters of Lady Mohun to Mrs. Howard occur in Brit. Mus. MSS. 22625 ff. 123 ff.; 22627, f. 78; 22629 ff. 11 ff., respectively. Two others have been reprinted in *The Private Correspondence of Sarah, Duchess of Marlborough*, ii, 86, 87. They give a fairly good picture of Lady Mohun's capacity and disposition.

BOCONNOC PARK HOUSE, CORNWALL

MAN OF *TON* 139

Lady Mohun's house seems to have been a place of resort for the Whigs, more especially those of less rigid morals.[1] She seems also to have entertained at Gawseworth Hall.[2] In 1718 she disposed of the ancestral seat of the Mohuns, Boconnoc in Cornwall,[3] which, with his other property, her husband had left her. The buyer was Thomas Pitt, who had just returned from India with the famous diamond, which he sold in 1717 to the Regent of France for one hundred and twenty-five thousand pounds.[4] Pitt paid Lady Mohun fifty-three thousand pounds for Boconnoc.[5] Gawseworth in Cheshire,

[1] Lady Cowper, *Diary*, p. 32.
[2] "Lewis Melville," *Lady Suffolk and Her Circle*, p. 48.
[3] Redding says of Boconnoc: ". . . the House was begun by Lord Mohun and finished by Governor Pitt." *An Illustrated Itinerary of the County of Cornwall*, p. 101. By no one else are any building operations by Lord Mohun at Boconnoc mentioned.
[4] Letter of Thomas Pitt to his son Robert, June 29, 1717, in *Hist. MSS. Comm. Reports*, xiii, pt. 3, 62, *MSS. of J. B. Fortesque*. It is interesting that Boconnoc finally descended to the great-great-grandson of Governor Pitt, his namesake Thomas Pitt, the second Lord Camelford, whose career was, as Gilbert notes (*Parochial History of Cornwall*, i, 70), much like that of Lord Mohun. Lord Camelford was killed in a duel by a Mr. Best on March 7, 1804; for the particulars, see Joseph Farington, *Diary*, ii, 199 ff.
[5] Lyte, *History of Dunster*, 494. The papers of Boconnoc appear to have been turned over to Pitt in the summer of 1718 (Thomas Pitt to his son Robert, August 12, 1718, *Hist. MSS. Comm. Reports, loc. cit.*). Lyte, however, and Harris

which Lord Mohun had inherited from the second Lord Macclesfield, Lady Mohun sold to her son-in-law, William Stanhope, the future Lord Harrington and Lord Lieutenant of Ireland.[1] Some time later—perhaps as a result of her sales of real estate—Lady Mohun took a third husband, Charles Mordaunt, a nephew of the Earl of Peterborough.[2] She died in the spring of 1725, being buried May 21, at Fulham.[3] Lady Mohun's daughter, Anne Griffith or Griffin, by her first husband, who had married William Stanhope, later first Earl of Harrington, died in childbirth in December, 1719, leaving twin sons.[4] As might be expected, Lady Mohun's marriage with Colonel Mordaunt was childless, as had been that with her second husband.

(*D. N. B.*, xv, 1235, art., "Pitt, Thomas"), give 1717 as the year of the transaction.

[1] Collins, *Peerage of England*, iv, 288, v, 534, n.; Nicholas, *Peerage*, i, 305–306.

[2] Charles Mordaunt was the son of Lewis Mordaunt, third son of John Viscount Mordaunt. After his first wife's death he married Anne, daughter of Scrope Viscount Howe. Collins, *Peerage of England*, iii, 329. It should be noted that Collins makes Lord Mohun's widow, "daughter of Thomas Gerrard Earl of Macclesfield," confusing her with the mother of the first Baroness Mohun and erring in the Christian name of Lord Macclesfield. Colonel Mordaunt's death occurred, it seems, in the spring of 1762, for a Charles Mordaunt was buried at Fulham on May 3, of that year. G. E. C., *Complete Peerage*, v, 323, n. *c*.

[3] *Ibid.*, v, 323.   [4] Collins, *op. cit.*, iv, 288.

MAN OF *TON*

With Mohun's turning his attention to affairs of state and to winning himself a place in the *chroniques scandaleuses* of the time, came, in fact, a comparative reformation in conduct. From the time of his above-mentioned [1] promise of an alteration in his fashion of life, upon his acquittal on his second trial for murder, to the date of his last duel, that is to say, from 1699 to 1712, — a period of thirteen years, — Mohun engaged in but two quarrels.

One of these is known to me only through casual references to it in an attack upon Mohun's character and in a defence of him, both published after his death.[2] Mohun would appear to have engaged in some dispute with a "Mr. Davenant" (perhaps Charles Davenant, the economist or Henry D'Avenant, later George I's envoy at Florence). The quarrel did not terminate in a duel, a fact which caused Mohun's enemies, such as Swift,[3] after his

[1] *Supra*, pp. 96 and 130.

[2] An article in the *Examiner*, November 13-20, 1712 (by Swift?), and a pamphlet, *A True and Impartial Account of the Animosity, Quarrel and Duel, between the late Duke of Hamilton, and the Lord Mohun* (London, printed and sold by A. Baldwin, 1712), p. 6. Notice that this is the Whig *True and Impartial Account*, there being a Tory pamphlet with nearly the same title.

[3] The *Examiner*, as cited above; the passage is quoted and commented upon in *A True and Impartial Account* ... p. 6, but there is credited to an article in the *Post Boy* of November 20.

death to asperse his courage. It was alleged, however, on the other hand, that Davenant admitted that Mohun had acted toward him like a man of honor and generosity.[1] I regret to say that I have been unable to discover the occasion of the trouble between Mohun and Davenant, or the circumstances accompanying it.

The other affair, which took place after Esmond's pretended encounter with Mohun at Lille, is better known to us. On May 27, 1712, the subject of debate in the House of Lords was the failure of the Duke of Ormonde, the successor of the Duke of Marlborough as commander-in-chief, to move against the French. Earl Poulet,[2] in answer to a speech of the Duke of Devonshire, said that no one could doubt of the Duke of Ormonde's courage, but that "he was not like a certain General, who led

[1] *A True and Impartial Account* . . . p. 24.
[2] John, first Earl Poulet, born in 1663. He was Privy Councillor to Queen Anne and a Commissioner of the Treaty of Union between England and Scotland. Later he was first Lord of the Treasury (August 8, 1710), and became Lord Steward, June 13, 1711. On October 26, 1712, he was elected a Knight of the Garter, at the same chapter as the Duke of Hamilton, but was not installed until August 4, 1713. He died May 28, 1743. He, like the Duke, named a son after the Queen. Lord Anne Poulet, born July 11, 1711, was several times a member of Parliament for Bridgewater. Collins, *Peerage of England*, iv, 13–14; *D. N. B.*, xlvi, 230–231, art. "Poulett, John, . . . First Earl Poulett," by J. M. Rigg.

JOHN, FIRST DUKE OF MARLBOROUGH

MAN OF *TON* 143

troops to the slaughter, to cause a great number of officers to be knocked on the head in a battle, or against stone walls, in order to fill his pockets by disposing of their commissions."[1] Marlborough, whose self-control was notable, although present at the time, restrained his anger at this gross insult, until the conclusion of the sitting of the House. He then sent Lord Mohun[2] to Lord Poulet, with instructions to tell the latter that the Duke wished an *eclaircissement* of some language used in the day's debate, and, therefore, requested him "to go and take the air in the country."[3] The Earl inquired of Lord Mohun as to whether he was conveying a challenge; Mohun replied that his message needed no explanation and that he would accompany the Duke.[4] Earl Poulet, being thus enlightened as to the meaning of the message and, perhaps, in cooler blood not unimpressed at the prospect of engaging with the foremost soldier of the period, is said to

[1] Cobbett, *Parliamentary History*, vi, col. 1137.

[2] According to one account, it was "at the Instigation of the Lord Mohun" that Marlborough sent his message to Earl Poulet. *The History and Proceedings of the House of Lords* . . . ii, 371, n.

[3] Tindal, *The Continuation of Mr. Rapin's History of England*, v, 509-510, n.

[4] Coxe says that Mohun responded, "I shall accompany the Duke of Marlborough, and your lordship would do well to provide a second." *Memoirs of the Duke of Marlborough*, iii, 309.

have displayed so much emotion that his countess [1] grew suspicious of some impending trouble. She confirmed her suspicions by eavesdropping when Lord Mohun waited upon the Earl, and immediately appealed to Lord Dartmouth, to whom she had previously communicated her apprehensions of a quarrel between her husband and some other nobleman.[2] As Lady Poulet wished, Lord Dartmouth posted guards at her door, requested the Duke of Marlborough not to stir from his house, and reported the affair to the Queen. The Queen sent to the Duke, desiring him to carry the business no further, whereupon he gave his word of honor that he would comply with her commands.[3] The quarrel was thus settled without a duel.

[1] The first Countess Poulet was daughter to Peregrine Bertie, of Waldershare, Kent, and a niece to Robert Earl of Lindsey, as well as a cousin to Robert Duke of Ancaster. Collins, *Peerage of England*, iv, 13–14.

[2] Five letters of Bridget Countess Poulet to Lord Dartmouth, May 29–31, 1712, *Hist. MSS. Comm. Reports*, xi, pt. 5, 309–310, *MSS. of the Earl of Dartmouth*.

[3] Tindal, *The Continuation of Mr. Rapin's History of England*, v, 509–10, n.

IX

STATESMAN

THAT Lord Mohun was, by any means, an outstanding figure among the Whig statesmen and politicians of his time no one could say; indeed, today his political activities are almost completely overlooked. He seems to have been, however, one of the most dependable of the Whig peers, generally in his place in the House of Lords and, so far as our knowledge informs us, a thoroughgoing and consistent supporter of the measures of his party.

Lord Mohun took his seat in the House of Lords July 4, 1698. He had come of age on April 11 of that year, but as he was then confined in the Tower awaiting trial for the murder of Captain William Hill, he did not take his seat until July 4, after pleading the Royal pardon for the crime. Parliament being prorogued on July 5, Mohun did not sit again until March 31, 1699. His taking his seat was delayed a second time by a personal affair; for during the previous part of the session he had been first in hiding and then in the Tower, charged with the murder of Captain Richard Coote. Being acquitted on his trial before the Lords on March 29, 1699, he began sitting at the next meeting of the session — that is, on March 31. From this date on to June 18, 1712, the last day but one of the sittings of the Parliament of 1711–12, and the last appearance of Lord Mohun in his seat in the House of Lords, he was among the most regular attendants upon the sessions of the Peers, missing, however, a number of days in 1710–11.[1]

It has been indicated that Lord Mohun's service in the House of Lords was in no way brilliant. He seems to have performed a number of routine duties, but in no such way as to secure therefrom promotion or position. He was named upon a number of committees, many of them for the purpose of dealing with legislation of no particular importance. His first duty of this sort was when, on March 31, 1699, he was placed on the committee to consider "An Act for the Encouragement of a new Invention, by *Thomas Savery*, for raising Water, and occasioning Motion to all Sorts of Mill-Work by the impellent Force of Fire."[2]

---

[1] *Journals of the House of Lords*, vols. xvi–xix, *passim*.
[2] *Ibid.*, xvi, 429. This bill was returned to the Lords from the House of Commons, after its passage there, by Mohun's old adversary, Francis Scobell.

Other committee appointments of a more important sort are as follows:

On April 24, 1699, to consider "An Act to enable posthumous Children to Inherit their Father's Estate."

On December 4, 1699, "to consider, whether, when Mr. Attorney General is heard on the King's Behalf, the Counsel of other Parties concerned may not be present."

On February 13, 1699/1700, to prepare and bring in a bill of the effect of the statute of the Twenty-second Year of Charles II, chap. 9, "intituled, 'An act, authorizing certain Commissioners of the Realm of *England* to treat with Commissioners of *Scotland*, for the Weal of both Kingdoms.'"

On April 1, 1701, "to inspect the Journals of this House [the Lords], in relation to the Proceedings of this House in Cases of Impeachment for Misdemeanors." . . .

On April 17, 1701, "to inspect the Journals, whether, upon any Address of this House the Lords to the King, there hath been no Answer returned; and report to the House."

On February 5, 1701/2, to draw and bring in a bill for settling Sir Thomas Cooke's bequest of £10,000 for a college at Oxford.

On March 13, 1701/2, to consider an act for the

better government of Balsal Hospital in Warwickshire.

On March 17, 1701/2, to consider the act to enable the officers of the city of London and the mercers to pay Sir Thomas Gresham's charities.

On March 31, 1702, to consider "An act for continuing and amending the Act made in the Eighth Year of His Majesty's Reign, intituled, An Act for the settling and adjusting the Proportions of fine Silver and Silk, and for the better making of Gold and Silver Thread, and to prevent the Abuses of the Wire-drawers."[1]

On January 12, 1703/4, the House ordered that Mohun be added to "the Earl of *Bathe's* Committee."[2]

On January 26, 1703/4, to consider of the allegations in the title of a bill for the better enabling of the officials of the city of London and the mercers to support Gresham College, and to examine the accounts and the raising of money for building the Exchange.[3]

[1] *Journals of the House of Lords*, xvi, 447, 480, 515, 641, 657; xvii, 27, 71, 74, 89.

[2] *Ibid.*, p. 363. A bill to enable the trustees of William Earl of Bath, a minor, to raise money to pay debts had been introduced November 24, 1703 (*Ibid.*, p. 338). The Bishop of Norwich and Lords Wharton and Somers were added to the committee at the same time as Lord Mohun.

[3] *Ibid.*, p. 385.

On February 2, 1704/5, "to consider the Method of passing Bills between the Two Houses."

On January 27, 1708/9, "to consider of the Method of keeping Records and Public Papers in Offices, how they are kept; and to consider of Ways to remedy what shall be found to be amiss." . . .[1]

On February 23, 1708/9, "to state Matters of Fact, as formerly ordered and adjudged, upon the Appeal of the late Earl of *Kildare*, and the Answer of Sir *Arthur Shaen*." [2]

On March 4, 1708/9, to consider "An Act to Explain a Clause in a Statute made in the Twenty-seventh Year of the Reign of King Henry the Eighth, enabling Tenants in Tail Possession to make Jointures to Wives; and enlarging the same, so as *Richard* Lord *Willoughby de Broke*, and other Tenants in Tail in Possession, may make Jointures to the Wives of their Eldest Sons or Grandsons." [3]

On December 15, 1711, to inquire out the author, printer, and publisher of "a Paper printed and published, contrary to a Standing Order of this House, intituled, '*The Earl of* Nottingham's

---

[1] *Journals of the House of Lords*, xvii, 645, xviii, 620.

[2] *Ibid.*, xviii, 642. The surviving executors and devisees of John Earl of Kildare had complained that Sir Arthur Shaen had several times proceeded contrary to previous orders of the House of Lords (*Ibid.*).

[3] *Ibid.*, xviii, 655.

Speech to the Honorable House of Lords; London, printed by J. Tomson, *near* Covent Garden, 1711.'"[1]

Mohun was first appointed on December 30, 1701, one of the "Lords Sub-committees ... to consider of the Orders and Customs of the House, and Privileges of the Peers ... and Lords of Parliament; and to peruse and perfect the Journal of the last Parliament, and also the Journal of this Parliament."[2] To the same standing sub-committee Mohun was reappointed November 9, 1703, October 4, 1704, October 27, 1705, December 4, 1706, November 6, 1707, November 18, 1708, November 15, 1709, December 8, 1711.[3] He was not placed on the sub-committee as named April 14, 1707,[4] nor was he a member of that appointed November 28, 1710.[5] Although he was named on November 16, 1699, as were all the other peers present, on the general committee upon privileges of peers and customs of the house,[6] he seems to have been completely passed over, even for this, on February 10, 1700/1, notwithstanding he is recorded as present on that day.[7]

---

[1] *Journals of the House of Lords*, xix, 343.
[2] *Ibid.*, xvii, 4. On March 17, 1702/3, Mohun certified the correctness of the Journals (*Ibid.*, p. 293).
[3] *Ibid.*, xvii, 332, 568; xviii, 9, 176, 335, 580; xix, 5, 338.
[4] *Ibid.*, xviii, 322.   [5] *Ibid.*, xix, 169.
[6] *Ibid.*, xvi, 477.   [7] *Ibid.*, p. 592.

STATESMAN

The first service of Lord Mohun on a committee of the peers to draw up an address to the King came when he was among the members of the upper house designated to investigate the facts regarding treaties of alliance with Holland and Sweden, and the treaty of partition with France and Holland, upon the results of which they were to address William III.[1] The address was accepted by the Lords March 20, 1700/1.[2] Mohun's next appointment of this sort was on the committee named April 16, 1701, to draw up an address to the King, desiring him to withhold any censure upon Lords Oxford, Portland, Halifax, and Somers, until the impeachments were tried.[3] It may be said here that on June 17, 1701, Mohun was among the fifty-six peers voting Lord Somers not guilty of the charges brought against him.[4] Likewise, he was one of the Lords who, on June 23, 1701, unanimously found Lord Oxford not guilty.[5] On December 31, 1701, Mohun was among the peers named to address the King upon the part of his speech from the throne relating to the recognition, by Louis XIV, of the Pretender as King of England.[6]

[1] *Journals of the House of Lords*, xvi, 622.
[2] *Ibid.*, pp. 628–629.   [3] *Ibid.*, p. 655.
[4] *House of Lords MSS.*, N. S. iv, 300; Grove, *Lives of . . . the Dukes of Devonshire*, p. 226, n.
[5] *House of Lords MSS.*, N. S., iv, 300.
[6] *Journals of the House of Lords*, xvii, 7.

152   A NOBLE RAKE

Two days later, on January 2, 1701/2, Mohun was on the committee to draw up the address to the King, assuring him of the peers' support of the royal measures to reduce "the exorbitant powers of France."[1] Mohun was also on the committee appointed January 21, 1701/2, to address the King on behalf of Colonel Baldwin Leighton, who apparently was held for debts due the military establishment, which he could not pay.[2] A committee was named by the Lords on November 9, 1702, to congratulate Queen Anne upon the recovery of Prince George of Denmark; of this, Mohun was a member.[3] Likewise he was among the peers appointed on November 19, 1702, to address the Queen concerning the debate upon the Bishop of Worcester.[4] Mohun was a member of the committee appointed February 9, 1702/3, to thank the Queen for her refusal of licenses to persons desiring to come to England from France.[5] On February 17, he reported the address for the committee. It runs thus:

We Your Majesty's most dutiful and loyal Subjects, the Lords Spiritual and Temporal in Parliament assembled, return Your Majesty our most humble Thanks, that you have been pleased out of Your great Care and Concern for the Peace and Security of Your Majesty's

---

[1] *Journals of the House of Lords*, xvii, 9.   [2] *Ibid.*, p. 21.
[3] *Ibid.*, p. 162.   [4] *Ibid.*, p. 168.   [5] *Ibid.*, p. 275.

Kingdoms, to be so strict and cautious in the granting of Licenses to the Enemies of Your Majesty and Your good People to resort hither from *France*, as to have granted such Licenses to Five Persons only.

And we do at the same Time humbly desire, that Your Majesty would be pleased to issue out Your Royal Proclamation, for the Discovery of any such as are or shall come from France without your Majesty's License, with such Reward to the Discoverers as to Your Majesty shall seem most proper; and that Your Majesty will also please to direct Your Attorney General, from Time to Time, effectually to prosecute all such Offenders.[1]

Mohun was among the members of the committee appointed January 13, 1703/4, to address the Queen upon "a Matter of the highest consequence, relating to the Privileges of this House" — the right of the Peers to arrest and keep in custody persons whom they wished to examine, as well as upon an address of the Commons to the Queen on December 23, 1703. He was one of the Lords chosen November 22, 1705, to urge the Queen to "maintain a good Correspondence with Her Allies . . . and to excite . . . all Her Allies, as much as possible to a vigorous Prosecution of the War." On December 3, 1706, Mohun was appointed to assist in drafting an address to congratulate the Queen upon "the great and glorious Successes of the Arms of Her Majesty."[2] He was named

[1] *Journals of the House of Lords*, xvii, 294.
[2] *Ibid.*, xvii, 367; xviii, 24, 175.

154 A NOBLE RAKE

among those committeemen who, on March 1, 1708/9, were charged to desire the Queen to maintain friendship among the Allies at the end of the war, and to oblige the French King to banish the Pretender and "own Her Majesty's Title."[1]

On November 10, 1703, Mohun was for the first time placed on the committee to address the Queen upon her speech from the throne. He was appointed to other committees with the like duty, on December 18, 1703, October 24, 1704, October 27, 1705, November 27, 1705, November 18, 1708, November 15, 1709,[2] December 7, 1711.[3]

It is unlikely that Mohun, in spite of his reformation and his regular attendance upon the sittings of the House, was so assiduous in his application to his duties in the House of Lords as he might have been. Still, it appears that he reported out the findings of various committees. On February 21, 1701/2, he presented the results of the consideration in committee of "An Act for punishing Officers or Soldiers who shall mutiny or desert in *England* or *Ireland*," a task probably resulting from his military rank. The amendments offered

---

[1] *Journals of the House of Lords*, xviii, 651.
[2] *Ibid.*, xvii, 334, 353, 568; xviii, 9, 32, 579; xix, 4.
[3] *Ibid.*, p. 336. All peers present were named on this committee.

by the committee were rejected by the House.[1] Mohun reported out on December 20, 1704, as fit for passage, with amendments, the act vesting the estate of Lord Howard of Escrick in trustees, to sell, for the payment of his debts.[2] On January 17, 1708/9, Mohun offered the report of the committee which had been considering the contested election of the representative peers of Scotland. The select committee had met on January 10, with Lord Mohun in the chair, and had considered the papers submitted to the House on December 23, 1708.[3] In his report, Lord Mohun described at length the documents produced in the case.[4] The election was considered at a number of sittings of the House, counsel for both sides being heard. On January 29, the voting on the various points at issue was concluded, and the committee was ordered to calculate, according to these decisions of the Lords, the number of valid votes cast.[5] On February 1, Lord Mohun reported for the committee, and the revised returns were presented.

[1] *Journals of the House of Lords*, xvii, 43.
[2] *Ibid.*, p. 606.
[3] *House of Lords MSS.* N. S., viii, 2–3; *Journals of the House of Lords*, xviii, 600.
[4] *Ibid.*, xviii, 605–606; Luttrell, *A Brief Relation of State Affairs*, vi, 396–397.
[5] *Journals of the House of Lords*, xviii, 623–624.

The name of the Marquis of Annandale was substituted for that of the Marquis of Lothian as a representative peer of Scotland.[1] On April 13, 1709, Mohun reported that the committee of the whole had considered, and had found fit to pass, "An Act for the Relief of the Non-Commission Officers and Soldiers of the respective Companies of the Three Regiments of Colonel *Thomas Handasyde*, Colonel *John Livesay*, and Lieutenant Colonel *Erle*, and the Four Independent Companies at *New York*, in *America*," which had been sent up from the House of Commons on March 25.[2] Mohun's connection with this bill is a curious coincidence, in view of Thackeray's transfer of Handasyde's Regiment from Jamaica to Lille in 1708, where its officers are present at Esmond's duel with Mohun.[3] Lord Mohun reported the private bill to provide for making possible the payment of the debts of William Heyward, out of the Committee of the whole House, on January 10, 1709/10, and, on January 11, recommended it as fit to pass with some amendments.[4]

Mohun seems to have taken a fairly prominent

[1] *Journals of the House of Lords*, xviii, 625–626. The actual emending of the returns took place on February 3.
[2] *Ibid.*, pp. 685, 706.
[3] See *supra*, p. 119, and *infra*, pp. 176 ff.
[4] *Journals of the House of Lords*, xix, 30.

part in the impeachment proceedings against Dr. Henry Sacheverell. When the impeachment was reported from the Commons, December 15, 1709, Mohun — like all the peers present — was named on the committee to consider the procedure and precedents therefor.[1] The trial began in Westminster Hall, on February 27, 1709/10, and continued up to March 16, 1709/10, when the votes upon the first article of the impeachment were taken. Voting upon the other articles and upon the question of Sacheverell's being guilty of high crimes and misdemeanors, as charged, continued until March 20, when the impeachment was sustained.[2] Mohun voted against Sacheverell.[3] He had attended every session during the proceedings.

On February 28, a committee of the Lords was appointed to inquire into the occasion of the disorders "by Dr. Sacheverell's coming to his trial." Lord Mohun was chairman of the select committee of investigation. During the sitting of this subcommittee, Lord North and Grey, a maimed veteran of Blenheim, who had incurred Mohun's hostility some years before, when he had won mili-

[1] *Journals of the House of Lords*, xix, 21.
[2] *Ibid.*, pp. 83–115, *passim*.
[3] *The History and Proceedings of the House of Lords* ... ii, 277; *Collection of the Parliamentary Debates in England* ... v, 266.

tary promotion over Mohun,[1] indiscreetly "reflected" upon the conduct of the inquiry. A Mr. Bendish was being examined on March 1 concerning the mob's making bonfires of chapel pews in Holborn and in Hatton Gardens, when Lord North and Grey said to Mohun:

"I do not know but this gentleman may instruct him what to say."

Mohun reported the remark to the Lord Steward, who laid it before the House on March 2, requesting Mohun to repeat the offensive language. The House thereupon voted to examine "the Matter of the late Disorders" at the bar, and various witnesses were then heard. In the meantime, Lord North and Grey had explained his observation, and

---

[1] William, sixth Baron North and second Baron Grey, was appointed captain and lieutenant colonel in the First Regiment of Foot Guards, February 14, 1702. He was commissioned colonel of the Lord North and Grey's Regiment of Foot, January 15, 1703. He served at Blenheim where he lost his right hand. Lord North and Grey became brigadier general on June 1, 1706, major general, January 1, 1709, lieutenant general, January 1, 1710; and on September 5, 1712, he was made governor of Portsmouth. He died in 1734. Lord North and Grey served at the siege of Ghent in 1708, and at the siege of Bouchain in 1711. (Dalton, *The Blenheim Bounty Roll*, p. 46, n. 1; Dalton, *Army Lists*, iv, 268, n. 6; Brodrick, *A Compleat History of the Late War*, pp. 110, 274–275, 348 ff.). Lord North and Grey had won on the field the promotion which Mohun sought by political intrigue at court.

had asserted that "he meant well nor did not intend to reflect upon the witnesses."[1]

Mohun acted as teller of the votes of the Lords on several occasions. With Lord Dartmouth he served as teller in the case of Grosvenor *v.* Coy on June 5, 1701. Later in the same month, he, like Lord Jeffreys, was a teller of the vote on the Deal bill. With Lord Dartmouth, Mohun acted as teller when the Public Accounts Commissioners bill was voted on, June 24, 1701. Mohun and the Earl of Stamford served when the question of censuring William Fuller's books was acted upon on January 19, 1701/2. With Lord Jeffreys, Mohun was a teller of the vote upon one of the motions made during the consideration of the Perjury bill, on February 16, 1701/2. He was a teller upon the previous question vote when a resolution censuring Sir George Rooke was before the House on January 14, 1702/3. When, on February 15 of the same year, a vote was taken as to adjourning the debate upon the Accounts Commissioners bill, Mohun acted as a teller.[2] He served in a similar capacity on January 21, 1708/9, with Lord Halifax, when the House voted as to whether

[1] *Journals of the House of Lords*, xix, 86–89; *House of Lords MSS.*, N. s., viii, 367–368.
[2] *Ibid.*, iv, 294, 365, 392, 409, 426; v, 210.

a peer of Scotland, who had a seat in the House of Lords as a peer of Great Britain by a patent passed after the Union, could vote in the election of the representative peers of Scotland. He again acted as a teller February 25, 1709/10, with Lord Conway, when the appeal of the inhabitants of Hammersmith against the Bishop of London, in the suit regarding the latter's assumption of the right of nominating the curate at Hammersmith, was voted upon. In the vote upon the previous question on the declaration that the allegedly criminal words in an impeachment for writing or speaking treasonably need not be specified in the impeachment, Mohun and Lord Ossulston acted as tellers. This vote, which concerned the preliminaries of the proceedings against Dr. Sacheverell, was taken on March 14, 1709/10.[1]

Mohun acted a number of times as one of the managers of conferences between the Lords and Commons. His first service of this sort was on May 3, 1699, when the amendments of the Upper House to a bill taxing paper, parchment, vellum, and the like, were under discussion.[2] A more important conference of which Mohun was a manager was that on April 9, and 10, 1700, when the Peers'

[1] *House of Lords MSS.*, N.S., viii, 2–3, 365, 343.
[2] *Journals of the House of Lords*, xvi, 462.

amendments to the Act for the Sale of Forfeited Estates in Ireland and for a Land-tax in England were the source of a disagreement between the two Houses. On February 17, 1700/1, Mohun acted as manager of the conference between the two Houses on the King's address, in which he had recommended that, in view of the Duke of Gloucester's death, Parliament act to secure the Protestant Succession. Mohun was appointed upon the committee named May 5, 1701, to draw a message reminding the Commons of their impeachment of Lords Portland, Oxford, Somers, and Halifax. On February 6, 1701/2, he acted as a reporter of the conference regarding the Lords' amendments to the Commons' bill for attainting the Pretender.[1] The effect of the amendment was to attaint the ex-Queen Mary of Modena.[2] When the Act for Abolishing Occasional Conformity was returned to the Commons with the Peers' amendments, on December 17, 1702, Mohun was made a manager of the conference. On December 18, he was chosen on the committee to draw up the reasons for the Lords' adherence to their amendments. He was a manager of a second conference on January 9,

[1] *Journals of the House of Lords*, xvi, 573–576, 600, 667; xvii, 28.
[2] Cobbett, *Parliamentary History*, v, col. 1334; see also *Journals of the House of Lords*, xvii, 20, 22, 29–31, 33–34.

1702/3, and possibly served as a manager subsequently, when Lords and Commons discussed the amendments further.[1] He was named a manager of the conference with the Commons on February 17, 1702/3, concerning the investigation of the public accounts and the Peers' management of the affair. On February 18, he was a member of the committee to consider what further should be done, and on February 22, he served as manager at another conference with the Commons upon the matter.[2]

Mohun also was a manager of the conferences February 28, March 7, and March 9, 1704/5, concerning the Commons' imprisonment of the Aylesbury electors.[3] He was appointed, as a result, to the committee to address the Queen to cause writs of error to issue regarding two of the unfortunate men.[4] A less important duty was that which devolved upon Mohun on March 1, 1704/5, when he was appointed to the committee for drawing up

[1] *Journals of the House of Lords*, xvii, 192, 195, 232, 264, 317. Mohun was probably not a manager of the conference of February 1, 1702/3, on which the Duke of Devonshire reported, February 24 (*Ibid.*, pp. 264, 305-314).

[2] *Ibid.*, xvii, 294-295, 297, 300.

[3] *Ibid.*, xvii, 681, 692, 694-695. Mohun was a manager of the first conference, and the same managers were reappointed for the subsequent conferences.

[4] *Ibid.*, p. 693.

the reasons for the Lords' disagreement to an amendment returned them with a naturalization bill by the Commons. On March 13, 1704/5, he was named a manager of the conference upon the Lords' insistence upon their amendments to the Militia Act. The preceding day he had been appointed to the committee to draw up the reasons of the Peers for their adhering to their amendments.

Mohun was a member of the committee appointed on December 6, 1705, to prepare the communication to the Commons designed to accompany the Peers' resolution that the Church, rescued by King William, was in a flourishing condition, and that he who alleged it to be in danger was an enemy to Queen, Church, and State.[1]

However busy Mohun may have been as a legislator, he seems not to have engaged often in debate. His first recorded speech was in December, 1703, when the Act for Abolishing Occasional Conformity was a second time before the House of Lords. His attack upon the bill was notable for its vigor:

" . . . And the Lord *Mohun*, a Peer eminently conspicuous for his Parts, and his Affection to the

[1] *Journals of the House of Lords*, xvii, 685, 698, 697; xviii, 44.

Protestant Succession, did not stick to say, that if they passed this Bill, they had as good tack the pretended Prince of Wales to it."[1] The result of the spirited opposition of such Whig leaders as the Bishop of Salisbury, the Duke of Devonshire, Lord Wharton, and Lord Haversham was that the bill was lost by a majority of twelve on its second reading.[2] Mohun's zealous Protestantism was further shown in his signing, with seven other peers, on February 16, 1701/2, the "Roll to contain the signatures of Lords to the Declaration in the Act of 1672 for preventing dangers which may happen from Popish Recusants," as well as the "Roll to contain signatures of Lords subscribing to the Association set out in the Act of 1695/6 for the better security of his Majesty's royal person and government."[3] On April 20, 1702, additional evidence of Mohun's "affection to the Protestant Succession" is afforded by the following entry of that day in the *Journals of the House of Lords:*[4]

[1] *The History and Proceedings of the House of Lords* . . . ii, 66; Tindal, *The Continuation of Mr. Rapin's History of England*, iii, 576.

[2] *The History and Proceedings of the House of Lords* . . . *loc. cit.* In Swift's letter of December 16, 1703, to the Reverend W. Tisdale, there is a description of the excitement concerning this bill (*Correspondence*, ed. by Ball, i, 38–39).

[3] *House of Lords MSS.*, N. s., iv, 464, and n.

[4] xvii, 104.

"*William Ireland* and *John Swaine*, were sworn to the Truth of Lord *Mohun's* Certificate of his Receiving the Sacrament.

"Then *Charles* Lord *Mohun* took the Oaths, and made and subscribed the Declaration, pursuant to the Statute 25° *Caroli* Secundi; and also took the Oath of Abjuration and subscribed the same."

Other peers followed the same procedure at this time.

Mohun's next reported participation in debate was, no doubt, due as much to personal enmity as to zeal for the opinions which he supported. It was on March 17, 1709/10, when the fourth article of the impeachment [1] of Dr. Sacheverell was under discussion by the Lords, that "The Duke of *Hamilton* having said something in Favour of Dr. *Sacheverell*, he was answer'd by the Lord *Mohun*, to whom his Grace readily reply'd." [2] The speeches seem not to have been preserved.

His next recorded appearance in debate was in a committee of the whole on January 12, 1710/11, for the consideration of the Earl of Scarsdale's resolution censuring Ministers for having advised the

[1] The fourth article charged that Dr. Sacheverell had suggested that the Queen's administration tended toward the destruction of the Constitution.

[2] *The History of the Reign of Queen Anne* . . . Year the Eighth, p. 320.

offensive operations in Spain which terminated in the unlucky defeat of Almanza.

The Lord *Mohun*, on the other Side [*viz.*, against the resolution], said, "He was against it, for several Reasons; 1*st*, Because he knew not who was meant by the Ministry; and he would not have a Censure pass upon Persons, who neither deserved, nor were intended to be censured. 2*dly*, Because the Advice of an Offensive War was, at that time, no ill Advice. 3*dly*, Because he would be just to all Mankind, and not censure any body that gives his Opinion to the best of his Understanding, and with an honest Intention."[1]

His oratorical effort was ineffectual, as the censure was voted.

Another sort of persuasion is recorded of Mohun. On November 29, 1704, Lord Haversham raised in the House the question of Scotland and the Protestant Succession. Lord Nottingham then spoke and

. . . having reflected on the late King *William* in Relation to the Treaty of Partition; the Lord *Somers* rose up, and said, "It was unbecoming a Member of that House to Sully the Memory of so great a Prince; and he doubted not but a Man who could reflect on King *William*, before his Successor, would do the same by her present Majesty, when she was gone. As to the Treaty mention'd by the Lord *N*——,[2] he added, That there was a noble Lord there present (meaning the Earl of

---

[1] *The History and Proceedings of the House of Lords*, ii, 327.
[2] Lord Nottingham.

J———y)[1] who was the principal Agent and Plenipotentiary in that Treaty; and whose Duty as well as Interest, it was to vindicate, both the Memory of his late most Gracious Master, and his own Conduct." In the mean time, the Lord M———n,[2] consulted with several Peers, whether they should move to send the Lord N——— to the Tower: but this being the first time the Queen did the House the Honour to come to hear their Debates, they thought fit to decline that Motion, out of meer respect to her Majesty.[3]

We have written evidence of Mohun's attitude on various questions that came before the House of Lords. These are in the protests signed by him and others upon the passing of acts to which they took serious exception. The first of the protests to which Mohun affixed his name was that of February 23, 1699/1700, against the passing of "An Act for continuing the Governor and Company of Merchants of London trading to The East Indies a Corporation."[4] The next protest which he signed was that of April 4, 1700, against the second reading of the bill in which provisions for selling forfeited Irish estates were tacked to a land-tax act

[1] The Earl of Jersey.
[2] Lord Mohun.
[3] *The History of the Reign of Queen Anne* . . . Year the Third, p. 179. See also *Journals of the House of Lords*, xvii, 586.
[4] *Journals of the House of Lords*, xvi, 525.

for England. The objection was rather to the annexing of foreign clauses to a supply bill than to the act itself.[1] It should be said here that Mohun was a signer on December 9, 1702, of the order and declaration to the effect that such a "tacking" was unparliamentary and tended toward destruction of the constitution. This order was reaffirmed on March 28, 1707, and on March 30, 1709.[2] On April 10, 1700, Mohun was one of twenty-one peers who protested at the passage of the same supply bill without the amendments proposed in the House of Lords but dropped at the request of the Commons.[3]

On January 19, 1702/3, Mohun was among the peers protesting against the clauses in the bill to enable Prince George of Denmark to enjoy his rank and fortune in case of his surviving the Queen.[4] The objections were that the terms of the clauses of the act were not revealed to the House, and that the saving clauses were not definite

[1] *Journals of the House of Lords*, xvi, 569; Rogers, *A Complete Collection of the Protests of the Lords*, i, 138 ff.; Cobbett, *Parliamentary History*, v, cols. 1218–1219: *The History and Proceedings of the House of Lords* . . . ii, 15–16 (where the year is given as 1699).

[2] *Journals of the House of Lords*, xvii, 185; xviii, 303, 692.

[3] *Ibid.*, xvi, 576; Rogers, *op. cit.*, i, 140; Cobbett, *op. cit.*, v, cols. 1219–1220.

[4] *Journals of the House of Lords*, xvii, 247.

enough.[1] Twenty-two peers, among them Lord Mohun, signed the protest of March 24, 1704, which alleged the imperfection of the papers submitted to the House regarding the machinations of Sir John Maclean, the Jacobite plotter.[2] This protest expresses the desire of its signers to censure the Earl of Nottingham for his supposed mismanagement of the case against Sir John.[3]

The next protest signed by Lord Mohun was that of January 11, 1710/11, against throwing out the petitions of Lords Galway and Tyrawley for a hearing before the House.[4] On the same day, he protested against the censure voted upon their insistence on an offensive campaign in Spain which led up to the battle of Almanza.[5] The next protest signed by Lord Mohun was that of January 12, 1710/11, against censuring the ministry for advising

---

[1] *The History and Proceedings of the House of Lords* . . . ii, 46–47.

[2] Rogers, *op. cit.*, i, 169 ff.; *The History and Proceedings of the House of Lords* . . . ii, 73–74.

[3] *Collection of the Parliamentary Debates in England*, iii, 462–463. For what appears to be evidence of Mohun's particular animus toward Lord Nottingham, see *supra*, 167.

[4] *Journals of the House of Lords*, xix, 190; Rogers, *op. cit.*, i, 198 ff.

[5] *Journals of the House of Lords*, xix, 191; Rogers, *op. cit.*, i, 200–201; Luttrell, *A Brief Relation of State Affairs*, vi, 678–679.

an offensive war in Spain in 1707.[1] As has been said, Mohun had spoken against this resolution.[2]

On May 28, 1712, Mohun was among the twenty-seven Lords who protested at the loss of the resolution to address the Queen regarding her sending orders to the Commander-in-Chief, the Duke of Ormonde, to direct him to move against the French.[3] He also signed the protest of twenty-six Lords on June 7, 1712, against the failure to add a clause to an address to the Queen, requesting that she take steps to cause her Allies to join in a mutual guarantee against France.[4] The reasons for both protests were expunged from the Journals of the Lords by a resolution of June 13, 1712.[5]

Mohun never held office under the Crown. He seems, in fact, unlike his father, not to have occupied any of the petty places to which the magnate of Boconnoc was entitled. Certain parliamentary distinctions did, however, fall to Lord Mohun, and had he outlived Queen Anne, very certainly he would have held office as a minister of state.

[1] *Journals of the House of Lords*, xix, 193; Rogers, *op. cit.*, i, 201. Mohun did not, like Lord Somers, sign every Whig protest drawn up during the bitter fight over the conduct of the Spanish campaigns.

[2] See *supra*, p. 166.

[3] *Journals of the House of Lords*, xix, 461.

[4] *Ibid.*, p. 474.

[5] *Ibid.*, pp. 480–481.

STATESMAN

On August 23, 1705, Mohun was one of the peers who attended the Queen to St. Paul's to the solemn thanksgiving for the victory over the French near Tirlemont on July 7.[1] When Parliament opened on October 27, of that year, Mohun was appointed a "Triour des Petic'ons de *Gascoigne*, et des autres Terres et Pais de per le Mer et des Isles." He received the same appointment on November 6, 1707, and November 18, 1708.[2]

On November 9, 1705,[3] the House of Lords began the consideration of "An Act for the better Security of Her Majesty's Person and Government and of the Succession to the Crown of England in the Protestant Line."[4] The act was finally passed by Commons and Lords, and was approved by the Queen on March 19, 1705/6.[5] Section eleven of this act named as "Lord Justices" to administer the kingdom in case of the Queen's death while her heiress was abroad, the Archbishop of Canterbury, Lord Chancellor, Lord Keeper, Lord Treasurer, Lord President, Lord Privy Seal, Lord High Ad-

---

[1] Luttrell, *A Brief Relation of State Affairs*, v, 585; see *Ibid.*, p. 575.
[2] *Journals of the House of Lords*, xviii, 8, 335, 580.
[3] *Ibid.*, pp. 20–21.
[4] *Statutes at Large of England and of Great Britain*, 4–5 Anne, cap. 8 (ed. 1811, vi, 509 ff.).
[5] *Journals of the House of Lords*, xviii, 162.

miral, and Lord Chief Justice of the Queen's Bench.[1] The twelfth section of the act provided for the nomination, by the heiress to the crown, of other Lords Justices to act with the Archbishop and the great officers of state. The list of these appointees was to be made out in triplicate and copies deposited with the Hanoverian minister in London, the Lord Keeper, and the Archbishop of Canterbury.[2] The bill was reintroduced into the House of Lords (having been passed by the Commons) with slight verbal changes, such as the substitution of "Great Britain" for "England,"[3] on February 7, 1707/8.[4] It was quickly passed and was approved by a Commission, the Queen being ill, on February 13, 1707/8.[5] The Electress Dowager Sophia of Hanover received from Lord Halifax a list of twenty-one names from which to choose her nominees as regents. Those upon whom she settled were the Archbishop of York, the Dukes of Somerset, Ormonde, Bolton, Marlborough, and Montagu; the Earls of Bridgewater, Manchester, Peterborough, Rivers, Stamford, Sunderland, Rad-

[1] Cobbett, *Parliamentary History*, vi, cols. 471–472.
[2] *Ibid.; Journals of the House of Lords*, xviii, 22.
[3] *Statutes at Large of England and of Great Britain*, 6 Anne, cap. 7 (ed. 1811, vi, 639 ff.).
[4] *Journals of the House of Lords*, xviii, 449.
[5] *Ibid.*, xviii, 460–461.

nor, and Oxford; and Lords Wharton, Mohun, Raby, Lexington, and Somers.[1] Queen Anne, however, not only outlived the Electress Sophia, but Lord Mohun as well; so that he missed the distinction of acting in a council of regency.

In the autumn of 1710, it seems that Mohun came close to office. A letter from the Duke of Shrewsbury to Robert Harley runs thus:

This morning [November 10, 1710] I have had a long discourse with her Majesty about the Admiralty. You know the objections she has to Lord Jer[sey], which are no ways to be overcome but by the sad reflection how few there are capable of that post. It is now plain by the late orders sent that Lord Raby can hardly be here in time, for it would be unjustifiable not to settle that Commission before the Parliament meets. Lord Rivers was thought on, but I believe he would not care for a place of so great attendance. She ordered me to write to you if you could propose anybody, for she seems in haste the Commission should be passed; and willing Lord Mohun should be one though not the first. I hope in your answer you will propose somebody better than has yet been thought on, or, if you cannot, you will have no ill occasion to press for Lord Jer[sey], or whoever you like best.[2]

---

[1] "Lewis Melville," *George I*, p. 146 and n. 1. "Melville" confuses the bill of 4–5 Anne with that of 6 Anne. He gives no source for his list of prospective Lords Justices.

[2] *Hist. MSS. Comm. Report*, *MSS. of the Marquis of Bath*, i, 200.

Someone better must have been found, for Mohun never served at the Admiralty. On December 13, Sir James Wishart and George Clarke were appointed commissioners of the Admiralty.[1]

From the preceding survey of Mohun's political and Parliamentary activities, it is plain that he did not stand high as a statesman. His interests were in party politics, and his lack of more than mediocre ability, together with his somewhat unsavory past, prevented him from laying claim successfully to the reward to which his zeal might have entitled him. Had he survived the Queen, however, no doubt, as a good Whig who had paid his court at Hanover in Lord Macclesfield's train, he would have had promotion and preferment.

But even though Mohun was not one of the more notable members of his party, he was sufficiently prominent to become, by 1707, a member of the famous Kit-Cat Club,[2] and to have his portrait as such painted by Sir Godfrey Kneller.[3] Among the other members of the club were the Dukes of

[1] Tindal, *A Continuation of Mr. Rapin's History of England*, iv, 195.

[2] For a brief account of this organization, see Aitken, *Life of Steele*, i, 96 ff.

[3] This portrait, dated 1707, is plate 23, in J. Faber's *The Kit-Cat Club Done from the Original Paintings by Sir Godfrey Kneller*, London, 1735. A reproduction serves as frontispiece to this book.

Somerset, Richmond, Grafton, Devonshire, and Marlborough, the Marquis of Wharton, the Earls of Godolphin, Halifax, and Stanhope, Lord Somers, Sir Robert Walpole, Sir John Vanbrugh, Sir Samuel Garth, Sir Richard Steele, William Pulteney, Joseph Addison, George Stepney, William Walsh, William Congreve, Arthur Maynwaring, and Jacob Tonson.[1]

[1] Faber, *op. cit.*

X

TWO DUELS IN A NOVEL

AT the mess of "Handyside's" Regiment, it is Esmond's intention, as it had been years before at the Grayhound Tavern,[1] to prevent a duel between Lord Mohun and a Lord Castlewood, by himself quarrelling with the former and taking the meeting on himself. He succeeds in forestalling his young cousin, who is still lame from his wound at Oudenarde, gives the lie to Mohun, and a duel is arranged immediately. The garden behind the house is suggested by Captain Roger Sterne of "Handyside's"[2] as the place. As becomes the hero of an historical novel, Esmond speedily disposes of his adversary, magnanimously wounding him in the arm, instead of killing him as he might. After the duel, "the gentlemen went back to their wine, and my Lord Mohun to his quarters, where he was laid up with a fever," and, between wound and illness, incapacitated for three months.

The meeting between Henry Esmond and Lord

[1] See *Esmond*, bk. I, chap. 14.
[2] As we learn later in bk. III, chap. 1.

TWO DUELS IN A NOVEL

Mohun is, of course, utterly unhistorical; there is not even the slightest basis in fact for it. On the day of the Allied occupation of the city of Lille (November 23, 1708),[1] Mohun was in his seat in the House of Lords, and, although absent on December 10, the day before the surrender of the citadel at Lille, was present on the fourteenth.[2] Up to the prorogation of Parliament on April 19, 1709, Lord Mohun had been absent from twenty-one scattered sittings of the Lords[3] and present at seventy-one sittings.[4] Of course, then, he could not have been at Lille during the winter, and certainly he was not incapacitated for three months.

Furthermore, in regard to Roger Sterne's part in the affair, Thackeray has again availed himself of his privilege as a writer of fiction. Roger Sterne, father of Lawrence Sterne, was commissioned ensign in Colonel Hans Hamilton's Regiment of Foot in 1710.[5] Although his first service was in Flanders,

---

[1] For data upon the siege of Lille, see Maycock, *Marlborough's Campaigns*, pp. 115–131, and cf. Brodrick, *A Compleat History of the Late War*, pp. 241–270.

[2] *Journals of the House of Lords*, xviii.

[3] *Ibid., passim.* Two of these absences occurred on days (January 31, 1708/9, and February 17, 1708/9), when the House adjourned to hear a sermon.

[4] *Ibid., passim.*

[5] *D. N. B.*, liv, 199–200, art., "Sterne, Lawrence," by Sir S. Lee. Thackeray relates the story of Sterne's marriage in

he obviously could not have been a captain in Handasyde's or "Handyside's," regiment in 1708. Moreover, Roger Sterne never attained the grade of captain, but died a lieutenant in Chudleigh's (late Hamilton's) regiment in March, 1731.[1]

Esmond returns to England soon after, with General Webb,[2] where he finds himself hailed as a hero for his taking on himself Lord Castlewood's

Esmond, bk. III, chap. 5. This incident, as well as the erroneous name of Roger Sterne's regiment, the novelist doubtless obtained from Lawrence Sterne's *Memoir* of himself. The fact that Roger Sterne's daughter, Mary, is said by her brother, in the same narrative, to have been born "in Lisle in French Flanders," in 1712, will account for Thackeray's connecting the elder Sterne and Handasyde's Foot with Lille, at all.

[1] Lee, *loc. cit.*

[2] General Webb's purpose, according to Esmond (bk. II, chap. 15), was to obtain the recognition due him for his services at Lille and Wynendael. It is worthy of note that Thackeray told the Reverend John Irvine that *Esmond* was "founded upon family papers," and that he dictated the Webb, Marlborough, and Cadogan incident to his amanuensis in the room in the British Museum allotted him for his work by Panizzi ("Melville," *Thackeray*, i, 338–339, 336). General John Richmond Webb, Thackeray's ancestor, was a subscriber to Thomas Brodrick's *A Compleat History of the Late War in the Netherlands* (London, 1713). In this work, which pretty certainly Thackeray consulted, occurs an account of the French attempt to carry a supply of powder into Lille (pp. 252 ff.). Brodrick reprints General Webb's report of the action at Wynendael; from this account (pp. 255 ff.) Thackeray most probably obtained the data for his story of the battle. "*An Account of the Battle of Wynendale, written by Major-General Webb himself*," is reprinted, with a plan of the

JAMES, FOURTH DUKE OF HAMILTON

TWO DUELS IN A NOVEL 179

quarrel with Mohun. At a dinner given by Rachel Viscountess Castlewood, a new figure and an important is introduced. This is James fourth Duke of Hamilton, "just created Duke of Brandon in England," "one of the greatest noblemen in the kingdom," as Esmond calls him.[1] The Duke, although a married man at the time, is noticeably struck by the charms of Beatrix Esmond. It is, therefore, no great surprise when we learn that, upon the death of his duchess, the Duke proposes marriage to Beatrix, who, ambitious as she is, accepts him.

Esmond gives, in the course of the narrative,[2] an account of the Duke's life which is, on the whole, fairly correct. It should be observed, however, that in reality the Duke was not a widower at his death, but that his second wife, whom he had married in 1698, outlived him many years, dying in 1744 (N. S.).[3] One ought to note, too, that the "earl of Arran," the Duke's eldest son and successor, was not thirty years of age in 1712, as Beatrix

---

battlefield, in *The History of the Reign of Queen Anne* . . . Year the Seventh, pp. 123–127. It differs from the narrative in Brodrick in details of punctuation and spelling, and occasionally in wording. See also *The History and Proceedings of the House of Lords* . . . ii, 245, where Cardonnel's ascribing the victory to the efforts of General Cadogan is mentioned.

[1] *Esmond*, bk. II, chap. 15.
[2] *Ibid.*, bk. III, chaps. 3, 4.
[3] G. E. C., *Complete Peerage*, iv, 147.

tells Harry,[1] but only nine, having been born January 5, 1702/3.[2] Three, not four, of the six daughters born to the two marriages of the Duke were living at the time of their father's death.[3] Thackeray probably mistook the Queen's godson, Lord Anne Hamilton, for a daughter.[4]

The Duke, too, was not forty-five or six, or yet merely "upwards of fifty," [5] in the last year of his life, but actually was in his fifty-fifth year, having been born April 11, 1658. His birthday, by a curious coincidence, was the same as Lord Mohun's.[6]

[1] *Esmond*, bk. III, chap. 4.

[2] Burke, *Peerage*, ed. 1921, pp. 1060–1061. There is a bare possibility that Thackeray may have been deceived into thinking that the Earl of Arran whom Swift mentions in the *Journal to Stella* was a son of the Duke of Hamilton, instead of a brother to the Duke of Ormonde. The Duke's heir, in any case, would probably have been known as Marquess of Clydesdale, rather than Earl of Arran. The Duke himself had borne the latter title.

[3] Burke, *Op. et loc. cit.* The Duke's two daughters by his first marriage died young.

[4] *Ibid.* Another royal godchild was Lord Anne Poulet, fourth son of Earl Poulet (see *supra*, p. 142, n. 2). The fourth Earl of Essex, who died in 1799, was named William Anne Holles Capel (Nicholas, *Peerage of England*, i, 221).

[5] *Esmond*, bk. iii, chaps. 3, 4.

[6] G. E. C., *op. cit.*, iv, 146; Burke, *op. et loc. cit.*; *D. N. B.* xv, 326, art., "Douglas, James, fourth Duke of Hamilton," by A. Vian. For Lord Mohun's birthday, see *supra*, p. 6. And, while coincidences are being mentioned, it is surely not out of place to point out that *The Injur'd Lovers* of William Mountford, whose death occurred at the very beginning of

TWO DUELS IN A NOVEL

The Duke, as Earl of Arran, had been envoy to Paris under Charles II and again under James II, but, contrary to Esmond's statement, had served William III in no diplomatic capacity.[1] The patent conferring upon him the titles which his mother had resigned, was signed August 10, 1698,[2] instead of in 1690, as Thackeray has it. Perhaps following Collins,[3] the novelist tells us that the Duke was installed as a Knight of the Garter at a chapter held in October, 1712. The fact is, that the Duke was elected to the order on October 25, 1712, but was never installed.[4] After her husband's death the

---

Mohun's career, was dedicated by its actor-author to James Earl of Arran, who years later, as Duke of Hamilton killed, and was killed by, the same Lord Mohun.

[1] G. E. C., *op. et loc. cit.* Some information as to the Duke of Hamilton's engaging in the Jacobite plots against William III came to Thackeray from Macpherson's *Original Papers*. Immediately following an entry concerning Marlborough's betrayal of the Brest expedition of 1694, with references to Macpherson, Thackeray has, in his MS. *Notebook for Henry Esmond*, p. 1:

"Lord Arran Son in law of Sunderland & S also in the plot."

[2] G. E. C., *loc. cit.*

[3] *Peerage of England*, ed. by Sir E. Brydges, i, 545. According to this work, the Duke was installed as a Knight of the Garter, October 26, 1712. Thackeray says that the Earl of Oxford and others were installed at the same time (*Esmond*, bk. III, chap. 4).

[4] G. E. C., *op. cit.*, iv, 147. The following account is from *The History of the Reign of Queen Anne* . . . Year the Eleventh, p. 272:

Duchess wrote the Earl of Oxford, mentioning the royal dispensations whereby knights who had died before installation had been registered in the order and had had their plates fixed in their stalls at Windsor.[1] This favor, for which the Duchess petitioned to perpetuate the distinction shown the Duke, was granted August 4, 1713. The plate was affixed to the Duke's stall only in 1836![2] It should be said that the Duke of Argyll was the first subject to receive both the Thistle and the Garter, but,

"On *Sunday* the 26th [*sic*] [of October, 1712] was held at Windsor Castle, 'A Chapter of the most Noble Order of the Garter, when the Queen, Sovereign of the Order, and several of the Knights Companions, habited in their Mantles, being present, *Henry*, Duke of *Beaufort*, Captain of Her Majesty's Band of Gentleman Pensioners; *James*, Duke of *Hamilton* and *Brandon*, Master General of Her Majesty's Ordnance; *Henry* Duke of *Kent;* John Earl Poulet, Lord Steward of Her Majesty's Household; *Robert* Earl of *Oxford* and Earl *Mortimer*, Lord High Treasurer of *Great Britain;* and *Thomas* Earl of *Stratford*, one of Her Majesty's Ambassadors Plenipotentiary at *Utrecht*, and first Lord Commissioner of the Admiralty, were Elected Knights Companions of the said most Noble Order, having been first introduced into the Chapter (except his Grace the Duke of *Hamilton*, who had formerly receiv'd the Honour of Knighthood, when he was invested with the Order of *St. Andrew* or the *Thistle*).'"

Thackeray remarks upon the Duke's election to the Order of the Garter at the same chapter as Lord Oxford (*Esmond*, bk. III, chap. 4).

[1] The letter was written perhaps in December, 1712; see *Hist. MSS. Comm. Reports, MSS of the Duke of Portland*, v, 257.

[2] G. E. C., *op. et loc. cit.*, n. *d.*

unlike the Duke of Hamilton, was not allowed to retain the two orders at once.[1]

When, at a dinner given in the winter of 1708/9, Thackeray has Henry St. John give the health of the Duke of Brandon,[2] he is setting forward by nearly three years Queen Anne's creation of a British dukedom for her Scottish favorite. The dukedom of Brandon was conferred upon the Duke of Hamilton on September 10, 1711.[3] In another place,[4] Thackeray appears, however, to date the British peerage in 1710.

Thackeray places the appointment of the Duke as Ambassador to France "a few days after" his installation as a Knight of the Garter. In reality, the Duke was named for the mission on August 29, 1712, nearly two months before his election, not installation, at Windsor.[5]

---

[1] G. E. C., *op. cit.* i, 11, n. *b*. Contemporary accounts allege that the Duke of Hamilton was asked to resign the Thistle (*The History of the Reign of Queen Anne* . . . p. 278). The Duke's illegitimate son, Charles Hamilton, asserted, however, that the Duke was not deprived of the Order of the Thistle, because of the Queen's intervention (*Transactions during the Reign of Queen Anne*, quoted by T. C. and W. Snow, *Esmond*, p. 540).

[2] *Esmond*, bk. II, chap. 15.

[3] G. E. C., *Complete Peerage*, iv, 146. T. C. and W. Snow incorrectly date the Duke of Hamilton's creation as Duke of Brandon in 1710 (*op. cit.*, 530). They do, however, observe Thackeray's anachronism in this passage.

[4] *Esmond*, bk. III, chap. 4. [5] G. E. C., *op. cit.*, bk. IV, 147.

Here and there through the novel, as is always the case when Lord Mohun is not on the scene, there are passing references to him.[1] The first significant allusion to him is made by the Duke of Hamilton himself, who remarks that he and Mohun are connected by marriage, though neither by blood nor friendship.[2] At the end of the same conversation, upon being asked when he intends to leave for Paris as ambassador, the Duke replies that he has law business to attend to first: "That ill-omened Mohun has come, or is coming, to London again: we are in a lawsuit about my late Lord Gerard's property;[3] and he hath sent to me to meet him."

On the eighteenth of November, 1712, Esmond is invited to a dinner at General Webb's house, in honor of the Duke of Hamilton. An hour before dinnertime, however, the Duke had sent Webb his excuses, alleging that "the most immediate busi-

[1] As in bk. II, chap. 15, when the ladies of Castlewood give Esmond a sword on his return to England, after his duel with Mohun at Lille; in bk. III, chap. 1, when Lord Castlewood announces his intention of forcing a duel with Mohun; in the same book and chapter, when Esmond introduces Roger Sterne by name; in bk. III, chap. 4, when Beatrix admits to Esmond that he has touched her heart by his taking her brother's quarrel with Mohun on himself.

[2] *Esmond*, bk. III, chap. 4.

[3] For the history of the Hamilton-Mohun law suits, see *infra*, pp. 190 ff.

The Reverend
Dr. J. Swift D.S.T.D.

ness" prevented his attendance. The dinner was, appropriately enough in view of the news which came at its end, "as dismal as a funeral." Another reference to Mohun occurs in the conversation: "Some one said the ill-omened face of Mohun had been seen at the theatre the night before, and Macartney and Meredith with him."

At last, all the guests leave, except Lord Bolingbroke and Esmond. As the former is building castles in the air with the accession of the Pretender as their foundation, Swift returns with a perturbed face and "the most dreadful news." Says he:

"Duke Hamilton is dead; he was murdered an hour ago by Mohun and Macartney; they had a quarrel this morning; they gave him not so much time as to write a letter. He went for a couple of his friends, and he is dead, and Mohun, too, the bloody villain, who was set on him. They fought in Hyde Park just before sunset; the Duke killed Mohun, and Macartney came up and stabbed him, and the dog is fled." [1]

Swift then suggests to Bolingbroke that he "send to every part of the country and apprehend" Macartney.

Esmond immediately verifies Swift's report by the weeping servants at the Duke's door, and then

[1] *Esmond*, bk. III, chap. 5.

sets out for Kensington, where he breaks the news — somewhat abruptly — to Beatrix. After she has retired, Lady Castlewood, Doctor Francis Atterbury, who is at the house, and Esmond discuss the affair. Esmond gives the story of the quarrel between Hamilton and Mohun and an account of their duel. He says:

"The two noblemen had long been at war with respect to the Lord Gerard's property, whose two daughters my Lord Duke and Mohun had married. They had met by appointment that day at the lawyer's in Lincoln's Inn Fields; had words, which, though they appeared very trifling to those who heard them, were not so to men exasperated by long and previous enmity. Mohun asked my Lord Duke where he could see his Grace's friends, and within an hour had sent two of his own to arrange this deadly duel. It was pursued with such fierceness, and sprang from so trifling a cause, that all men agreed at the time that there was a party, of which these three notorious brawlers were but agents, who desired to take Duke Hamilton's life away. They fought three on a side, as in that tragic meeting twelve years back, which hath been recounted already, and in which Mohun performed his second murder. They rushed in, and closed upon each other at once without any feints or crossing of swords even, and stabbed one at the other desperately, each receiving many wounds; and Mohun having his death-wound, and my Lord Duke lying by him, Macartney came up and stabbed his Grace as he lay on the ground, and gave him the blow of which he died."

TWO DUELS IN A NOVEL

Esmond adds:

"Colonel Macartney denied this, of which the horror and indignation of the whole kingdom would nevertheless have him guilty, and fled the country, whither he never returned."[1]

Esmond's comment upon the affair is that it had at its bottom "a paltry quarrel that might easily have been made up." Lord Mohun's character was such, he thinks, that the Duke might have refused his challenge; but the Duke's "spirit was so high that those who wished his death knew that his courage was like his charity, and never turned any man away, and he died by the hands of Mohun, and the other two cut-throats that were set upon him." He goes on to say:

"That party to which Lord Mohun belonged had the benefit of his service, and now were well rid of such a ruffian. He, and Meredith, and Macartney were the Duke of Marlborough's men; and the two colonels had been broke but the year before for drinking perdition to the Tories. His Grace was a Whig now and a Hanoverian, and as eager for war as Prince Eugene himself. I say not that he was privy to Duke Hamilton's death: I say that his party profited by it; and that three desperate and bloody instruments were found to effect that murder."[2]

---

[1] *Esmond*, bk. III, chap. 6.
[2] *Ibid.*

As Esmond and Dean Atterbury walk away from Kensington after their conversation with Lady Castlewood, they hear the street-criers hawking their broadsides, recounting the story of the duel. Early the next morning Esmond drives away one of them who is crying his wares beneath Beatrix's open window.[1]

With the death of Lord Mohun, naturally references to him, and to those associated with him, grow fewer. A year and a half after the Hamilton-Mohun duel, Doctor Atterbury reports to the Jacobite conspirators, of whom Esmond is one, how "Mr. Aymé," the surgeon of Long Acre, had cupped the dying Queen Anne, and had caused her to rest more easily.[2] It was at his bath that Lord Castlewood had died after his duel with Mohun; and there that Lord Warwick and several of the other participants in the affair that had served

[1] *Esmond*, bk. III, chap. 6.
[2] *Ibid.*, bk. III, chap. 11. This circumstance is historical. "Mr. *Ayme* Surgeon in *Long-Acre*, and her Majesty's Cupper in Ordinary, being immediately sent for upon the Queen's falling ill, July 29, 1714, perform'd his Office between Twelve and One in the Afternoon, in the Presence of Dr. *Arbuthnot*, Serjeant-Surgeon *Dickens*, and the Lady Masham" (A. Boyer ... *The Political State of Great Britain* ... second ed., viii, 628; this passage, which they quote, is by T. C. and W. Snow erroneously ascribed to Boyer's *Annals*, a work which comes down only to the end of 1712).

Thackeray as a source had actually repaired at its conclusion.[1] Then a few days later, as Esmond and Lord Castlewood gallop over Castlewood Downs on their way to save Beatrix from the Pretender, Henry notes the spot where fourteen years before Esmond and Mohun had been overturned in the latter's pony carriage, and his sinister influence upon the house of Esmond had begun vigorously to be asserted.[2] No further mention of Lord Mohun occurs in *Esmond*.

[1] *Esmond*, bk. I, chap. 14, and see *supra*, pp. 75 and 88.
[2] *Esmond*, bk. III, chap. 13.

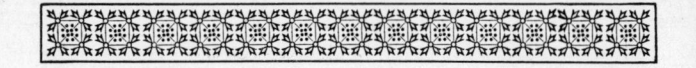

XI

LAWSUITS

AS one would expect who has followed Thackeray's treatment of historical fact up to this point in *Henry Esmond*, the novelist has dealt very freely with the circumstances of the actual duel between Lord Mohun and the Duke of Hamilton in transferring them to his fiction.[1] This will be evident from a perusal of the following account of the events which led up to the meeting and of the duel itself.

James fourth Duke of Hamilton married as his second wife the Honorable Elizabeth Gerard, only daughter of Digby fifth Lord Gerard of Bromley and his wife Elizabeth, youngest of the three daughters of Charles first Earl of Macclesfield, and sister of the second and third earls of Macclesfield. The events incident to the marriage and those

[1] I certainly do not agree, therefore, with T. C. and W. Snow, who assert that Thackeray's account is not at variance with "the contemporary narratives, where they agree, except in two points," these being the number of combatants on each side and the cousinship of the Duchess of Hamilton and the first Lady Mohun (*Esmond*, p. 547).

LAWSUITS

resultant from it are thus recounted by a contemporary:

Upon the Death of the Lord *Digby Gerrard* the Lady *Elizabeth Gerrard* his wife was left Guardian to her Daughter, who having about 60000*l.* to her Portion, when the late Duke *Hamilton* courted her for a Wife, he offer'd to content himself with the said Portion; and to prevent all future Contests and Disputes at Law, promis'd to give the Lady *Gerrard* a general Release of the Guardianship two Days after Marriage; for the Performance of which Promise he bound himself in a Bond of 10000*l.*

After the Consummation of the Marriage the Lady *Gerrard* call'd upon her Son-in-Law to give her the said Release, which he declined to do, and on the contrary, sought Relief in the Court of Chancery against his said Bond for 10000*l.* which the Lady *Gerrard* so highly resented, that in the general Opinion, it broke her heart; and enclined her, by her Will, to bequeath the all she had to her Brother the late Lord *Brandon Gerrard* Earl of *Macclesfield*; leaving only a Legacy of Five Shillings to her Daughter, and a Diamond Neck-lace, in Case her Husband should consent to give the said Release: Whereas tis very probable, that if the late Duke of *Hamilton* had perform'd his Promise, he would have inherited all the Estate of the *Macclesfield's* Family.

But upon his Non-performance, the late Earl of *Macclesfield*, as was hinted before, constituted the late Lord *Mohun*, who had married his Niece, Daughter to the present Lady *Charlotte Orbey*, his Sole Heir in Consideration of the Affection and Value he had for him;[1] so that

---

[1] Burke, who tells us in his *Landed Gentry of . . . Great Britain*, that Lord Mohun was descended from the Gerrards,

on the Decease of the said Earl, the Lord *Mohun* took Possession of his Estate, except that Part of it which the Earl left to his Brother the Lord *Fitton Gerrard*, last Earl of *Macclesfield*, who dying afterwards without Issue, the whole Estate of the *Macclesfield's* Family, to the Value of above 4000*l. per. Annum.* fell to the late Lord *Mohun*.

The late Duke of *Hamilton* thinking himself injur'd by the Wills of the Lady *Gerrard*, and the late Earl of *Macclesfield*, chose rather to forfeit his Bond of 10000*l.* than not [to] vindicate his Claim to so considerable an Estate; in pursuance of which he exhibited a Bill in Chancery against my Lord *Mohun* to oblige him, as Executor of the Lady *Gerrard*, to give an Account of her Guardianship.[1]

The death of the second Earl of Macclesfield certainly enhanced Lord Mohun's fortunes, which seem to have been considerably straitened by the debts of his father and grandfather.[2] Probably, too, his own life up to 1701 had not been one of economy. Luttrell[3] reports the property left by the Earl to Lord Mohun to have been worth twenty thousand pounds. Another story brings the

and hence inherited by right of birth from Lady Gerard, is of course, in error (iv, 463, art., "Digby of Osbertstown").

[1] *A True and Impartial Account of the Animosity, Quarrel and Duel, between the late Duke of Hamilton, and the Lord Mohun* . . . (printed by A. Baldwin, London, 1712), pp. 25 ff.

[2] See *supra*, p. 11, and cf. *The History of the Reign of Queen Anne.* . . Year the Eleventh, p. 304.

[3] *A Brief Relation of State Affairs*, v, 106–107.

LAWSUITS

value up to fifty-one thousand pounds.[1] Gawseworth, in Cheshire, which had been acquired by the Earl of Macclesfield after a long law suit with the Fittons, was a part of Lord Mohun's inheritance.[2] It appears also that, upon the death of Fitton third Earl of Macclesfied, in 1702, Mohun inherited the other property of the Macclesfield family.[3] This, according to one source, amounted to four thousand pounds a year;[4] the estates which passed from the second to the third earl at the former's death were reported at the time to be worth six thousand pounds a year.[5] In any event, it is certain that Mohun profited to a considerable extent from the property, personal and real, which he inherited from the family of the first Baroness Mohun.

It is perhaps no wonder then that the Duke and Duchess of Hamilton strove vigorously to recover what they could of the latter's mother's fortune, and that Lord Mohun busied himself equally in the attempt to retain what he had been bequeathed.

[1] Letter from John Coke to Thomas Coke in 1701 (*Hist. MSS. Comm. Reports*, xii, pt. 2, p. 446, *MSS. of Earl Cowper*).
[2] Collins, *Peerage of England*, v, 534, n.
[3] *A True and Impartial Account of the Animosity* ... p. 26. Gilbert in his *Parochial History of Cornwall* has confused the second and third earls, for he says that Fitton Earl of Macclesfield left part of his estates to Mohun in 1701 (i, 67).
[4] *A True and Impartial Account of the Animosity* ... *loc. cit.*
[5] Luttrell, *A Brief Relation of State Affairs*, v, 106–107.

Mohun was forced to defend himself against attacks from two quarters, for not only was suit brought by the Duke and Duchess, but the Crown as well laid claim to the property involved. The second earl, who, when Lord Brandon, had been attainted for treason, although later pardoned, had failed to record his pardon. Hence, according to the Crown attorneys, the property left him could not be inherited by him, but escheated to the Crown.[1] This second claim, which rested upon a mere technicality,[2] seems not to have been pressed very hard, and Lord Macclesfield's oversight was finally remedied by permission of the Judges of Queen's Bench.[3] Any title which the Crown may have had was finally disposed of, after Lord Mohun's death, when, at the petition of his widow, the House of Lords confirmed by a special act the reversal of Lord Macclesfield's attainder, and thereby cleared the title of Lady Mohun to the property inherited from her husband which she was proposing then to sell.[4]

[1] Luttrell, *op. cit.*, v, 307; *Hist. MSS. Comm. Reports*, iv, 233, an abstract of an opinion in the *MSS. of the Marquess of Bath*.
[2] It was, however, taken with considerable seriousness at the time; see Luttrell, *op. cit.*, v, 307, 360.
[3] *Ibid.*, v, 363.
[4] *Journals of the House of Lords*, xx, 322, 386, 387, 388–389, 392, 396. The petition was offered March 27, 1716; the bill

LAWSUITS

Improved though Lord Mohun's fortunes were by his acquisition of the property of the Earls of Macclesfield, it involved him in litigation which descended to his widow at his death.[1] Perhaps the first complication was the arrest, on December 15, 1701, of Thomas Sheperd, Mohun's steward, and

was brought in June 20; on June 22, the Duchess of Hamilton and her aunt Lady Charlotte Orby, mother of the first Baroness of Lord Mohun, petitioned for a hearing in opposition to the bill, but were denied it; the bill passed the Lords on June 23, and was signed by King George I on June 26, after the Commons had concurred in it. Previously the Lords had been informed (on March 27) of the King's approval of the action proposed. Cf. Boyer ... *The Political State of Great Britain* ... xi [Jan.-June, 1716], 689-690, 692.

[1] Lady Mohun having successfully brought actions for ejectment against them in the Court of Exchequer, the Duchess of Hamilton, her aunt Lady Charlotte Orby, her uncle or cousin, John Elrington, and Elizabeth, Lord Mohun's daughter, appealed the case to the House of Lords on April 14, 1714, on writs of error; but as no counsel appeared for the plaintiffs on the day set for arguing the writs, their petition was dismissed, and the judgment of the lower court affirmed on June 7, 1714 (*Journals of the House of Lords*, xix, 657, 674, 688-689, 690, 691, 693, 708). As has been noticed above (p. 194, n. 4), the Duchess Dowager of Hamilton and Lady Charlotte Orby petitioned the Lords on June 22, 1716, to be heard against the bill then pending to confirm the reversal of the attainder of the second Earl of Macclesfield; but their plea was rejected (*Ibid.*, xx, 388-389). What were the grounds of the case involved in Lady Mohun's appeal on a writ of error from the Court of Exchequer to the House of Lords on May 8, 1713, which was decided against her on June 3, because of the non-appearance of her counsel, I do not know (*Ibid.*, xix, 531, 541, 558).

his imprisonment at Macclesfield on a charge of trespass brought by the agents of the third Earl of Macclesfield, but probably without his knowledge. By direction of the House of Lords, to which Lord Mohun complained of this infringement of his peer's privilege, Sheperd was released.[1]

It was probably at a time shortly after the death of the third Earl of Macclesfield that the servants of the Duchess of Hamilton attempted to take possession of the house at Gerard's Bromley, but were driven away by the persons resident therein, aided by the tenantry.[2]

During the ten or eleven years through which the legal contest of the Duke and Lord Mohun dragged on, both sides are said, in their turn, to have won the advantage, although from such reports as are preserved, Lord Mohun would seem to have gained more points than his opponent. On January 27, 1702/3, a suit in chancery between the Duke and Mohun was decided for the latter.[3] The suit was brought to compel Lord Mohun as heir and execu-

---

[1] *Journals of the House of Lords*, xvii, 12–13 (January 7, 1701/2); *MSS. of the House of Lords*, N. S., iv, 417.

[2] Letter of the Duchess of Hamilton to the Earl of Sunderland, undated (*Hist. MSS. Comm. Reports*, vii, 49, *MSS. of the Duke of Marlborough*).

[3] So Luttrell, *op. cit.*, v, 263. As Mohun appealed from the decision in chancery to the House of Lords, he cannot have considered himself actually to have won the suit.

LAWSUITS

tor of Charles Earl of Macclesfield to deliver to the plaintiffs a pair of diamond pendants and a necklace left by the Earl to the Duchess on condition that she gave no trouble to his executor. Mohun, who had now become executor of Lady Gerard's estate, had refused to turn the jewels over to the Duchess, unless the Duke would give him the release for which he had bonded himself to his mother-in-law, the late Lady Gerard. The Court of Chancery decreed that the Duke and Duchess were not to "trouble" Mohun, and that the jewels were to be delivered to a master in chancery to be resigned to them after they had signed the release. Lord Mohun appealed the case to the House of Lords on November 9, 1703; and, after a long delay, on account of the Duke's illness, the hearing took place on January 28, 1703/4. The decree of the Court of Chancery was reversed, and the jewels were left in Lord Mohun's care until the Duke and Duchess executed the general release of him from all claims on the property inherited from the Earl of Macclesfield. They were allowed until February 1, 1704, to sign the instrument in question. The petition of the Duke and Duchess, on February 1, 1703/4, to be heard before a date should be set for the execution of the release, was rejected by the Lords.[1]

[1] *Journals of the House of Lords*, xvii, 333, 336, 341, 363,

On January 28, 1705/6, a hearing took place in chancery for property worth two thousand pounds a year, of Lord Macclesfield's estate, with Lord Mohun as defendant and Sir Thomas Orby as plaintiff. Sir Thomas claimed the property as an heir at law (presumably on behalf of Lady Charlotte Orby, his wife).[1] The case went over to January 30.[2] The Duke and Duchess of Hamilton did not relax their efforts to gain some share of Lady Gerard's, or Lord Macclesfield's, estate. A decree in chancery was made in favor of the Duke on May 20, 1710.[3] On November 22 of the same year, however, in a chancery hearing it was Lord Mohun who secured the decision.[4] The Duke and Duchess petitioned the House of Lords on January 29, 1711/2, asking leave to proceed in the Court of Chancery against Lord Mohun without regard to his privilege of Parliament. The

---

388, 391; *Hist. MSS. Comm. Reports, MSS. of the House of Lords*, N. S., v, 221 ff.; Luttrell, *op. cit.*, v, 385.

[1] Luttrell, *op. cit.*, vi, 11. The diarist says that Sir Charles Orby (who had been Mohun's guardian) was a partner to the suit, but it is more probable that Sir Thomas Orby, second husband to the mother of the first Lady Mohun, was the person involved.

[2] What the ultimate decision was, I do not know. Probably it was in favor of Lord Mohun.

[3] Luttrell, *op. cit.*, vi, 585.

[4] *Ibid.*, vi, 657.

LAWSUITS

Lords, however, on February 8, rejected the petition.[1] On February 11, of the same year, Lord Mohun appealed to the House of Lords, as heir and executor of Lord Macclesfield, from two decrees in chancery (of June 18 and November 19, 1711) against him and in favor of Peter Minshall (or Minshull)[2] and his sisters, Elizabeth and Jane. The two latter respondents petitioned the Lords in their turn to allow them three months for the preparation and submission of their answer, as Peter Minshall was then in Spain.[3] The hearing of the appeal was deferred until the sitting of Parliament next after Michaelmas. As Parliament, after successive prorogations, did not begin to sit regu-

---

[1] *Journals of the House of Lords*, xix, 366, 371, 372, 373; Luttrell, *op. cit.*, vi, 724. We learn from a letter of the Earl of Mar to his brother, dated February 14, 1711/2, that the Scotch peers, angered at a resolution of the House of Lords regarding the Duke of Hamilton and his English peerage, by agreement absented themselves for two days from the sessions of the House. During these two days the Duke's petition came up and was rejected (see *Hist. MSS. Comm. Reports, MSS. of the Earl of Mar*, p. 497. In the index, "Mohun" should be read for "Mahon"; the text gives "Mahoun").

[2] It is not without interest that one recalls that in June, 1713, Edward Minshull, "formerly of Stoke, in Cheshire," suing Richard Steele for £250 lent him, secured a judgment for that sum with three guineas' damages (Aitkin, *Life of Steele*, i, 391–392). No doubt Edward Minshull was a relative of Peter.

[3] *Journals of the House of Lords*, xix, 375, 396.

larly until April 9, 1713,[1] the appeal was not heard then, since Lord Mohun had been dead nearly five months. The appeal was revived on July 9, 1715, on the petition of Elizabeth Lady Mohun, who asserted that the Minshalls had taken possession of the estate in question, and had enjoined her from executing the judgment in ejectment which she had obtained.[2] After investigation of Lady Mohun's charges, the House of Lords ordered, on July 29, that she be put in possession of the estate.[3] On August 4, 1715, Alice and Jane Minshall, as administrators of Thomas Minshall, deceased, on their behalf and that of their brother Peter, petitioned the House of Lords that they again be allowed sufficient time to hear from their brother (who was still in Spain) and to prepare their defence, notwithstanding that possession of the estate over which the litigation had arisen, had been awarded Lady Mohun. The petition was tabled and no further action seems to have been taken.[4]

[1] *Journals of the House of Lords*, xix, *passim*.
[2] *Ibid.*, xx, 98.
[3] *Ibid.*, xx, 133.
[4] *Ibid.*, xx, 146.

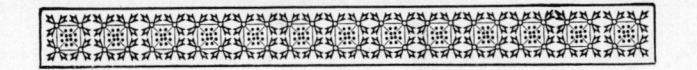

XII

A QUARREL AND A CHALLENGE

THE reference already noted [1] of the Duke of Hamilton, in Thackeray's novel, to his law business with Lord Mohun does not depart from fact, for, in the early part of November, 1712, the two noblemen were engaged in another chancery hearing. It is said that the main cause was finally nearing a settlement when, on November 11, 1712, the Duke and Lord Mohun met at the chambers in Chancery Lane of one Mr. Orlebar,[2] a master in Chancery. That day everything passed peaceably.[3] The next hearing occurred before Mr. Orlebar on November 13, between six and seven in the evening.[4] In the course of the business a deposition by

---

[1] *Supra*, p. 184.

[2] Was this Mr. Orlebar the Richard Orlebar of Queen Anne's time whose letters are now among the MSS. of Richard Orlebar, Esq., of Hinwick House, County Bedford? See *Hist. MSS. Comm. Reports*, iii, 274 ff.

[3] *A True and Impartial Account of the Animosity* ... p. 27.

[4] *Ibid.*; also *A Particular Account of the Tryal of John Hamilton, Esq., for the Murder of Charles Lord Mohun, and James Duke of Hamilton and Brandon*, published by Order of the Right Honourable Sir Richard Hoare, Kt., Lord Mayor

Richard Whitworth, who had been a steward for Lady Gerard and for the Earl of Macclesfield,[1] was read. The Duke commented upon the evidence, saying that Whitworth had neither truth nor justice in him.[2] To this observation Lord

of the City of London. Testimony of Rice Williams, footman to Lord Mohun.

[1] See *A True and Impartial Account of the Animosity* ... pp. 27–28. Richard Whitworth of Adbaston, County Stafford, was father to Charles Lord Whitworth, Ambassador at the Russian Court. It might be noted that another son, Richard Whitworth, Jr., was a cornet in Lord Macclesfield's Regiment of Horse (see Dalton, *Army Lists*, iii, 354, iv, 268, n. 1). Edward Whitworth was an ensign in Lord Mohun's Regiment of Foot in 1706 (Dalton, *op. cit.*, v, 265).

[2] *Tryal of John Hamilton*, testimony of Williams and of Mr. Gawin Mason, the Duke's secretary. Mason swore that the Duke said that Whitworth "had quite forgot himself about a Year" before, and was not to be believed, and that Lord Mohun who was "in Wine" had replied as Williams testified. One of the Duke's lawyers, Mr. Thornhill, testified before the Privy Council on November 18, that the Duke objected of the admission of Whitworth's deposition (who had been excused on account of his age two years before), saying he did not believe the deponent would speak the truth, "upon which Lord Mohun said as true as his Grace" (*Lord Dartmouth's Minutes* in *Hist. MSS. Comm. Reports*, xi, pt. 5, 311, *MSS. of the Earl of Dartmouth*). There were various accounts of the immediate grounds of the quarrel. The *Post Boy* reported that Whitworth had appeared a year before as a witness for the Duke and had then been impeached for his senility by Lord Mohun. The Duke commented on his lawyer's recalling this fact, whereupon Mohun retorted. To this reply the Duke answered that he did not believe Lord Mohun (November 20–22, 1712). Both the *Post Boy* and Swift [?] in the *Examiner*

A QUARREL AND A CHALLENGE 203

Mohun retorted sharply that his witness had as much of either as the Duke. The Duke did not respond; but soon after, on the adjournment of the hearing, he went away. As Lord Mohun passed the Duke in leaving Mr. Orlebar's chambers, neither spoke to the other.[1] Before the adjournment of the hearing, Saturday, November 15, was fixed for the next meeting at the master's, in spite of Lord Mohun's request that it be set for the following Monday, because of his desire to go into the country for a day or two.[2]

---

assert, as did Mason, that Mohun was drunk at the hearing before the Master in Chancery (in the issues for November 18-20, 1712, and November 13-20, 1712, respectively). See also the Tory *True and Impartial Account of the Murder of . . . the Duke of Hamilton . . .* pp. 3-5.

Gawin Mason possibly was not a disinterested witness, even setting aside his relationship to the Duke. He had apparently sued Colonel Baldwin Leighton in the Court of Queen's Bench for possession of the wardenship of the Fleet, but had lost his case. He had then appealed to the Lords on a writ of error. The writ was argued February 21, 1710/1, and decided against Mason. See *Journals of the House of Lords*, xix, 198, 216, 232. Colonel Leighton had earlier been assisted by Mohun, who probably did not in this case show much favor toward a friend of the Duke of Hamilton. See *supra*, p. 152.

[1] *Tryal of John Hamilton*, testimony of Rice Williams.

[2] *A True and Impartial Account of the Animosity . . .* p. 28. According to General Maccartney, Mohun told him of an engagement to dine at "Ashly" on Saturday (*A Letter from Mr. Maccartney to a Friend of His in London.* printed for A. Baldwin, London, 1713).

Lord Mohun is said by one witness [1] (his footman) to have gone then to White's Chocolate House, and afterwards to the Queen's Arms in Pall Mall for supper, after which he went home, leaving orders with his servants that no one should be admitted the next morning except Lieutenant General George Maccartney.[2] On its face, however, this account of Lord Mohun's actions after leaving Mr. Orlebar's chambers does not agree with that given by one of the chief actors in the approaching duel. General Maccartney later said that at about nine o'clock in the evening of November 13, Lord Mohun appeared at his (Maccartney's) lodgings "prodigiously wearied out with his lawyers," but unable to eat or drink until he had unburdened himself to his friend. Mohun complained of the Duke's having previously browbeaten his witnesses, and asserted that the Duke's language and manner that evening had been such as to cause him to believe himself aimed at by them.[3] Maccartney attempted to calm his visitor,

---

[1] *Tryal of John Hamilton*, testimony of Rice Williams.

[2] For a brief sketch of Maccartney's career, see *Appendix B, infra*, pp. 257–265.

[3] "Particularly he said of Mr. *Whitworth*, that he was a vile old Rogue, not to be credited, nor fitting for any honest Man to employ; saying this in such an Air and Manner, as if I had produced corrupt Evidence." (Lord Mohun's

A QUARREL AND A CHALLENGE 205

who, however, refused to be pacified, but desired the general to take a message from him to the Duke. Said Mohun:

"Tell him, in the civillest manner you can, that though I have had reason to complain of his Grace's hard Usage of my Council and Evidence several times before now, yet I would not make theirs any Concern of mine; and though the severe Reflections he made this Evening seem'd to be directly levell'd at myself, yet I leave them to his Grace's own Explanation; and if I am out of the Question, then I only wish that for the future we may meet on better Terms, and leave the Scolding to the Lawyers; or both by Consent absent ourselves from their Meetings; but if his Grace have any particular Prejudice to my Person or Manners, he may find other Opportunities of telling me his Mind, and I shall be always ready to attend him." [1]

Maccartney then agreed to carry Lord Mohun's message if he persisted in his desire to send it after they had supped. The two then had supper "abroad with company." [2] When they parted Mohun told Maccartney he was only the more confirmed in his resolution, and requested the general not to neglect him.

There is an apparent discrepancy in the accounts

account of the event, as quoted by General Maccartney in *A Letter from Mr. Maccartney.*)

[1] *Ibid.*

[2] This agrees in part with Rice William's evidence concerning his master's doings, as summarized, *supra*, p. 204.

of Lord Mohun's movements given by the general and by the footman. Perhaps, however, Williams, the servant, was not in a position to observe all his master's doings on the evening in question. That Mohun in some way communicated with Maccartney appears established by his orders to admit no one except the general on Friday morning, November 14. Possibly after going to White's, Mohun visited Maccartney's lodgings without the notice of the domestic, and thence went to supper at the Queen's Arms.

On Friday morning, Mohun went early to Maccartney's lodgings,[1] and pressed the General to carry out his instructions of the night before. Having learned that nine was the Duke's hour for company, Maccartney went in Mohun's coach to the Duke's house. As the Duke had gone out, with the intention of returning at eleven, Maccartney left his name, and called at that hour, only to find the Duke absent again. Since a message had been left for Maccartney in which he was desired to return in half an hour, he did so, but the Duke was still not at home. Then Maccartney went to dinner with Lord Mohun, at the Globe Tavern in the Strand, where Colonel Joseph

[1] *A Letter from Mr. Maccartney; Tryal of John Hamilton*, testimony of Rice Williams.

A QUARREL AND A CHALLENGE

Churchill and Sir Robert Rich were of the party.[1] Some time earlier Mohun and Maccartney had gone to the Duke of Marlborough's house, where they had spent about half an hour.[2] While at the tavern, Maccartney learned that a gentleman from the Duke of Hamilton — his secretary, Gawin Mason — was searching for him; so, as soon as he had dined, Maccartney made his fourth journey of the day to the Duke's house, arriving about four o'clock in the afternoon.

Maccartney gave the Duke, who received him "with a good deal of civility," Lord Mohun's message. The Duke, however, according to Maccartney's account, did not receive it with cordiality, but said that Mohun had been very much in the wrong the night before, and that he had been abroad that morning in search of a certain friend, to send Lord Mohun to tell him so. Not finding this gentleman and hearing of the repeated calls of Maccartney, Mohun's intimate friend, at his house, he had suspected that the general came

[1] *Tryal of John Hamilton*, testimony of Rice Williams.
[2] *Ibid.* If the two friends visited the Duke of Marlborough, it is obvious why Maccartney says nothing of their call in his letter, especially when the Tories had proclaimed the meeting of the Duke and Lord Mohun a "political duel" instigated by the Whigs, among whom Marlborough was now a chief figure. Cf. *Esmond*, bk. III, chap. 6; and see Tindal, *A Continuation of Mr. Rapin's History of England*, iv, 297–299.

from Lord Mohun, and so he had sent to say that he was now at home. "And now, Sir," continued the Duke, "be pleased to tell my Lord *Mohun* I will meet him when and where he pleases."

On hearing this bellicose message, Maccartney asserted later that he attempted to persuade the Duke that the affair might be settled without a duel, but the Duke persisted in demanding a meeting. It was then arranged that the Duke with a friend should meet Maccartney an hour later at the Rose Tavern in Covent Garden.[1] Maccartney agreed to this, saying that, if he could, he would bring Lord Mohun, in the hope still of accommodating matters between the two peers. Returning to his friend, Maccartney reported only a part of the Duke's discourse, being afraid of angering his friend still more. He then sought and obtained from Mohun full power to act for him, so that he might proceed as freely as possible in his projected reconciliation.

The two went next to the Rose, where, in about a quarter of an hour, the Duke of Hamilton arrived with a companion, dressed very plainly, to avoid notice. The Duke, who was alone in a room when Maccartney first met him, called in his friend im-

---

[1] For comments on the Rose Tavern and the various references to it in *Esmond*, see *supra*, p. 73, n. 2.

A QUARREL AND A CHALLENGE 209

mediately. This proved to be Lieutenant Colonel John Hamilton of the Scots Foot Guards.[1] Maccartney states that up to the entrance of Colonel Hamilton, he had still some hope of settling the

[1] John Hamilton was commissioned lieutenant in the Scots Foot Guards on March 1, 1689 (N.S.). He was promoted to captain lieutenant, September 30, 1690, and became captain, ranking as lieutenant colonel, on September 1, 1691. From 1691 to 1694 he served in Flanders (Dalton, *Army Lists*, iii, 44, 45, n. 18, iv, 21, v, 219). According to Maccartney, he and Hamilton had quarrelled over the former's promotion to a majority over the latter's head (see *A Letter from Mr. Maccartney;* Maccartney became a major on November 13, 1695, according to Dalton, *op. cit.*, iv, 69). Colonel Hamilton was forced to sell his commission in the Guards, as the result of his testimony regarding Maccartney's part in the Duke's death. Chichester asserts that he was driven from the army in 1714, upon the accession of George I (*D. N. B.*, xxxiv, 443 ff., art., "Maccartney, George"). In the life of Maccartney in an earlier edition of this work, Chichester had dated Hamilton's dismissal after the General's trial in 1716. The later date is that given also by Vian in his life of the Duke of Hamilton (*D. N. B.*, xv, 326 ff.). Vian alleges that Colonel Hamilton left England to escape prosecution for perjury. Boyer, who records Colonel Hamilton's death on October 17, 1716, places his dismissal from the army in 1714, but says nothing of his flight from England, and remarks that after his retirement he was allowed a pension of two hundred pounds a year. Colonel Hamilton's death was due to an internal hemorrhage, which Boyer piously regarded as a manifestation of the divine vengeance because of his charges against General Maccartney. By a curious coincidence, the Dowager Duchess of Hamilton, mother of Lord Mohun's victim, died on the same day as Colonel Hamilton. (Boyer, *The Political State of Great Britain*, xii [July–Dec., 1716], 472.)

affair peaceably; but upon seeing the latter he could expect nothing except a duel, since he himself and the colonel had been on bad terms for a long time.[1] Accordingly, finding the Duke still bent on a duel, and desirous of settling nothing besides the time and place of the meeting, the general returned to Lord Mohun and told him all that had been said. Mohun responded that he had thought his friend "overwise and managing," conjured him to secrecy, and proposed that they spend the night together at the Bagnio,[2] in order to guard more thoroughly against the betrayal of their plans. The Duke had suggested to Maccartney that the four — he and Mohun, Hamilton and Maccartney — should meet for the duel in Hyde Park before eight o'clock the next morning.[3] This being agreed upon, they left the tavern.

Two other accounts of the meeting of the Duke and Maccartney, although given by the same person, differ from each other, as well as from the general's story. According to one statement by Isaac Sisson, drawer at the Rose,[4] the Duke's companion stayed in another room while Mac-

[1] *A Letter from Mr. Maccartney;* see the preceding note.
[2] *A Letter from Mr. Maccartney.*
[3] *Ibid.*
[4] At the inquests; see *The Substance of the Depositions taken at the Coroner's Inquest* . . . *on the Body of Duke Hamilton:*

A QUARREL AND A CHALLENGE

cartney and the Duke were together. After Maccartney had consulted with Lord Mohun, the Duke and his friend left the tavern in company. In another account [1] Sisson said that the gentleman with the Duke (whom he could not identify as Colonel Hamilton) left the tavern on Maccartney's appearance; after the general had gone several times between the Duke and Mohun, the Duke's friend returned and went away with him. It will be noticed that in Maccartney's narrative Colonel Hamilton is indicated as present at the whole of the interview at the Rose, whereas the drawer at one time describes him as attending the Duke to the tavern and seemingly remaining, but in a room by himself, until the conclusion of the Duke's business. On the other occasion, he is said to have arrived with the Duke, to have gone away, and returned in time to accompany the latter at his departure. Of Sisson's two stories, the first, given at the inquests, seems the more credible, agreeing as it does the more nearly with General Maccartney's account of the meeting. This statement was made a few days after the event, when its circumstances

---

And . . . on the Body of my Lord Mohun, printed for A. Baldwin, London, 1712.

[1] At Colonel Hamilton's trial for murder; see *The Tryal of John Hamilton*.

were fresher in the witness's mind and, too, when Colonel Hamilton's friends had had less opportunity of influencing the testimony. Possibly, after having served the Duke and Maccartney with wine, and having left them alone at their request,[1] Sisson paid no particular attention to what was going on, and did not notice Colonel Hamilton's entering the room where Maccartney and the Duke were. That Colonel Hamilton went to the Rose with the Duke, left the tavern with him, and dined that night at his house with him, cannot be doubted.[2] What part he took in arranging the details of the duel cannot be definitely settled. According to Maccartney, these matters were managed by the Duke himself.[3] That, as he stated on his trial, Colonel Hamilton did not know that a duel was contemplated until he came into the field, is incredible.[4]

After leaving the Rose Tavern, Lord Mohun and Maccartney went together to the play.[5] They supped later at the Queen's Arms, the Duke of

[1] *Tryal of John Hamilton*, testimony of Sisson.

[2] *Ibid.*, testimony, respectively, of John Lesly (or Lesley), the Duke's footman, and of Joseph Hipsley, his porter.

[3] *A Letter from Mr. Maccartney.* See *supra*, p. 210.

[4] *Tryal of John Hamilton*, Colonel Hamilton's statement in his own defence.

[5] *Ibid.*, testimony of Rice Williams.

A QUARREL AND A CHALLENGE

Richmond, Sir Robert Rich,[1] and Colonel Churchill completing the party.[2] About one o'clock Saturday morning, Lord Mohun arrived at the Bagnio, whither, earlier in the night,[3] Maccartney had sent his own servant with a portmanteau. The general reached the house later and had a bed in the same room with his friend. The servant who assisted Lord Mohun in disrobing afterwards described him

---

[1] Sir Robert Rich, who had dined with Mohun and Maccartney the night before, was the head of the elder branch of the family of which Mohun's earlier friend, Lord Warwick, had been a member. His wife was Mohun's stepdaughter. Sir Robert Rich, Bart., was at this time a captain in the Grenadier Guards. In June, 1708, he had wounded Sir Edmund Bacon seriously in a duel. Later he sat for years in Parliament, was Groom of the Bedchamber to George II, and died February 1, 1768, being then Governor of Chelsea Hospital and a field marshal. (See *D. N. B.*, xvi, 1020–1021, art., "Rich, Sir Robert," by W. R. Williams.)

[2] *Tryal of John Hamilton*, testimony of Rice Williams. Doubtless to mislead the footman, who had already displayed some suspicion as to what was in the air, Maccartney sent him to his lodgings after supper; when he returned to the Queen's Arms, the party had broken up, and he was unable to find his master that night.

[3] *Ibid.*, testimony of Richard Cook, servant at the Bagnio. Charles Chabiner, another servant, testified that Maccartney's servant had brought the portmanteau and engaged a room for two gentlemen at eleven o'clock Friday morning. This would have been impossible, had Mohun suggested lodging at the Bagnio only late on Friday afternoon, as Maccartney asserted (*A Letter from Mr. Maccartney*). Perhaps it should have been Friday night instead.

as walking in "a melancholy posture" and as fetching a deep sigh when he lay down.[1] Another attendant noted that Mohun "spoke not a word," whereas Maccartney jested as he undressed.[2] Neither of these servants testified to bringing wine for either of the guests.[3]

As they had directed, Maccartney and Mohun were called early Saturday[4] morning.[5] After a pot of tea they set off in a coach which they had bespoken, bidding the coachman hasten to Kensington.[6] On reaching Hyde Park, Lord Mohun ordered him to enter, telling the gate-keeper they were going to Price's lodge. Mohun then asked the coachman where they could get "something

---

[1] *Tryal of John Hamilton*, Cook's testimony.

[2] *Ibid.*, Chabiner's testimony.

[3] Swift [?] charged that Maccartney was "forced to keep up his Patron's Courage with Wine, till within very few Hours of their meeting in the Field" (*Examiner*, November 13-20, 1712).

[4] Burke places the duel on Sunday, November 15 (*Peerage*, ed. 1921, p. 1061); Collins dates it in 1713 (*Peerage*, i, 545). The narrative of the affair in *The History of the Reign of Queen Anne* . . . Year the Eleventh, dates the meeting both on Sunday (p. 297) and on Saturday (p. 299) — the latter day being given in its account of Colonel Hamilton's testimony before the Privy Council.

[5] *Tryal of John Hamilton*, testimony of Cook and Chabiner. Mohun desired to be called at six, Maccartney at half-past six.

[6] *Ibid.*, Chabiner's testimony.

A QUARREL AND A CHALLENGE 215

that was good," to which he responded, "At the house near the Ring." Coming near the Lodge, Mohun and Maccartney got out of the coach, bidding Pennington, the coachman, get some burnt wine at the tavern while they took a little walk. Pennington ordered the beverage, but the drawer demurred at preparing it, since, as he said, few gentlemen came so early to the Park save to fight. Being told that two persons were at his coach inquiring for him, Pennington returned to his vehicle to find the Duke of Hamilton and Colonel Hamilton there. On learning whom Pennington had driven to the Park, the Duke asked as to the direction in which they had gone, and with his companion set out after them. The coachman, now becoming suspicious himself, hastened to the house to obtain assistance in parting the duellists. Without waiting for the men who were called to prevent the duel, he ran back to a tree some fifty yards from where the four duellists had halted. Pennington was followed by the drawer, John Reynolds, and Joseph Nicholson, a laborer, provided with staves.[1]

The Duke of Hamilton had risen early on the

[1] *The Substance of the Depositions taken at the Inquests*, testimony of John Pennington, John Reynolds, and Joseph Nicholson.

morning of Saturday, November 15, for by six o'clock he had sent his footman, John Lesly, to Colonel Hamilton's lodgings at the Golden Peruke in Charing Cross, to bid the latter dress, as the Duke intended calling upon business. Another member of the ducal household, one Ferguson, was despatched about seven o'clock to secure Paul Bouffier, the surgeon, to attend the Duke if it were necessary.[1] Bouffier not being ready, however, sent his man Robert Talbot with Ferguson. They did not reach Hyde Park until after the duel and just before the Duke died.[2] Bouffier, it may be said, went later to the Duke's house, to find that its master had been brought home a corpse.[3] The Duke must have followed his messenger to Colonel Hamilton closely, since the Colonel, who was getting up when Lesly reached his lodgings, only finished fastening his buttons in the coach.[4] In his

[1] At about a quarter past eleven on the preceding night Bouffier had been sent for by the Duke of Hamilton. Learning from the servant who had brought the message that the Duke was not ill, Bouffier had desired to be excused until morning. (*Tryal of John Hamilton*, Paul Bouffier's testimony.)

[2] *Ibid.*, testimony of Ferguson and Robert Talbot.

[3] *Ibid.*, Bouffier's testimony.

[4] The version of Colonel Hamilton's testimony before the privy Council, contained in *A True and Impartial Account of the Murder of his Grace the Duke of Hamilton and Brandon, by Mr. Mackartney*, printed by J. Morphew, London, 1712 (the Tory *True and Impartial Account*). In his evidence before

A QUARREL AND A CHALLENGE 217

hurry Colonel Hamilton forgot an article indispensable for the errand on which he and the Duke were going. Seeing that his friend had no sword with him, the Duke halted his coach at the corner of St. James's Square by the Earl of Portland's dwelling and sent his footman to his own house for a certain mourning sword. When the servant returned with the weapon, which he handed to Colonel Hamilton, the Duke ordered Andrew Clark, his coachman, to drive to the upper end of St. James's Street. Thence they went toward Kensington, as far as Hyde Park, where the Duke left the coach near Price's Lodge, bidding his servants and Colonel Hamilton's boy await them at the "Corner of the White Pales," or Kensington Gate. They then walked away on the grass between the two ponds.[1]

the Council, as preserved in *Lord Dartmouth's Minutes*, Hamilton said that the Duke assisted him in putting on his shirt (*Hist. MSS. Comm. Reports*, xi, pt. 5, 313, *MSS. of the Earl of Dartmouth*). In his deposition at the inquests upon the Duke and Lord Mohun, Lesly stated that on his return from his errand he found the Duke just setting out in his coach. (*The Substance of the Depositions*.)

[1] *Ibid.*, deposition of John Lesly (or Lesley).

XIII

THE LAST DUEL

HAVING learned from their hackney-coachman in which direction Lord Mohun and Maccartney had gone, the Duke and Colonel Hamilton followed them and came upon them near the left part of the Ring, by a ditch. The Duke cried to Mohun: "My Lord, have I come [in] time enough?" To which Maccartney answered: "Time enough." They then jumped the ditch into the nursery, and prepared to fight.[1] The Duke is reported to have said to Maccartney: "Let the event of this be what it will, you are the occasion of it." To this remark Maccartney responded: "I had a commission for it."[2] Lord Mohun then made the suggestion that the two seconds should

[1] *The Case at Large of Duke Hamilton and the Lord Mohun*, printed for E. Curll, London, 1712. The report herein contained of Colonel Hamilton's testimony before the Privy Council presents certain details in addition to those given in *Lord Dartmouth's Minutes* (*Hist. MSS. Comm. Reports*, xi, pt. 5, 313–314, *MSS. of the Earl of Dartmouth*).

[2] *Lord Dartmouth's Minutes*, loc. cit., testimony of Colonel Hamilton.

THE DEATH OF THE DUKE OF HAMILTON

THE LAST DUEL

not engage, to which the Duke replied that he left them to themselves.[1] Maccartney is reported to have remarked: "We will take our shares." The Duke answered: "Here's my friend; he will take his share in my dance."[2]

The four men drew thereupon, and the Duke and Mohun began fighting furiously, without parrying or feinting. The combat did not last long.[3] The Duke closed with Lord Mohun, who seized the former's sword-blade. They fell, Mohun underneath, and in a ditch, the Duke above him and with a knee on his body. As they lay on the ground, Maccartney and Colonel Hamilton, who seem, at least, to have exchanged passes,[4] turned to care for

---

[1] *Lord Dartmouth's Minutes, loc. cit.*, testimony of Colonel Hamilton; also, *A Letter from Mr. Maccartney to a Friend of His in London.*

[2] *Lord Dartmouth's Minutes, loc. cit.*

[3] The Duke of Richmond, who concealed General Maccartney after the duel, is reported to have said that "Duke Hamilton was run through the Right Arm at the first thrust, and at the same Time he ran Ld Mohun through the Breast sideways. This made 'em close, and so they fell to stabbing till both fell." (Letter signed "Fletcher," and dated November 22–30, 1712, in *The Letters of Thomas Burnett to George Duckett*, ed. for the Roxburghe Club by D. Nichol Smith, p. 17.)

[4] No eyewitness testified to having seen the seconds fighting. Both alleged, however, that they fought, and each professed to have got the better of the other. It is certain, at any rate, that Colonel Hamilton was wounded in some manner in the foot.

them. At this point, it is pretended, came the alleged act of treachery which won Maccartney the undying hatred of the Tory party. Hamilton declared on oath later that, as he was supporting the Duke whom he had lifted off Lord Mohun, Maccartney came up with a sword and thrust at the helpless nobleman.[1] The popular version, as fostered by the Tory pamphleteers, was that Maccartney had leaned over Colonel Hamilton from behind and had stabbed the Duke.[2]

Upon Maccartney's alleged assault upon the wounded Duke, Colonel Hamilton asserted that he had opened his principal's clothing, but saw no blood upon his breast. He then asked the Duke how he did, to which the reply was: "I am wounded." He next took up his own sword to

[1] *Lord Dartmouth's Minutes*, *loc. cit.*; also *The Case at Large*. Cf. also the letters of Colonel Hamilton and the Earl of Sutherland, as reprinted in Appendix F, *infra*, pp. 277–281.

[2] *A True and Impartial Account of the Murder* . . . (Tory). This story was founded, no doubt, upon the statement of Henry Amy, one of the surgeons who examined the Duke's corpse. Amy declared that the wound in the Duke's breast, because of its direction, must have been given from an arm that reached over or was above him. (*Tryal of John Hamilton*, testimony of Henry Amy.) Swift, in the *Journal to Stella*, November 15, 1712, says that, as the Duke was over Lord Mohun, the latter shortened his sword and "stabbed him in at the shoulder to the heart." *Prose Works*, ed. T. Scott, ii, 392–393.

protect himself against another attack by the general. Then he led the Duke to a tree, where the latter fell and called for his coach. One Ferguson, a servant of the Duke, came up and took charge of his master, bringing a surgeon, who opened the Duke's coat and found a large wound on the left side, which did not bleed. This Colonel Hamilton believed to be the wound which Maccartney had dealt. Hamilton then assisted the Duke into a coach which had been secured.[1]

But the four witnesses of the duel — John Reynolds, drawer, Joseph Nicholson, laborer, John Pennington, hackney-coachman, and William Norris, groom, — saw nothing of an attack by General Maccartney upon either the Duke of Hamilton or his second, after the fall of the two principals. They witnessed Lord Mohun fall on his back, with the Duke upon him, and the two seconds run to aid them. Reynolds appears to have arrived at the spot where the peers lay, at almost the same time as Colonel Hamilton and Maccartney. Nicholson was at his heels.[2] They found each second with

[1] *Lord Dartmouth's Minutes*, *loc. cit.* It will be noted that in various particulars Colonel Hamilton's testimony agrees exactly with that given by other and disinterested witnesses as summarized *infra*.

[2] Nicholson was about four yards behind Reynolds, who was that distance from the seconds when they reached Mohun

his own sword in his right hand and grasping his principal's sword hand with the left. Reynolds demanded the swords of the seconds, and obtained them without difficulty. At the request of the seconds the two men tried to bend or break the blades but succeeded in bending only Maccartney's. Reynolds secured the Duke's weapon, but Lord Mohun would not yield his unless his adversary were disarmed also. Reynolds then carried the four weapons some distance away. The seconds swore that their principals were killed, and Colonel Hamilton added, "We've made a fine Morning's work on 't." General Maccartney then took Nicholson by the hand, and bade him note that the seconds had striven to part the duellists, and to remember that he "in the Grey Cloaths and Silver Lac'd Hat" said so. While Reynolds assisted Colonel Hamilton in trying to remove the Duke from the field, Nicholson helped the general care for Lord Mohun. They could not lift him; so they turned him on his face in order to prevent his bleeding inwardly. Then, with the aid of Mohun's footman, who had come up, Nicholson and others

and the Duke (*The Substance of the Depositions taken at the Coroner's Inquest . . . on the Body of Duke Hamilton: And . . . on the Body of my Lord Mohun*. Nicholson's testimony). Reynolds was thirty to forty yards from the spot, when the two men fell (*Ibid.*, Reynold's deposition).

THE LAST DUEL 223

put the dying man into the hackney coach, this operation being directed by General Maccartney. Pennington, the coachman, inquired as to who would pay him for taking Mohun's body to his late home in Marlborough Street, and was told by Maccartney that the footman would pay; whereat Pennington asked the general for his own fare for the latter's ride to the Park, and secured a half-crown.

By this time Lord Mohun had probably died. The footman, Rice Williams, and Pennington then took his body to Marlborough Street.[1] Lord Mohun, it might be added, was buried November 25, at St. Martin's in the Fields.[2] No monument or tablet at present marks his grave.

In the meantime, Reynolds had been helping Colonel Hamilton in tending the dying Duke.[3]

---

[1] Lady Mohun, who was absent at the time (*Lord Dartmouth's Minutes*, p. 312, testimony of Brown, Lord Mohun's valet), is said to have been very indignant at her return, over the carelessness of her household, who had placed their dead master's bloody corpse on her best counterpane and spoiled it. *Memoirs of the Celebrated Persons Forming the Kit-Cat Club*, pp. 120 ff.

[2] G. E. C. *Complete Peerage*, v, 323. According to one historian, he "was, with great Pomp, inter'd under the Altar of the Church in [*sic*] St. Martins in the Fields, near his Fathers'." *The History of the Reign of Queen Anne, Digested into Annals*, Year the Eleventh, p. 312.

[3] Thus Reynolds (*The Substance of the Depositions* and *The Tryal of John Hamilton*); but Colonel Hamilton swore before

They raised him to his feet, and with their support he managed to walk a short distance, until, overcome by weakness, as Colonel Hamilton stated, he sank down at the foot of a tree and called out for his coach. It was at this moment that Ferguson arrived with Talbot, the surgeon's man. Some examination seems to have been made of the Duke's wounds, but nothing could be done for him; he had no perceptible pulse then, and died in a short time.[1] His body was placed in a coach which had been sent for,[2] and was taken to his house. There the surgeons who were summoned —

the Privy Council that no one of the crowd which speedily gathered came to the assistance of the Duke. (*Lord Dartmouth's Minutes, loc. cit.*)

[1] According to Mr. Roujat, formerly surgeon-general to William III, Robert Talbot told him, when he was called to the Duke's house after the body had been borne there, that "the Duke was dead before he was put into his Coach" (*A True and Impartial Account of the Animosity* . . . p. 37). Swift, in his *Journal to Stella*, November 15, 1712, says that the Duke died on the grass before he could be helped to Price's Lodge. *Prose Works*, ed. T. Scott, ii, 392–393. The account in the *Gazette*, November 15–18, 1712, states that the Duke died as he was being carried to his coach; the *Post Boy*, on November 15–18, reports that he died "soon after he was brought home," but in the next issue (November 18–20), that he "expired soon after he was put into the coach."

[2] Not the Duke's own coach in which he had driven to the Park, since that was awaiting him at the White Pales by Kensington Gate, where Colonel Hamilton found it on his way from the scene (*infra*, p. 230).

THE LAST DUEL

Mr. Roujat and Mr. Bouffier (who had finally forsaken his bed) — confirmed the opinion of the latter's man, and pronounced the Duke dead.[1]

According to one surgeon who examined the Duke's body,[2] he "had receiv'd a wound by a Push which had cut the Artery and small Tendant of his Right Arm; another in his Right Leg, Eight Inches long, which he suppos'd to be by a Slash, it being very large; another small one in his Left Leg, near the Instep; and a fourth on his Left Side, between the second and third Rib, which ran down into his Body, most forwards, having pierc'd the Skirt of his Midriff, and gone through his Caul." The severed artery in the Duke's arm was the immediate cause of his death, the surgeons agreed;[3] he might have lived two or three days with the wound in his breast.[4] It should be emphasized here that all the surgeons who examined the Duke's body agreed that his death was caused, not by the

[1] *The Case at Large of Duke Hamilton and the Lord Mohun*, iii; *Tryal of John Hamilton*, testimony of Paul Bouffier.

[2] Henry Amy, whose name appears in *Esmond* (*supra*, pp. 75 and 188).

[3] Amy and Bouffier (their respective testimony as given in the *Tryal of John Hamilton*), and Mr. Roujat (*The Case at Large*, iii).

[4] *Tryal of John Hamilton*, testimony of Henry Amy. It should be noted that Roujat's account of the Duke's wounds, as given in *The Case at Large*, does not include the third of those noticed by Amy.

wound in his side which was attributed to General Maccartney's sword, but by that in his right arm which Lord Mohun had given him and which had severed the artery and a tendon.[1] The charge made later that Maccartney had caused the Duke's death was controverted, therefore, by the testimony of the medical men.[2]

The same surgeon examined Lord Mohun's corpse, and found that "he had a Wound between his short Ribs, quite through his Belly; another about three Inches wide in the upper part of his Thigh; a large Wound about four Inches wide in his Groin, a little higher, which was the Cause of his Immediate Death; and another small Wound on his Left Side; and, That the Fingers of his Left Hand were cut."[3]

After having seen the body of Lord Mohun on its way to his late friend's house, General Maccartney took thought to his own safety. He left Hyde Park on foot by the Kensington Gate, pas-

[1] Amy's testimony, *Tryal of John Hamilton;* Bouffier's testimony, *Ibid.;* Roujat's statement, *The Case at Large.*

[2] This is pointed out in *A True and Impartial Account of the Animosity* . . . pp. 38–39.

[3] *Tryal of John Hamilton*, testimony of Henry Amy. Mr. La Fage, the surgeon called in by Lord Mohun's chaplain, does not mention the second and fourth wounds noted by Amy, and says that "Three Fingers of his Right Hand [were] almost cut off." (*The Case at Large.*)

CHARLES, FIRST DUKE OF RICHMOND

sing the Duke of Hamilton's coach and servants, "with his Waistcoat Buttons all bloody and in a very melancholy Posture." [1] Maccartney's movements, after the Duke of Hamilton's people had seen him disappear toward Kensington, are to be traced fairly exactly. It would seem that probably he sent a message to the Duke of Richmond, from the house of the friend in Chelsea with whom he took refuge,[2] for that nobleman later admitted having brought the general to his house on the day of the duel. He remained at the Duke's until about two o'clock the next day — Sunday, November 16. It must have been by aid of the Duke that Maccartney escaped to Belgium, where he was by December 4.[3]

---

[1] *Tryal of John Hamilton*, testimony of Andrew Clark, coachman of the Duke of Hamilton, and of John Lesly.

[2] *A Letter from Mr. Maccartney* is addressed to this friend. Tindal says that from Hyde Park Maccartney "walked to *Kensington*, and thence to *Chelsea*, went from thence to the Duke of *Richmond's* house in the *Privy-Garden*, near *Whitehall*; lay there that night, and, early the next morning, crossed the *Thames;* and thence in a disguise, went over to *Flanders*" (*A Continuation of Mr. Rapin's History of England*, iv, 298, n. 2).

[3] Maccartney's defence of himself — *A Letter from Mr. Maccartney to a Friend of His in London* — is dated from Ostend, December 4–15, 1712. The part of the Duke of Richmond in concealing Maccartney and in assisting his flight is drawn from *Lord Dartmouth's Minutes* for November 26. On that date the Duke of Richmond was called before the

Maccartney's flight to the Continent was dictated by a commendable prudence. He was sought through England with all the vigor that could be commanded by the Ministry, the family and countrymen of the Duke of Hamilton, and by an angered Queen, in whose favor the slain nobleman appears to have succeeded to the place once held by the Duke of Marlborough. A proclamation for his arrest was issued by the Ministry, November 24, 1712, in which a reward of five hundred pounds was offered by the Queen for his apprehension. To this the Duchess of Hamilton added three hundred pounds.[1]

Privy Council for examination, as information had been received that the general had been seen at the Duke's house the day before. The Duke denied Maccartney's presence there on November 25, but admitted it as to November 15 and 16. The Duke remarked, during his examination, that he hoped Maccartney "was safe now." Notwithstanding his denial of a knowledge of Maccartney's whereabouts, the Duke's house was ordered searched (*Lord Dartmouth's Minutes*, p. 314). Possibly Maccartney's flight was accomplished in a female disguise (see the transcription of the proclamation for his arrest and the appended notice, as given in Appendix E, *infra*, pp. 273-277. A fairly accurate account of the general's flight is found in *The History of the Reign of Queen Anne Digested into Annals*, Year the Eleventh, p. 312.

[1] *Lord Dartmouth's Minutes;* see also Swift, *Journal to Stella*, November 16, November 18, 1712 (T. Scott's ed. of Swift's *Prose Works*, ii, 394, 395). The Duchess had at first intended to offer a reward of five hundred pounds, but reduced the amount to three hundred for fear of seeming pre-

THE LAST DUEL 229

It was at first reported that Maccartney had escaped to Ireland.[1] A few days later, what would appear to be positive evidence came to London of his presence in Holland.[2] Swift, however, was not thoroughly convinced yet that the general was beyond the vengeance of his party.[3] The Scotch peers voted an address to the Queen, desiring that she should attempt the extradition of Maccartney, wherever he might find refuge.[4] The general, however, remained safely abroad, entering the service of the Elector of Hanover and returning to England with the troops brought in by that prince after his accession to the English throne.[5] On

---

sumptuous if she offered as much as the Queen (letter from Ferdinand Fairfax to the Countess of Oxford, undated, in *Hist. MSS. Comm. Reports, MSS. of the Duke of Portland*, v, 258). The text of the proclamation is reprinted from "a contemporary newspaper" (*The Evening Post*, December 24–30, 1712) by H. B., in *Notes and Queries*, ser. II, x, 481–482. It should be noted that both Chichester (*D. N. B.*, xxxiv, 443 ff.) and Dalton (*Army Lists*, iii, 45, n. 13) are at fault in saying that the Duchess of Hamilton offered only two hundred pounds for Maccartney's arrest. For the text of both the royal proclamation and the Duchess of Hamilton's advertisement, see Appendix E, *infra*, pp. 273–276.

[1] Swift, *Journal to Stella*, December 26, 1712 (*Prose Works*, ii, 405).
[2] *Ibid.*, January 4, 1712/3 (*Prose Works*, ii, 410).
[3] *Ibid.*, January 7, 1712/3 (*Prose Works*, ii, 412).
[4] H. Manners Chichester in *D. N. B.*, xxxiv, 443 ff. (ed. of 1909), art., "Maccartney, or Macartney, George."
[5] E. Solly in *Notes and Queries*, ser. VI, xii, 177–178.

April 20, 1716, "being lately arrived from beyond Sea," Maccartney applied for a writ of error in the Court of King's Bench, for the reversal of his outlawry, as he desired to be tried on the indictment against him.[1] The writ was issued, and on May 14, he was arraigned in court, preliminary to his trial.[2] On June 13,[3] the general was tried in Westminster Hall, before the Court of King's Bench, and was found not guilty of murder, but guilty of manslaughter.[4] After being "branded" with a cold iron, he was released, and, shortly after, was restored to his places in the British army.[5]

Colonel Hamilton, like Maccartney, escaped from the scene of the duel. Following the same course as the general through Hyde Park, he reached the Duke's coach before Maccartney was out of sight. On his way, Hamilton met Lesly, the footman, to whom he told the news of his master's being mortally wounded. Hamilton entered the

[1] A. Boyer ... *The Political State of Great Britain* ... xi (January–June, 1716), 504.

[2] *Ibid.*, p. 641.

[3] The trial had been set first for June 6, but evidently had been postponed (see Maccartney's petition to George I, reprinted by Dalton, *George I's Army*, i, 253, n. 3).

[4] For contemporary accounts of General Maccartney's trial for the murder of the Duke of Hamilton, see Appendix B, *infra*, pp. 261–264.

[5] Dalton, *loc. cit.;* Chichester, *loc. cit.*

THE LAST DUEL

coach and was first driven to Kensington Gravel Pits, thence to St. Giles's Pound, and next to Holborn Bridge, where the coachman, stopping, said he would take him no further.[1] Accordingly, Hamilton alighted and went into the Rose Tavern.[2] Thence he seems to have gone to the Half Moon Tavern in Cheapside,[3] where he summoned one Woodward, a surgeon, who dressed the wound in his foot which he had received from Maccartney.[4] Later, he gave himself up, and deposed concerning the facts of the duel at the inquests upon the Duke and Lord Mohun, November 15–22, inclusive.[5] He also testified before the Privy Council, November 21.[6] He was committed to Newgate on November 27,[7] and being indicted for murder, was tried at the Old Bailey, December

---

[1] *The Case at Large of Duke Hamilton and the Lord Mohun*, ii, testimony of Andrew Clark, the Duke's coachman, at the Coroner's inquest; *The Substance of the Depositions*, testimony of John Lesly and of Clark.

[2] This, it should be remembered, was not the Rose Tavern in Covent Garden, where the details of the duel had been settled the day before.

[3] Ned Ward refers to the Half Moon Tavern, but places it in the Strand. *The London Spy*, pt. ix, p. 215.

[4] *Lord Dartmouth's Minutes*, testimony of Mr. Woodward before the Privy Council.

[5] *The Substance of the Depositions*.

[6] *Lord Dartmouth's Minutes*.

[7] The *Post Boy*, November 27–29, 1712.

12, 1712. Found not guilty of murder, he was convicted of manslaughter, but, pleading his clergy, was released.[1]

[1] *Tryal of John Hamilton.* Hamilton was defended by Serjeant Thomas Pengelly, legal advisor to the Duke of Somerset. Serjeant Pengelly's brief and notes thereon are still extant (*Hist. MSS. Comm. Reports*, vii, 681, 690, *MSS. of the Rev. T. W. Webb*). Cf. *infra*, p. 263, n. 1.

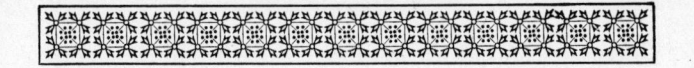

XIV

FACT AND FICTION

AS Mr. Edward Solly very aptly has said,[1] the account of the Hamilton-Mohun duel "as given in *Esmond* is certainly not history, but a very well-written piece of fiction." To the emphasizing of this point of view so seldom taken by pretended Thackeray authorities and *soi-disant* students of the English novel, I shall devote the remainder of this study.[2] I shall indicate specifically wherein

[1] In *Notes and Queries*, ser. VI, xii, 131–132.

[2] Apart from the fact of its figuring so prominently in *Esmond*, I believe myself justified in giving the detailed account above of the Hamilton-Mohun duel and its causes and results, since nowhere does such a narrative exist, and since so great a degree of inaccuracy occurs in those versions of the affair that are to be found. For instance, Chancellor tells us that there was "an arranged plot" to kill the Duke, that the *six* duellists met *just before sunset* near the Ring in Hyde Park where, after the Duke had wounded Mohun mortally, Maccartney stabbed him to death! These, says Chancellor, "are incidents which have become almost part of the country's history." (*The London of Thackeray*, pp. 42–43). W. C. Sidney recounts how the park keepers, hearing the clashing of swords, hastened to the spot whence the sounds came, and found there the Duke of Hamilton and Lord Mohun "weltering in their blood." Colonel Hamilton, according to Sidney,

Thackeray has deviated from historical fact, and, as well, whence he derived such incidents as occur both in the novel and in the earlier literature upon the subject.

Thackeray doubtless did not err in ascribing enmity to the Duke of Hamilton and Lord Mohun. Contemporary accounts mention their hostility.[1] It would be most improbable, too, that the parties to a series of fiercely contested lawsuits over property, which had dragged along for more than ten years, could be other than enemies. Especially would this be the case when the persons involved were opposed in politics and in nationality. The relationship which Thackeray gives the two peers is, of course, incorrect. The Duke and Mohun were not brothers-in-law. They had married cousins, one the daughter of Lord Gerard of Bromley, the other of James Manwaring. The second Duchess

remained on the spot and was arrested, whereas General Maccartney "immediately took to his heels and fled." Mohun, who had been thrice tried by the Lords for murder before he came of age, had been grossly insulted at a chance meeting by the Duke, had "there and then angrily challenged him to a duel," says Sidney, in relating the origin of the quarrel (*England and the English in the Eighteenth Century*, i, 251–252). Other errors of fact are noted, *infra*, p. 244, n. 2.

[1] See *A Letter from Mr. Maccartney to a Friend of His in London*, for Lord Mohun's statement regarding his feelings about the Duke's attitude toward his own witnesses and lawyers, and cf. *supra*, 204, n. 3.

FACT AND FICTION 235

of Hamilton's mother and the first Lady Mohun's mother were sisters, being daughters of the first Earl of Macclesfield, and sisters of the second and third earls.[1] Their suit had to do with the property of Lady Gerard or that of the last two Earls of Macclesfield, rather than with that of Lord Gerard. That Lord Mohun came to London in the autumn of 1712, especially on account of his suit with the Duke, I do not know; that he sent to the Duke, desiring to meet him is improbable. The hearing at which the quarrel arose was the second, at least, at which the Duke and Lord Mohun were present, and a third was set for the day of the duel.[2]

Possibly in order to increase the dramatic suddenness of the overthrow of Beatrix Esmond's ambitions, the novelist has taken liberties with the date and time of day of the duel. It actually occurred on November 15,[3] before eight o'clock in the morning, whereas Thackeray places the meeting on November 18, — "three days after the 15th of November,"[4] — apparently about four o'clock

[1] See *supra*, pp. 190 ff.
[2] *A True and Impartial Account of the Animosity* . . . p. 28.
[3] It is perhaps worth noting that Burke, in his *Landed Gentry . . . of Great Britain*, places the duel on "Sunday, 13th, November, 1712" (iv, 463).
[4] Thackeray's virtual pointing out of his change of date is inexplicable.

in the afternoon — "just before sunset." The change in hour can doubtless be attributed to Thackeray's desire for a dramatic surprise: Swift's breaking in upon the peaceful dreams of Lord Bolingbroke and Esmond with the startling tidings of the affair. Too, a time in the afternoon permitted Esmond to find Beatrix engaged with the goldsmith,[1] a thing which would have been hardly probable in the early morning.[2]

In order to shorten the time between the quarrel and the duel and to make the latter more of a surprise, Thackeray has changed, as well, the time of the meeting of Mohun and the Duke at the "lawyer's in Lincoln's Inn Fields" from an evening two days before the actual engagement took place, to the morning of the same day. The preliminaries are hurried through in the novel, whereas, in fact, the day before the duel was devoted to mat-

[1] In regard to this situation and to the other references of the novelist (as in bk. III, chap. 4) to the plate which was being prepared for the Ambassador, it should be noted that "Her Majesty was pleas'd to give him [the Duke] out of the *Jewel* Office 1700 Ounces of Silver for Plate for his Extraordinary Embassy to the Court of *France*." *The History of the Reign of Queen Anne, Digested into Annals*, Year the Eleventh [September, 1712], p. 391.

[2] But one wonders how, if four duellists barely escaped being prevented from fighting in Hyde Park, between seven and eight in the morning, six men could manage a duel in the same place at four o'clock in the afternoon!

HENRY, FIRST VISCOUNT BOLINGBROKE

FACT AND FICTION

ters connected with it. By this shortening of the time between the quarrel and the resulting engagement, Thackeray intended, no doubt, to emphasize the ferociousness with which Mohun and his friends were animated.

The dinner given in his honor by General Webb, which the Duke's business prevents him from attending, is appropriately — and significantly — gloomy. The remark is made that Mohun had been seen the night before at the theatre. As has been shown, he did appear at the playhouse on the night previous to the historical duel.[1] He had then as his companion General George Maccartney, as in the novel, but there was no third person. Thackeray's introduction of Lieutenant General Thomas Meredyth [2] as a companion of Lord Mohun, and a second of his in the memorable duel with the Duke of Hamilton, is utterly unhistorical. Probably it results from the names of Maccartney and Meredyth having been linked in the circumstances of their retirement from the army. Why Thackeray did not make free with the name of Brigadier General Phillip Honeywood,[3] who was

[1] *Supra*, p. 212.

[2] For a brief sketch of Meredyth's career, see Appendix C, *infra*, pp. 265–268.

[3] Phillip Honeywood, son of Charles Honeywood, of Charing, Kent, and Markshall, Essex, was commissioned

involved with the other two generals in the same affair, is not clear. It is equally inexplicable why Thackeray saw fit to bring another pair of seconds into the duel. Perhaps he felt that the impression which he certainly seeks to give of the political grounds of the affair would be increased, did he set three desperate men upon the Duke of Hamilton.[1] It is interesting, though not important, to note

ensign in Stanley's Regiment of Foot, June 12, 1694. He became a captain in the Royal Fusiliers, on April 1, 1696, and was commissioned captain in the Earl of Huntingdon's Regiment of Foot, March 10, 1702. He was brevetted major, December 1, 1703. Honeywood received the colonelcy of Townshend's Regiment of Foot, May 27, 1709. In 1710 he became a brigadier general. Like Maccartney and Meredyth, he was forced to sell his regiment and retire, in December, 1710, and, like them, he reëntered active service on the accession of George I. Honeywood was commissioned colonel of a regiment of horse, July 22, 1715. On November 5, 1714, he had been appointed a groom of the King's bedchamber. He commanded a brigade at the battle of Preston in 1715, and was wounded. In 1719, he saw service at Vigo. He was transferred to the colonelcy of another cavalry regiment, May 29, 1732. General Honeywood commanded a division at the battle of Dettingen in 1743. He became colonel of the King's Dragoon Guards, April 18, 1743. For his services he was created a Knight of the Bath. At the time of his death, on June 17, 1752, he was governor of Portsmouth, with the rank of general. See Dalton, *Army Lists*, iv, 30, n. 11; *George I's Army*, i, 115, n. 1. In the latter work, Dalton reproduces a portrait of General Sir Phillip Honeywood, K. B. And see Boyer . . . *The Political State of Great Britain* . . . viii, 442.

[1] Again, the use of two pairs of seconds may be but a recollection of the French-Coote duel upon which Thackeray

FACT AND FICTION

that the names of the seconds, save Maccartney and Meredyth, are not mentioned in the novel.

At least two hints for Doctor Swift's announcement to Bolingbroke and Esmond of the deaths of the Duke and Mohun come from *The Journal to Stella*. Writing to his *amie* in Dublin, on the day of the duel, Swift tells her of the "accident." "The dog Mohun,"[1] as Swift calls the Duke of Hamilton's adversary, evidently suggested the doctor's words in the novel, regarding Maccartney: "The dog is fled." His suggestion that Bolingbroke should set a hue and cry in operation appears derived from Swift's statement, when writing to Stella on November 16: "I design to make the ministry put out a proclamation (if it can be found proper) against that villain Maccartney."[2] A third suggestion is taken from *The Journal to Stella* for Esmond's conduct upon hearing of the duel. Esmond goes at once to the Duke's house to learn what he can, and has the news confirmed by the weeping domestics. Swift tells Stella that he sent his servant to St. James's Square, where the Duke's porter (Joseph Hipsley) "could hardly answer for

modelled his Mohun-Castlewood fray. One might infer this to be the case, from Esmond's reference to the "three on a side" of the latter event.

[1] *Prose Works*, ed. T. Scott, ii, 392–393.
[2] *Ibid.*, ii, 394.

tears."[1] It should be noted, too, that as Esmond goes to console Beatrix, the Duke's betrothed, so Swift visited the Duchess of Hamilton.[2] Another debt of Thackeray to the *Journal*, perhaps, is to be found in Esmond's receiving from the Duke the offer of a secretaryship of embassy.[3] Swift wrote Stella that the Duke had the "greatest mind in the world" to take the doctor with him to France, although he did not dare reveal this desire.[4] A last borrowing from the *Journal* comes when Esmond drives away a street-vender who is crying his broadside accounts of the duel under Beatrix's open window.[5] Swift tells Stella that he would not suffer the Duchess of Hamilton to be moved from the lodging to which she was taken, since the proposed place "had no room backward, and she must have been tortured with the noise of the Grub Street screamers mention[ing] her husband's murder at her ears."[6]

---

[1] *Prose Works*, ed. T. Scott, ii, 392–393.

[2] *Ibid.* But one wonders why it was that, at least an hour and a half after the Duke's death, Beatrix Esmond, the Duke's betrothed, should not have been already informed of the death of her lover.

[3] *Esmond*, bk. III, chap. 5.

[4] *Prose Works*, ii, 392–393.

[5] *Esmond*, bk. III, chap. 6.

[6] *Prose Works*, ii, 393. The account being hawked was probably the quarto sheet with the title, "A full and true Account of a Desperate and Bloody Duel: which was Fought

FACT AND FICTION

The account of the fighting between the Duke and Mohun, which Esmond gives, perhaps owes something verbally to a pamphlet of the time, wherein the statement is made that, upon engaging, "my Lord Duke and the Lord *Mohun* did not Parry, but gave Thrusts at each other."[1] Another narrative, which Thackeray perhaps had seen, tells us that the principals in the affair "fought desperately like wild beasts, not fencing or parrying."[2]

As one would suspect, Esmond, as a Tory, a personal friend and admirer of the Duke of Hamilton, and a prospective relative by marriage, having, too, reason for animosity toward Lord Mohun, the evil genius of the house of Esmond, swallows completely the Tory accounts of the termination of the duel.[3] Indeed, his doing so goes far toward

---

this Morning in *High-Park* [*sic*] between My Lord *Moon* and Duke *Hambilton*. With an Account how my Lord *Moon* was kill'd on the Spot, and Duke *Hambilton* receiv'd a Mortal Wound, of which he Dy'd in a few Hours after he receiv'd The Wound. *Enter'd in the* Stamp-Office, *according to the late Act of Parliament. London*, Printed by *Edw. Midwinter*, at the *Star* in *Pye-Corner*, price one I penny."

[1] *A True and Impartial Account of the Animosity* . . . pp. 7–8. The quotation above, as the author of the pamphlet states, comes from the *Post Boy* of November 18–20, 1712.

[2] *A Strict Enquiry into the Circumstances of a Late Duel* . . . printed for J. Baker, London, 1713, pp. 18 ff.

[3] The existence of Jacobite hopes for a restoration of the male line of James II as a result of the Duke of Hamilton's

establishing the realism of character and of atmosphere in this portion of the novel.

That General Maccartney did stab the Duke of Hamilton as he lay helpless in the arms of his second is a belief which, to the modern student, rests upon very dubious foundations. The duel was witnessed by four men, none of whom had any interest in the combatants.[1] Their stories of the affairs agree in so far that in none of them is any attack by Maccartney upon the Duke even suggested. The only person alleging such an assault was Colonel John Hamilton, the Duke's second and kinsman, and an enemy of General Maccartney.[2] Colonel Hamilton attempted in no way,

embassy (see *Esmond*, bk. III, chap. 6) is confirmed by Haile, who says: "It was generally believed that Hamilton was to have brought secret powers to treat for James's adoption by Queen Anne, provided she were left in possession during her life-time" (*Queen Mary of Modena*, p. 436). See also, *infra*, p. 247, n. 1.

[1] One of the park-keepers testified at General Maccartney's trial, in 1716, that Lord Bolingbroke had attempted to bribe him to swear that Maccartney had killed the Duke (see Appendix B, *infra*, p. 262).

[2] On the day of the duel it would seem that rumors of foul play were afloat, for Swift, writing to Stella on November 15, says: "I am told, that a footman of Lord Mohun's stabbed Duke of Hamilton; and some say Macartney did so too" (*Journal to Stella*, in *Prose Works*, ed. T. Scott, ii, 392–393). Lord Chesterfield, in his letter to Bishop Chenevix in 1758, asserts, however, that Colonel Hamilton's first accusation of

FACT AND FICTION

however, to secure Maccartney after the pretended wound was given the Duke, but allowed him to minister to Lord Mohun and to leave the field unmolested.[1] Furthermore, it is said that, on Maccartney's trial for the murder of the Duke and Lord Mohun four years later, Colonel Hamilton "practically broke down" in his testimony.[2] The famous fourth Earl of Chesterfield, who attended

General Maccartney was made on November 18, three days after the duel. See T. Scott's edition of Swift's *Prose Works*, vol. x, pp. xxii–xxiii. It is not impossible that the rumors which had been stirring suggested to Lord Bolingbroke and Doctor Swift, as a means of discomfiting the Whigs and ruining Maccartney, and, through him, Marlborough, the story which Colonel Hamilton related at the inquests and before the Privy Council. Earl Stanhope quotes a letter from Lord Bolingbroke to the Duke of Argyll, dated November 19, 1712 (the day after Colonel Hamilton's testimony before the Privy Council), in which the duel is described but without any imputation of treachery to Maccartney (*History of England*, ii, 275).

[1] An excellent and convincing defence of Maccartney occurs in the pamphlet, *A Strict Inquiry into the Circumstances of a Late Duel*. . . . A correspondent of George Duckett, whose account of the duel has already been drawn upon (*supra*, p. 219, n. 3), says, "Coll. Hamilton has . . . deposed before the Councill, that Macartney run Duke Hamilton through while he was upon the Ground. This oath is wondrous Strange and I think a true picture of a —— man I woud not keep company with" (*The Letters of Thomas Burnett to George Duckett*, Roxburghe Club, p. 17). Here evidently was a contemporary who was impressed by the incredible features of Colonel Hamilton's story.

[2] Edward Solly, *Notes and Queries*, ser. VI, xii, 177–178.

General Maccartney's trial, later said [1] that there did not appear "the least ground for a suspicion of" his assassination of the Duke of Hamilton; "nor did Hamilton, who appeared in court, pretend to tax him with it." [2]

After repeated references in preceding passages to General Maccartney's return to England and his subsequent trial, it seems certainly not necessary to dwell long on the fact that Esmond was sadly wrong in asserting that "Colonel Macartney" never came back to England when he had reached an asylum abroad. The last fourteen years of General Maccartney's life were actually passed in Great Britain and Ireland, in the peaceful enjoyment of high military appointments.[3]

Notwithstanding the fact that Mohun and the Duke were known to have been engaged for years

[1] In a letter to Doctor Chenevix, Bishop of Waterford, May 23, 1758, quoted by T. Scott in his edition of Swift's *Prose Works*, vol. x, pp. xxii–xxiii.

[2] Notwithstanding General Maccartney's practical exoneration from the charge of murdering the Duke, writers of later times have repeated the old libellous tale concerning his part in the duel. Among these are Burke, *Extinct Baronetcies*, ed. of 1838, p. 360; Collins, *Peerage*, i, 546; "Melville," *Some Aspects of Thackeray*, pp. 205–207; Chancellor, *The London of Thackeray*, pp. 42–43. Ebsworth, curiously enough, says that Maccartney "had severely wounded the Duke's second, Colonel Andrew Hamilton, and fled abroad." *Roxburghe Ballads*, viii, 231.

[3] For an account of General Maccartney's life, see Appendix A, *infra*, pp. 257 ff.

FACT AND FICTION

in lawsuits about the most embittering of causes, — an inheritance, — and that they were known to have exchanged offensive remarks at the last hearing of the pending cause, yet the story was soon circulated, and widely believed, that the duel between the two noblemen was the result of a Whig plot to remove the newly nominated ambassador to France. Of course, the allegation of Colonel Hamilton that General Maccartney had given the Duke his death wound [1] as the latter lay in his second's arms, fitted very well into such a tale. The two charges — the one relating to the underlying motive for the duel, the other concerning unfair practice in it — are inseparable in the literature dealing with the affair. And as is to be expected, a large amount of printed matter concerned with the duel appeared in the few months following it,[2] and it caused much discussion.[3] There is

---

[1] That the wound which was the immediate cause of the Duke's death was not that alleged to have been given by General Maccartney was the opinion of all the surgeons who examined the Duke's body. See *supra*, p. 226.

[2] For the interchange of letters between Colonel John Hamilton and the Earl of Sutherland, see Appendix F, *infra*, pp. 277–281. In the last of these (No. 3), it should be observed that Colonel Hamilton has remembered details which do not appear in the earlier versions of his story, and has given them a sinister interpretation which they need not necessarily possess.

[3] For example, see Swift, *Journal to Stella*, *loc. cit.*; letters of Sir Richard Bradshaigh to George Kenyon, November 15

no evidence to-day extant, however, which would implicate the Duke of Marlborough, or any member of his party as such, in the death of the duke. That Lord Mohun and Maccartney called upon the Duke of Marlborough on the morning of November 14, 1712, is of no significance, unless it can be proved that they saw the Duke and that they discussed the possibility of a duel. Nowhere was any capital made of this visit, and nowhere was any sinister meaning attached to Mohun's and Maccartney's dining and supping that same day with Colonel Joseph Churchill, the general's fellow lodger.[1] Thackeray, it should be noted, makes Esmond avoid charging Marlborough with complicity in the alleged plot, but asserts — what any one would admit — that the Duke's party "profited by it."[2]

and 18, 1712, *Hist. MSS. Comm. Reports*, xiv, pt. 4, 448–449, *MSS. of Lord Kenyon*; letter of F. Cholomondeley [?] to George Kenyon, November 15, 1712, *Ibid.*, p. 449; letters of Doctor William Stratford of Christ Church, Oxford, to Edward Harley, on November 17, 22, and 27, 1712, *Hist. MSS. Comm. Reports, MSS. of the Duke of Portland*, vii, 113, 113–114, 114; letter of Ferdinand Fairfax to the Countess of Oxford, December [?], *Ibid.*, v, 258; letter of the Earl of Kinoull to the Earl of Oxford, December 27, 1712, *Ibid.*, v, 256–257; letter of Robert Lowther to the same on the same day, *Ibid.*, v, 256.

[1] *Tryal of John Hamilton*, testimony of Rice Williams.
[2] *Esmond*, bk. III, chap. 6.

FACT AND FICTION

Esmond's remark that Mohun's party, having had his services, were well rid of him, perhaps was suggested to Thackeray by the quotation in a pamphlet either of an observation made after Mohun's death: "*The* Whigs *had lost a Man they had reason to be asham'd of*," or of the coffee-woman's remark that Mohun "*like* Sampson, *did more good at his death, than he did in all his Life*."[1]

That, as Esmond declares, Lord Mohun, General Maccartney, and General Meredyth (who was not concerned in the actual duel) were "the Duke of Marlborough's men" is true enough, if it be interpreted properly.[2] Mohun, as has been seen,

---

[1] *A Strict Enquiry* . . . p. 40 [wrongly paged]. There is a *double entendre* in the second quotation, if one desires so to interpret it. In this connection may be quoted a passage from a contemporary letter to George Duckett: " . . . I will assure you that I am heartily sorry for my Ld Mohun, but I believe tother went to France for some more ends than we know of. My only Comfort is what I will tell you by a Story. Bull the Druggist is broke and soon after another Druggist broke thereabouts too. So a gentleman met the Latter and asked him whether he was broke. Yes, says he, I am. I am sorry for it, says tother. Why faith, says he, the only comfort I have is that my neighbor Bull is broke too, and that makes me more easy in my Misfortune." (*The Letters of Thomas Burnett to George Duckett*, Roxburghe Club, p. 18.)

[2] In bk. III, chap. 10, of *Esmond*, Thackeray speaks of Marlborough's friends in the army as "broke and ruined." This might well refer to the historical Meredyth, Maccartney, and Honeywood.

carried the Duke's challenge to the Earl Poulet in 1710.[1] Generals Maccartney and Meredyth had both enjoyed conspicuously the favor of the Duke when he was commander-in-chief.[2] Together with General Honeywood (who is not mentioned in *Esmond*), they had lost their regiments in 1710, for too noticeable partisanship.[3] That, however, this nobleman and a high army officer could have been concerned in such an assassination plot as Esmond suggests, seems out of the question to an impartial modern student. Also, when Thackeray has Esmond class Maccartney and Meredyth with Mohun as "notorious brawlers" and "cut-throats," he does these officers a gross injustice. So far as my investigations have gone, I have found neither Lieutenant General George Maccartney nor Lieutenant General Thomas Meredyth ever concerned in any duel or other serious escapade.[4] That Mac-

[1] *Supra*, p. 143.

[2] See Appendices B and C, respectively, *infra*, pp. 257 ff. and 265 ff.

[3] *Loc. cit.*, It was, therefore, nearly two years before the duel that Maccartney and Meredyth had been deprived of their regiments, instead of the year previous, as Esmond says (*Esmond*, bk. II, chap. 6).

[4] It is true that Maccartney was indicted for his conduct toward an elderly widow, when he was drunk; but Chief Justice Sir John Holt called the indictment "vexatious." (Chichester, *D. N. B.*, *loc. cit.*). It seems likely also that he was extravagant. Swift's charge (in the *Examiner*, Novem-

FACT AND FICTION

cartney was not averse to a "job" is clearly proved; that he was an assassin is not. Meredyth's record is better than Maccartney's, for he seems to have discharged his offices faithfully.

Esmond's expressed opinion that the Duke of Hamilton might well have refused Lord Mohun's challenge, because of the latter's previous career of profligacy and crime, could hardly apply to the reformed Lord Mohun of history, who had acted only a year and a half before as the Duke of Marlborough's friend. And in any case, for the Duke of Hamilton to have refused the challenge of a notorious bravo, such as Thackeray paints Mohun as being (and as the young Lord Mohun was),[1]

---

ber 13–20, 1712), that Maccartney "made an Offer to the late King to murder a certain Person who was under his Majesty's Displeasure," appears to be a libel. Swift adds that William "disdained the Motion, and abhorred the Proposer ever after." Maccartney was promoted, however, between 1689 and 1697, from captain to major to lieutenant colonel in the Scots Foot Guards, a fact which does not argue any loss of favor between those years at any rate. Lord Chesterfield, long after Maccartney's trial in 1716 (at which he was present), said, in commenting upon Swift's *History of the Four Last Years of Queen Anne:* "though Maccartney was very capable of the vilest actions, he was guiltless of that [the attack on the Duke]." (Swift's *Prose Works*, ed. T. Scott, vol. x, p. xxii; cf. *supra*, p. 244).

[1] Thomas Hearne, writing November 24, 1712, calls Mohun "ye greatest Debauchee and Bully of ye Age," but attributes to him "a strange Trembling and Consternation"

would have been all the more impossible. Esmond's comment on the Duke of Hamilton's high spirit and courage is perhaps based upon a contemporary pamphlet's allusion to him as "a fiery and brave man with strength and experience."[1]

It would seem that Thackeray has made free with Lord Mohun's life to a greater degree in the latter part of *Esmond* than in the earlier. He has overlooked Mohun's "reformation," keeping him still the roistering bravo of his youth. He has distorted the life of his villain, giving him a part in events in which he was not, and could not have

---

after the duel had been arranged. (*Remarks and Collections*, ed. by C. E. Doble, Oxford Historical Society, iii, 483.) Lord Mohun was charged with cowardice almost immediately upon his death. Swift [?] in the *Examiner*, for November 20, 1712, accused him of having quarrelled with the Duke in the hope of regaining the character for courage which he had lost in his encounter with Davenant (see also *A True and Impartial Account* . . . p. 6). Swift suggested also that Maccartney was forced to keep up his friend's courage with wine (*Ibid.*, p. 24, where this is denied). The author of the Tory *True and Impartial Account of the Murder* remarks "that His Lordship in the course of his many Adventures never dealt in Quarrels with Men of Honour . . . his Lordship never being easily provok'd to draw his Sword, unless heated with Wine, or prompted to it by pernicious Counsel" (p. 3); and he goes on to say that General Maccartney supplied both of these. It must be said, indeed, that on the occasion of each escapade in which he was concerned and about which we have complete data Mohun had been drinking more or less heavily.

[1] *A Strict Enquiry*. . . .

been, concerned. Of the closing events of Mohun's life, the novelist has accepted an interpretation which the facts of history, as they appear to the student, will not bear out, but yet which is in perfect harmony with the point of view of the pretended witness of these occurrences. And Thackeray has even involved persons in these matters who had no part in them at all. Again, in spite of his twisting of fact, and even of probability here and there, he has, however, managed to obtain and preserve that verisimilitude, that plausibility, which makes *Henry Esmond* one of the most nearly perfect presentations in literature of the life and actions and thoughts of a past age.

APPENDICES

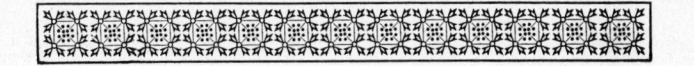

APPENDICES

A

Adelaide Duchess of Shrewsbury

Adelaide Duchess of Shrewsbury was a daughter of the Marchese Andrea Paleotti of Bologna, and, through her mother, a great-great-granddaughter of Robert Earl of Leicester, Queen Elizabeth's favorite. She was married to the Duke at Augsburg, on August 20, 1705.[1] This was apparently her second marriage, her first husband having been a noble of the household of Maria Christina, Queen of Sweden, in which the uncle of the Duchess was chancellor. It was alleged that she had engaged in an intrigue with the Duke before their marriage, which, being detected by her brother, had resulted in their union because of the fraternal threats.[2] She is said also to have been the mistress of an Italian, Brachiano. The Duke and his new Duchess arrived in London on January 1, 1705/6. By January 5, they had taken a house in St. James's Street, and had waited on the Queen. A bill to naturalize the Duchess was introduced into the House of Lords on January 17. It was passed, and received the Queen's approval on February 16.

---

[1] According to Luttrell, *A Brief Relation of State Affairs*, v, 595, and Ward in *D. N. B.*, lv, 305, art., "Talbot, Charles, Duke of Shrewsbury," the marriage was at Augsburg, not at Rome.

[2] Lady Cowper, *Diary*, p. 8.

The Duchess is alleged to have acted as her husband's intermediary in his correspondence with the Pretender. Her free manners and naïveté attracted much ill-natured criticism during her first years in England. Swift, however, who took pleasure in her company, called her "indeed, a most agreeable woman, and a great favorite of mine," and said, when it was proposed to make the Duke "Governor of Ireland," that "the Duchess will please the people there mightily." She can hardly, therefore, have been stupid. Upon the accession of George I, she asked for, and finally secured, on November 8, 1714, the post of Lady of the Bedchamber to the Princess of Wales. She was much admired by George I for her wit. It is certain that she was an amiable and vivacious woman. She outlived the Duke, dying June 29, 1726.[1]

The Duchess's brother Ferrante was hanged at Tyburn on March 28, 1718, for murdering his servant.[2] I have seen neither *The Life, Actions, and Amours of Ferdinando Marquis of Paleotti*, nor *A Particular Account of the Life . . . of the Marquis Paleotti*, both published in London in 1718.

---

[1] As sources for the above account of the Duchess and her career, see G. E. C., *Complete Peerage*, vii, 143–144, vi, 89; *D. N. B.*, xvi, 122 ff., art., "Dudley, Sir Robert," by Sir S. Lee; Ward in *D. N. B.*, *loc. cit*; Luttrell, *op. cit.*, vi, 1, 2; "Lewis Melville," *The First George*, i, 150–151; *Journals of the House of Lords*, xviii, 68, 74, 75, 76, 78, 90, 107; Hutton, *Country Walks about Florence*, p. 289; Lady Cowper, *Diary*, pp. 8 ff., 12, 13, 14–15, 20–21, 47, 113, 197; Swift, *Journal to Stella*, T. Scott's ed. of *Prose Works*, ii, 217, 254, 256, 309, 357, 361, 384, 399.

[2] Letter of Lieutenant General Dillon to the Duke of Mar, dated April 4, 1718, in *Hist. MSS. Comm. Reports, Stuart MSS. of the King of Great Britain*, vi, 249.

B

LIEUTENANT GENERAL GEORGE MACCARTNEY

George Maccartney was born in Belfast about 1660, being eldest son of George Maccartney, of the Maccartneys of Blackett in Scotland, who had settled in Ireland in 1650. George Maccartney the younger was educated in Ireland and France.[1] His first army service was, perhaps, in Holland, for among the Irish ensigns given in "A List of Officers from Holland" in 1689 is one "Mackarly."[2] At any rate, in 1689, he was a captain in the Scots Foot Guards. On November 13, 1695, he was commissioned major, and on May 30, 1697, he became a lieutenant colonel. Maccartney received his commission as colonel of a regiment of foot on January 29, 1704.[3] In the latter part of 1705, Maccartney sought the colonelcy of the Cameronian Regiment, the commander of which, General Ferguson, had just died; but, in spite of his having influential friends close to the Duke of Marlborough, he failed to secure it.[4] Maccartney bore apparently a rather ill character among the more sedate of Marlborough's officers, be-

[1] *D. N. B.*, xxxiv, 443, art., "Maccartney, or Macartney, George," by H. Manners Chichester.

[2] *Hist. MSS. Comm. Reports, Laing MSS. in the University of Edinburgh*, i, 460.

[3] Cf. Luttrell, however, who says under January 8, 1703/4, that Maccartney had then received his commission (*A Brief Relation of State Affairs*, v, 378). Probably Dalton, from whom the date of 1704 is taken (*Army Lists*, v, 224), was beginning the year with January 1.

[4] Letters of Major J. Cranstoun to Robert Cunningham, dated October 20, 1705, and February 11, 1706 (*Hist. MSS. Comm. Reports*, xv, *MSS. of the Duke of Portland*, iv, 265-268, 284 ff.).

cause he had not only squandered his wife's fortune, but had run his regiment in debt.[1] Generals Palmes, Cadogan, and Meredyth were among his friends.[2] He was commissioned brigadier general on December 25, 1705, at the same time as Lord Mohun. In the summer of 1706, a battalion of Maccartney's regiment was transferred from Flanders to Spain.[3] There they were engaged in the battle of Almanza, April 25, 1707,[4] and were among the four thousand men rallied, after the allied defeat, by Generals Shrimpton and Maccartney, Colonel Britton, and others, who marched them off the field. This force was surrounded by the French during the night following the battle, and surrendered to them.[5] According to Dalton,[6] Maccartney was promoted to major general on January 1, 1709, although Luttrell reports the rise in rank under September 6, 1707.[7] In December, 1708, Maccartney was named to command an expedition against the French in Canada. This projected invasion fell through ultimately, after Maccartney had been relieved of the command, but he had taken the precaution of collecting his pay in advance, a fact which was the subject of censure by a committee

---

[1] *Hist. MSS. Comm. Reports*, xv, *MSS. of the Duke of Portland*, *loc. cit.* General Maccartney had married the widow of General Douglas.

[2] *Ibid.*

[3] The same to the same, January 10, 1706 (O. S.), *Ibid.*, iv, 311.

[4] Where their Lieutenant Colonel, Ramsey, was killed (Brodrick, *Compleat History*, p. 195). Brodrick gives an account of the battle of Almanza (pp. 193 ff.), as does Parnell in *The War of the Succession in Spain* (pp. 210 ff.).

[5] *An Account of the Earl of Galway's Conduct* . . . p. 85; MacKinnon, *Coldstream Guards*, i, 311–312, n. 1.

[6] *Army Lists*, iii, 45, n. 13.   [7] *Op. cit.*, vi, 209.

of the Commons in 1713.[1] Maccartney had expected the governorship of Jamaica, but failed to obtain it.[2] Apparently it was at this time that Maccartney felt first the Queen's displeasure. He had engaged in some prank with an old woman as its butt.[3] As the result, he seems to have been removed from the command of the Canadian expedition and to have lost his regiment as well.[4] Maccartney then served in Flanders as a volunteer.[5] He evidently recovered the Queen's favor, as in January, 1709/10, he was appointed colonel of Sir Thomas Pendergasse's regiment.[6] In the same year, he acted as engineer at the siege of Douai,[7] and was promoted to lieutenant general.[8] In December, 1710, however, he, like his friends, Lieutenant General Thomas Meredyth and Brigadier General Phillip Honeywood, was forced to sell his regiment at half price and leave the army. The reason for these drastic measures was such indiscreet acts as drinking damnation and confusion to the new ministry, and to those who had any hand in turning out the old.[9] Marlborough expostulated with

---

[1] Cobbett, *Parliamentary History of England*, vi, cols. 1179 ff.
[2] *Ibid.*
[3] Chichester in *D. N. B.*, xxxiv, 443.
[4] *Ibid.*; Cobbett, *loc. cit.* [5] Chichester, *D. N. B.*, xxxiv, 444.
[6] Luttrell, *A Brief Relation of State Affairs*, vi, 535. Sir Thomas had been killed at Malplaquet the preceding September. Brodrick, *Compleat History*, p. 312.
[7] Chichester in *D. N. B. loc. cit.* Brodrick mentions the service of Maccartney's regiment at the siege of Douai, but says nothing of its colonel's engineering duties. See the *Compleat History*, p. 326.
[8] Early in May, 1710. *The History of the Reign of Queen Anne, Digested into Annals*, Year the Ninth, p. 415.
[9] Tindal, *A Continuation of Mr. Rapin's History of England*, iv, 195; Swift, *Journal to Stella*, December 10, 1710, in T. Scott's edition of the *Prose Works*, ii, 71; Swift in the *Examiner*, December 14, 1710,

the Queen upon the loss of these officers, but without effect.[1] How Maccartney existed for the next two years without employment, we do not know; it was said in 1712 that Lord Mohun had supported him.[2] Early in 1710/11, it was reported that "General Macknarty" was intending to enter the service of the Czar of Russia.[3] He acted as second to Lord Mohun in his duel with the Duke of Hamilton on November 15, 1712, and fled to Holland, after the deaths of the duellists, pursued by charges of having himself assassinated the Duke. He later took refuge in Hanover, where Lord Mohun had been in 1701, on a diplomatic mission with the Earl of Macclesfield.[4] Returning to England with the foreign troops brought in by George I, in 1715/16,[5] he was

Ibid., ix, 127; Luttrell, *op. cit.*, vi, 664. Grove says that the generals asserted that they had merely drunk "a health *to the Duke of* Marlborough and *confusion to all his enemies.*" *Lives of . . . the Dukes of Devonshire*, p. 35 [*Life of the second Duke*]. This distinction, which is really only nominal, was alleged at the time in extenuation of the offence (*The History of the Reign of Queen Anne, Digested into Annals*, Year the Ninth, pp. 278–279).

[1] On January 17, 1711. *D. N. B.*, x, 335, art., "Churchill, John, Duke of Marlborough," by Sir L. Stephen.

[2] Swift [?], the *Examiner*, November 13–20, 1712; and see also *A True and Impartial Account of the Murder of his Grace the Duke of Hamilton* . . . pp. 5–6.

[3] Newsletter dated January 23, 1710/11, *Hist. MSS. Comm. Reports, MSS. of the Marquess of Downshire*, i, pt. 2, 693.

[4] Constance Russell, in *Notes and Queries*, ser. VI, xii, 131. Probably General Maccartney had been presented to the Elector or to the Electoral Prince, or to both, during his service with the army. Three younger brothers of the Elector were also in the Allied armies, one under Marlborough. Perhaps, too, the general had accompanied Marlborough to Hanover in 1704.

[5] E. Solly, *Notes and Queries*, ser. VI, xii, 177–178. These were Dutch soldiers to the number of six thousand (Collins, *Peerage of England*, i, 546, n. z).

arrested on the indictment against him for the murder of the Duke of Hamilton,[1] and on June 13, 1716, was tried in the Court of King's Bench. Being convicted of manslaughter, — by the direction of the court, it has been said,[2] — he was burned in the hand with a cold iron. A contemporary newspaper story of the trial runs thus:

"Yesterday June 13 General Mackartney's Tryal came on, at the King's Bench Bar, before the Rt. Hon. the Lord Chief Justice Parker, &c. and a numerous Appearance of the Nobility. The Prosecutor's Witnesses contradicted one another, and swore to many Particulars which they had never done before, to prove him guilty of the wilful murder of the late Duke of Hamilton; but the General's Evidence was so clear and satisfactory both to the Bench and the Jury, that after the General, supported by his own Innocence, and the Integrity of his Judges, had made a very Handsome Speech in his own Defence, the Jury went out, and immediately return'd with their Verdict, that he was Guilty only of Manslaughter."[3]

Another account is that of the annalist Abel Boyer:

"On *Wednesday*, the 13th of *June* [1716], at the King's Bench Bar at *Westminster*, came on the Tryal of Lieutenant General *Mackartney*, for the pretended Murder of the late Duke of *Hamilton*. The Main Evidence

---

[1] Dalton reprints a petition of Maccartney to the King, asking that the Attorney General be directed to "confess" his plea of not guilty on the indictment against him for the murder of Lord Mohun. *George I's Army*, i, 253, n. 3.

[2] Collins, *op. cit.*, i, 546.

[3] The *Flying-Post*, June 12–14, 1716.

against him was Colonel *Hamilton*, who deviated from his former Depositions, for whenas he swore, some years before, that General *Maccartney* gave the late Duke his mortal Wound, he now only averr'd, That he saw his Sword over the Duke's Shoulder. But all he had advanc'd to charge Mr. *Maccartney* was fully confuted by the Testimony of two Park-Keepers who stood firm to their former Depositions, *viz.* That they had taken the Swords from Gen. *Maccartney*, and Col. *Hamilton*, when they went to the Relief of Duke *Hamilton* and Lord *Mohun*; and even a Footman of the late Duke ran counter to Part of the Colonel's Evidence. But what fill'd the Court and all the Spectators with Amazement, was the Deposition of one of the Park-Keepers, who said, he was offer'd two handfulls of Gold, and a Place of 100*l.* a Year, by the late Ld. *Bolingbroke*, if he would swear, That Mr. *Maccartney* kill'd Duke *Hamilton:* So that a more villainous Contrivance to take away a Man's Life was scarce ever laid open in *Westmins*ter-*Hall!* Two or three Surgeons were also examin'd as to the Nature of the Wounds of which the Duke dy'd; after which General *Maccartney* spoke for himself, with a great deal of Temper, and pleaded, among other Things, That having had a long Intimacy with the Lord *Mohun*, the latter desired him to wait on Duke *Hamilton*, about a Law-Affair, and that he never imparted to him the Design of a Duel,[1] 'till they came into *Hyde-Park*, where

---

[1] Yet in his account of the events leading up to the duel, in his *Letter*, dated less than three weeks after the affair, Maccartney certainly shows that he not only knew a meeting was contemplated, but even discussed the arrangements for it with the Duke. Cf. *supra*, p. 210.

the two Principals interchang'd mortal Wounds, before Colonel *Hamilton* and himself could prevent it. He modestly complain'd of the inveterate Malice and Barbarity of his former Prosecutors, who, through Party Hatred and Revenge, had charged him with a most odious and detestable Crime, of which he was intirely innocent; and who, not having it in their Power to take away his Life, had wounded him in what he valued above Life itself, his Honour; and obliged him to wander out of his native Country, loaded with Infamy. Hereupon, he call'd several Noblemen, and Officers of Distinction to his Reputation, who all gave him a very good Character, and said, among other things, that to their Knowledge, he had been instrumental in making up several Quarrels.[1] The Duke of *Richmond* said in particular, that after the Unfortunate Affair between Duke *Hamilton* and Lord *Mohun*, General *Maccartney* having taken Refuge in his House, he found him so confident of his own Innocency, that he had much ado to perswade him to consult his Safety, by yielding to the Malice and Perversity of the Times, and flying beyond Sea. In the last Place, the Lord Chief Justice *Parker*, with his usual Eloquence and Integrity [2] summ'd up the

[1] Maccartney's counsel was Sergeant Thomas Pengelly, who had already defended Colonel Hamilton (*supra*, p. 233, n. 1). His brief in General Maccartney's case and notes for his client's defence are still preserved. Among the latter is the following: "It's necessary for you prove your peacefull disposition by the many reconciliations you have made." *Hist. MSS. Comm. Reports*, vii, 690, *MSS. of the Rev. T. W. Webb*.

[2] When one recalls that later this upright judge, then curiously enough Earl of Macclesfield, was impeached and found guilty of corruption in his office of Lord Chancellor, Boyer's praises seem rather empty.

Evidence; and took Notice that Col. *Hamilton's* Depositions were inconsistent, and therefore carried a Face of Unsincerity.[1]

"This memorable Tryal lasted about 6 Hours, after which the Jury brought in a Verdict, whereby General *Maccartney* was acquitted of the Murder, and declared only guilty of Manslaughter; and having, the next Morning, appeared again at the *King's Bench Bar*, he receiv'd Judgment accordingly; and the Formality of being burnt in the Hand, was immediately executed upon him with a Cold Iron, to prevent the late Duke's Relations lodging an Appeal."[2]

Maccartney did not long await restoration to his military posts. On June 30 he kissed hands for the colonelcy of the Royal Scots Fusiliers, succeeding the Earl of Orrery in command of the regiment. His commissions as colonel and as lieutenant general were antedated to June 12.[3]

General Maccartney seems to have been high in personal favor with George I.[4] He was made governor of Portsmouth on April 15, 1719. In 1722 he was a mem-

---

[1] Although the Lord Chief Justice's charge favored the prisoner, yet he is not reported by Boyer as directing a verdict of manslaughter, as Collins asserts (*supra*, p. 261, n. 2).

[2] ... *The Political State of Great Britain* ... xi [January–June, 1716], 745 ff.

[3] *Ibid.*, xii [July–December, 1716], 108–109; Dalton, *George I's Army*, i, 202, 247.

[4] Letters of J. Menzies to L. Inese, June 18–29, 1716; of the same to the Duke of Mar, August 5–16, 1717, *Hist. MSS. Comm. Reports, Stuart MSS. of the King of Great Britain*, ii, 242, iv, 525; newsletter, November 15, 1717, *Hist. MSS. Comm. Reports, MSS. of the Duke of Portland*, v, 539.

ber of the board to examine the half-pay officers.[1] He was appointed colonel of the First Regiment of Carabiniers on March 9, 1726/7. From 1726 on, he commanded the Forces in Ireland. General Maccartney died in London, July 7, 1730.[2]

[Where no other source is cited in the preceding account, I have drawn upon Dalton's *English Army Lists* and his *George I's Army*.]

C

LIEUTENANT GENERAL THOMAS MEREDYTH

Thomas Meredyth was a son of Arthur Meredyth of Dollardstown, County Meath. He was commissioned captain in the Duke of Leinster's Regiment of Horse, on April 23, 1691; he was brevetted colonel of horse, June 1, 1701, and, on the same day, was appointed adjutant general of the forces. On February 12, 1702, he became colonel of a regiment of foot on the Irish Establishment (as did Mohun at the same time). Meredyth was commissioned brigadier general on August 25, 1704;[3] his commission was probably antedated to January 1, 1704.[4] He had been wounded in the cheek at Schellenberg on July 2, 1704. In the summer of 1706, General Meredyth directed the siege of

[1] *Hist. MSS. Comm. Reports*, xi, pt. 4, 138, *MSS. of Marquess Townshend*.
[2] G. Ormerod, *Notes and Queries*, ser. II, iii, 179.
[3] Dalton, *Army Lists*, v, 17.
[4] Dalton, *Blenheim Bounty Roll*, p. 4, n. 14; and *George I's Army*, i, 160, n. 1.

Dendermond, which finally capitulated September 5.[1] He was then appointed governor of the city.[2] Meredyth's commission as major general was dated January 1, 1707/8,[3] although, when writing on October 18, 1707, Narcissus Luttrell reports Meredyth's promotion, and on December 2, 1707, calls him "major general."[4] Either early in December, 1707, or on February 20, 1707/8, Meredyth was appointed governor of Tynemouth Castle.[5] He was appointed Gentleman of the Horse to the Duke of Somerset, Master of the Horse to the Queen.[6] At the battle of Oudenarde, Meredyth was again wounded.[7] On March 8, 1708/9, he was seated on petition in the House of Commons as member for Midhurst.[8] Meredyth appears to have received his commission as lieutenant general only in May, 1709,[9] although the promotion was as of January 1, 1709.[10] On

[1] According to Brodrick, the Duke of Marlborough's brother, Lieutenant-General Churchill, was put in command of the besiegers on August 29, 1706. *Compleat History*, p. 173.

[2] Luttrell, *A Brief Relation of State Affairs*, vi, 55, 87. Brodrick says, however, that when the army went into winter quarters after November 6, 1706, Major General Lauder commanded in Dendermond (*op. cit.*, p. 177).

[3] Dalton, *Army Lists*, v, 153.

[4] *Op. cit.*, vi, 224, 241.

[5] *Ibid.*, vi, 241; Dalton, *Blenheim Bounty Roll, loc. cit.*

[6] Letter of Joseph Addison to the Earl of Manchester on March 30, 1708, *Hist. MSS. Comm. Reports*, viii, 97, *MSS. of the Duke of Manchester*.

[7] Luttrell, *A Brief Relation of State Affairs*, vi, 325.

[8] *Ibid.*, p. 416.

[9] *Ibid.*, p. 445, under date of May 26, 1709; see also a letter of George Tilson to Horatio Walpole, May 10, 1709, *Hist. MSS. Comm. Reports*, xi, pt. 2, 49, *MSS. of the Marquess Townshend*.

[10] Dalton, *Blenheim Bounty Roll, loc. cit.*

APPENDICES

May 1, 1710, Meredyth was commissioned colonel of the Scots Fusiliers.[1] Early in December of that year, together with Generals Maccartney and Honeywood, Meredyth was forced to sell his regiment at half price, and was relieved of his military duties.[2] He was dismissed, also, as Gentleman of the Horse.[3] His regiment was given to the Earl of Orrery.[4] In the late winter of 1711/12, Meredyth entrusted his fortune of ten thousand pounds to one Stratford, a friend of Doctor Swift, to invest for him; but Stratford lost this money while speculating on tips given him by Swift, who was, of course, intimate with the Tory ministers.[5] On the accession of George I, Meredyth was restored to his place in the army. He was commissioned colonel of a regiment on October 4, 1714.[6] When, in the same month,

---

[1] This colonelcy had been offered by the Queen to Samuel Masham, brother of the favorite, and only by giving the Queen the choice between himself and Masham, did Marlborough secure the right of naming the commanding officer, General Meredyth. Stephen in *D. N. B.*, x, 334, art., "Churchill, John, Duke of Marlborough." Sir Leslie, however, dates the transaction in 1709.

[2] Tindal, *A Continuation of Mr. Rapin's History of England*, iv, 195; Swift, *Journal to Stella*, December 10, 1710, T. Scott's ed. of the *Prose Works*, ii, 71, and in the *Examiner*, December 14, 1710, and January 4, 1710/11, respectively, *Prose Works*, ix, 127, 148; Luttrell, *op. cit.*, vi, 664, under date of December 12, 1710.

[3] Luttrell, *op. cit.*, vi, 673, under date of January 2, 1710/11.

[4] *Ibid.*, p. 679. In turn, Lord Orrery's colonelcy was taken from him and given to General Maccartney when that officer was reinstated in the army in 1716 (see Appendix B, *supra*, p. 264).

[5] Swift, *Journal to Stella*, March 1, 1711/12, T. Scott's ed. of the *Prose Works*, ii, 346.

[6] According to Boyer, on October 11, 1714, the King signed "a Commission for Lieutenant-General *Thomas Meredyth* to be Colonel of the Regiment lately commanded by Major-General *William Newton*, deceased." ... *The Political State of Great Britain* ... viii, 338.

the Privy Council of Ireland was dissolved, Meredyth was among the new members appointed.[1] In 1716 he was governor of Londonderry.[2] General Meredyth died in 1719, and was buried June 19, in St. Patrick's Cathedral, Dublin. Like Cadogan, Meredyth seems to have been a favorite of Marlborough, a fact which created some jealousy and occasioned a certain number of complaints.[3]

[Where no authority is given above, I have utilized Dalton's valuable *Blenheim Bounty Roll*, *English Army Lists*, and *George I's Army*.]

D

PAMPHLETS, ETC., ON THE HAMILTON–MOHUN DUEL

The pamphlets dealing with the Hamilton-Mohun duel which I have examined may be divided into three classes:

I. The non-political, such as: "A full and true Account of a Desperate and Bloody Duel: which was Fought this Morning in *High Park* [sic] between My Lord *Moon* and Duke *Hambilton*. With an Account how my Lord *Moon* was Kill'd on the Spot, and Duke *Hambilton* receiv'd a Mortal Wound, of which he Dy'd in a few Hours after he receiv'd the Wound. . . . Printed by *Edw. Midwinter*, at the Star in Pye-Corner, price one I penny."

---

[1] . . . *The Political State of Great Britain* . . . viii, 339.

[2] Dalton, *George I's Army*, ii, 153.

[3] Letters of Major J. Cranstoun of the Cameronian Regiment to R. Cunningham, October 1, 1705, and October 20, 1705, *Hist. MSS. Comm. Reports*, xv, *MSS. of the Duke of Portland*, iv, 255, 265.

"The Lives and Characters of *James* Duke *Hamilton* and *Brandon* . . . and *Charles* Lord *Mohun;* Who were unfortunately Kill'd by each other in *Hyde-Park*, on *Saturday* the 15th of this Instant *November*, 1712. Together with a true and particular Account of that Unfortunate Action; and also an Elegy on Their Deaths . . . *London:* Printed by J. Read near Fleet-street."

"*The Substance of the Depositions taken at the Coroner's Inquest the 17th, 19th, and 21st of November, on the Body of Duke* Hamilton: *And the 15th, 18th, 20th and 22d, on the Body of my Lord* Mohun. London. Printed *for* A. Baldwin *in* Warwick Lane. 1712. (Price One Penny.)"

"A Particular *Account* of the *Tryal* of *John Hamilton*, Esq; *For the Murder of* Charles *Lord* Mohun, *and* James *Duke of* Hamilton *and* Brandon, *at the* Sessions-House *in the* Old-Baily, *on* Friday *the twelfth of* December, 1712. *Publish'd by Order of the Right Honourable Sir* Richard Hoare, *Kt. Lord Mayor of the City of* London."

"A Full and Exact Relation of the Duel Fought In *Hyde Park* on *Saturday*, *November* 15, 1712. Between His Grace *James*, Duke of *Hamilton*, And the Right Honourable *Charles*, Lord *Mohun*. In a Letter to a Member of Parliament. *London:* Printed for E. *Curll*, at the *Dial* and *Bible* against *St. Dunstan's* Church in *Fleetstreet*, 1713. . . . Pr. 2*d*."

II. The Tory accounts, such as: "The Whole Lives, Characters, Actions, and Fall of D. *Hamilton* and L. *Mohun*. With an Exact Account of the Bloody Duel which they Fought on *Saturday* morning the 15th of *November*, 1712. in *Hide-Park*, where my Ld. *Mohun* was instantly Kill'd, and Duke *Hamilton* Dy'd in two Hours after at his own House. . . . With a full Relation of the Ground and Cause of this Bloody Quarrel. Together with two Elegy's on the Death of these two Great Peers. *London* Printed, and *Newcastle* Reprinted by J. White."

"The case at Large of Duke *Hamilton* and the Lord *Mohun*. Viz. I. A Full and Exact Relation of the Duel Fought in *Hyde-Park* on *Saturday*, *Nov.* 15. 1712. With the Grounds and Management of the Quarrel. II. The Authentic Depositions at large, taken at the Coroner's Inquest, and at the Earl of *Dartmouth's* Office, before a Committee of Council. III. The Particular Wounds of the *Peers*, upon Searching their Bodies by Dr. *Roujat*, Mr. *Bussiere*, and Mr. *la Fage* . . . *London*; Printed for E. *Curll*, at the *Dial* and *Bible* against *St. Dunstan's* Church in *Fleetstreet*. 1712. Price 6*d*."

"*A True and Impartial Account of the Murder of his Grace the Duke of Hamilton and Brandon, by Mr. Mackartney*. London, Printed and Sold by John Morphew near Stationer-Hall, 1712."

To the above may be added Swift's *The History of the Last Four Years of the Queen*.

III. The Whig accounts, such as: "A True and Impartial Account of the Animosity, Quarrel and Duel, between The late Duke of Hamilton, and The Lord Mohun: with the reports of Three Eminent Surgeons, who open'd the Bodies and examin'd the Wounds. And Some Previous Reflections on Sham-Plots, &c. *London:* Printed and Sold by *A. Baldwin*, near the *Oxford-Arms* in *Warwick-Lane*. 1712. Price 6*d*."

APPENDICES

"A Strict Enquiry into the Circumstances of a late Duel, with Some Account of the Persons Concern'd on Both Sides. Being a Modest Attempt to do Justice to the Injur'd Memory of a Noble Person Dead, and to the Injur'd Honour of an Absent Person Living. To which is added, The Substance of a Letter from General *MacCartney* to his Friend. *London:* Printed for *J. Baker*, at the *Black-Boy* in *Pater-Noster-Row*. 1713. (Price 6*d*.)" Professor W. P. Trent, to whose profound knowledge of the period I have had recourse, kindly informs me that this pamphlet is Defoe's. Its acute reasoning and excellent style certainly point to an author of more attainments than those of the average hack.

"A Letter from Mr. Maccartney to a Friend of His in London. Dated at Ostend, Dec. 4–15. 1712. Giving a Particular Account Of what pass'd before and at the Unfortunate Duel between His Grace the D. of Hamilton and L. Mohun. London. Printed for A. Baldwin in Warwick-Lane. 1713. Price 6*d*."

In the Yale University Library is the following pamphlet, which I have not seen, and the description of which I owe to the kindness of Miss Anne S. Pratt, Reference Librarian at Yale:

"A Defence of Mr. Maccartney, By a Friend. Non talia audivimus. The Second Edition. London: Printed for A. Baldwin, near the Oxford Arms in Warwick-Lane, MDCCXII. (Price Six-pence.)." I am informed by Professor Trent that John Oldmixon is probably the author of this pamphlet. There is no copy in the British Museum or Bodleian Libraries, and it is not listed among Oldmixon's works in Mr. G. A. Aitken's bibliography given in his life of this writer in the *D. N. B.*, xiv (ed. of 1909), 1009–1013.

The account of the duel in *The History of the Reign of Queen Anne, Digested into Annals*, Year the Eleventh, pp. 296 ff.

To the above may be added Bishop Gilbert Burnet's *History of His Own Times;* Nicholas Tindal's *Continuation of the History of England by Mr. Rapin de Thoyras;* and Bishop White Kennett's *Complete History of England*.

It will be noticed that to certain of the works listed above pieces of verse are appended. As one would suspect, the deaths of the Duke and Lord Mohun inspired the ballad-mongers and occasional hack poets. A non-partisan ballad is "An Excellent Ballad of the Lord Mohun and Duke Hamilton. With an Exact Account of their Melancholy Deaths. . . . Printed and Sold in Alder-mary Church-yard, Bow-Lane, London," which is printed in *Roxburghe Ballads*, viii, 232–233. A ballad with Tory leanings is "*Duke Hamilton and Lord Mohun*," which was reprinted by J. P. A. in *Notes and Queries*, ser. VI, xii, 330–331, and is to be found also in *Roxburghe Ballads*, viii, 234. Another piece of Tory verse is "The Lord M——n's Ghost to the D—— of R——nd," which is in vol. i of *A Collection of Broadsides* in the British Museum (Pressmark, 1870., d. 1). Whig comments in verse on the duel are reprinted by J. W. Ebsworth from *Political Merriment*, iii, 48 and 50 (ed. of 1715) in *Roxburghe Ballads*, viii, 233. Ebsworth also quotes a stanza from a Whig satirical song "of about 1713," called "The Raree Show" (*Ibid.*, p. 235). Swift alludes to Maccartney in his poem, "Horace, Book II,

Ode 1, Paraphrased." I have not seen "The Lord Mohun's Vindication," Edinburgh, 1712 (see Maggs Brothers' Catalogue No. 477, item 542).

IV. The British Museum possesses the following contemporary newspapers in which matter relating to the Hamilton-Mohun duel occurs:

The *Gazette*, November 15–18, 1712.

The *Post Boy*, November 15–18, 18–20, 20–22, 22–25, 27–29, December 11–13, 13–16, 1712.

The *Examiner*, November 13–20, 1712 (editorial by Swift[?]).

The *Evening Post*, November 20–22, 1712.

The *Flying-Post*, December 4–6, 1712: "The Romantick History of Fairy-Land," by "Bob Hush" [Sir Robert Walpole?].

E

ROYAL PROCLAMATIONS

THE *POST BOY*, NOVEMBER 25–27, 1712; THE *GAZETTE* NOVEMBER 25–29, 1712

London, Nov. 27. Yesterday, the following Proclamation was Publish'd.

BY THE QUEEN,

A Proclamation, for Seizing and Apprehending George Maccartney, *Esq; commonly call'd Lieutenant-General* Maccartney.

ANNE R.

Whereas on Saturday the Fifteenth Day of this instant November, James Duke of Hamilton and Duke of

Brandon, and Charles Lord Mohun, in high Contempt and open Defiance of Our Laws, pursuing their Private Animosities, Fought a Duel in Hyde-Park; and John Hamilton, Esq., was Second to the said Duke, and the said George Maccartney was Second to the Lord Mohun; and the said Duke and Lord Mohun were kill'd: And whereas by an Inquisition taken the Seventeenth Day of this instant November, before Charles Lowe, Gent. Coroner of the Liberty of the Dean and Chapter of the Collegiate Church of St. Peter of Westminster, on the View of the Dead Body of the said Duke, it is found, That the said Charles Lord Mohun, on the said Fifteenth Day of November, did Murder the said Duke, and that the said George Maccartney and John Hamilton, at that time were present, aiding, abetting, assisting, and maintaining the said Lord Mohun to Commit the said Murder; and that the said George Maccartney is fled for the same: And by another Inquisition taken before the said Coroner, on the View of the Dead Body of the said Lord Mohun, it is found, that the said Duke did Murder the said Lord Mohun, and that the said George Maccartney and John Hamilton were present at, aiding, abetting, assisting, and maintaining the said Duke to commit the said Murder; but the said John Hamilton hath voluntarily surrendred himself, in order to his Tryal; We desiring to manifest Our utmost Displeasure against such Horrid and Impious Practices, and to deter all others from committing the like for the future, and that the said George Maccartney may be brought to speedy Justice, do, by the Advice of Our Privy-Council, issue forth this Our Royal Proclamation, hereby commanding and requiring all Our Justices of the Peace, and all other Our Officers, and other Our Loving Subjects, That they do use their utmost Diligence, in their several Places and Capacities, to discover, seize, and apprehend the said George Maccartney, and, being apprehended, to carry him forthwith before the next Justice of the Peace, whom We do hereby Require to Commit him to the Gaol of the County, where he shall be so Taken, charg'd with the Murder of the said Duke, and to give immediate Notice thereof to One of Our Principal Secretaries of State. And We do hereby Promise and Declare, That whosoever shall Discover and Apprehend the said George Maccartney, and bring him before such Justice of the Peace, shall Have and Receive the Reward of Five Hundred Pounds for so doing, whereof Our High Treasurer is hereby Authorized and Requir'd to make Payment. And we do hereby Publish and Declare, That if any Person or Persons, after the Issuing of this Our Royal Proclamation, shall, directly or indirectly, Conceal, Harbour, Keep or Maintain the said George Maccartney, or shall be aiding or assisting to him in making his Escape or preventing his being Taken or Arrested, such Person or Persons, so Offending, shall be prosecuted for the same with the utmost Severity of the Law.

Given at Our Court at Windsor, *the Twenty-Fourth Day of* November, *In the Eleventh Year of Our Reign.*

GOD SAVE THE QUEEN.

The *Post Boy*, November 29 — December 2, 1712;[1]
the *Gazette*, December 2-6, 1712

"London, Dec. 2.

"Whereas, by an Inquisition taken the 17th Day of November last, upon view of the dead Body of James Duke of Hamilton and Brandon; it was found that George Maccartney, Esq., was aiding and assisting the Lord Mohun to commit the Murder on the said Duke; and, That the said Maccartney is fled for the same. And whereas it hath since appear'd upon Oath, that the Wound whereof the said Duke dyed, was given him by the said Maccartney. And Her Majesty having been graciously pleas'd to issue out Her Royal Proclamation, for apprehending the said Maccartney, promising a Reward of Five Hundred Pounds, to such Persons as shall apprehend him. Her Grace the Duchess of Hamilton and Brandon, doth hereby promise, that whosoever shall discover the said George Maccartney, commonly called Lieutenant-General Maccartney; so that he be apprehended and brought to Justice, shall Receive from her Grace a Reward of Three Hundred Pounds (over and above what is promis'd by Her Majesty) to be paid by Sir Richard Hoare, Goldsmith,[2] at the Leather Bottle in Fleetstreet."

The *Post Boy*, December 18-20, 1712

Whereas it has been industriously reported, That Mr. Mackartney has made his Escape, and is now in Hol-

---

[1] This advertisement appeared in the *Post Boy* as late as February 10-12, and 17-19, 1712/13.
[2] Lord Mayor of London at the time.

land; this is to inform the Publick, That the said Report is false; and that whenever he is either taken, or has made his Escape, Notice shall be given in the Gazette, this Paper, and all other Prints. And for the more easy apprehending him, the following Description is given: He is a well-set middle-siz'd Man, of a dark, ruddy Complexion, dark Eyes, dark Eye-brows, has a wide Mouth, and good Teeth, generally wearing a black Peruke, but of late has appear'd in Woman's Cloaths, and other Disguises.

F

LETTERS OF THE EARL OF SUTHERLAND AND COLONEL JOHN HAMILTON [1]

I

THE *POST BOY*, FEBRUARY 7–10, 1712/3

London, Feb. 10. Hearing there is a Report spread abroad, That the Earl of Southerland has heard me say, That Mr Mackartney did not kill his Grace the Duke of Hamilton; I think it my Duty to do Justice to that Noble Earl and myself, by declaring the said Report to be False; and that, that Noble Earl and I never had any Discourse upon that Subject. I further think myself oblig'd in Honour and Conscience, to declare, That I saw Mr Mackartney stabb his Grace the Duke of Hamilton, while I had his Grace in my Arms, after I had disarm'd the said Mr. Mackartney,

[1] My thanks are due my friend Professor George W. Sherburn of the University of Chicago for calling my attention to these letters.

and given him his Life: but going to part the Two Lords, I threw down Mr Mackartney's Sword and my own, the former of which Mr Mackartney took up, and stabb'd his Grace with; this I have more fully declar'd upon Oath, before the Lords of Her Majesty's most Honourable Privy Council, and am ready to satisfy any body of the Truth of this from my own Mouth. In witness whereof, I here sign my Name,

JOHN HAMILTON.

II

THE *POST BOY*, FEBRUARY 12–14, 1712/3

Being much surpriz'd to see in the *Post Boy* of Tuesday last in the Paragraph from London, a Declaration said to be subscrib'd by Colonel Hamilton, in which the said Colonel affirms, That he and I never had any Discourse upon the Subject of the Duel between the Duke of Hamilton and Lord Mohun, I do upon this Occasion declare, That when the Colonel was in Custody of a Messenger in Dartmouth Street, I went to condole with him the Loss of those Noble Lords, and the unhappy Circumstances that he and Lieutenant-General Mackartney were involv'd in upon that Account; I then ask'd him whether the Lieutenant-General and he fought? He told me they did, and that by beating down General Mackartney's Sword he received that Wound in his Leg, which I then saw his Surgeon dress; he told me at the same time that he had disarm'd the Lieutenant-General, but upon seeing both the Lords

APPENDICES

fall, he went to the Duke's Assistance, and threw down both the Swords, one of which Mr Mackartney took up, and made a Poke (that was his Expression) at his Grace: What! said I, had my Opposite made a Thrust at my Principal, I should have made no more scruple to have run him thro' than killing a Frog; he answer'd, nor he neither, had he then had a Sword, and the Duke not in his Arms. I ask'd if he was sure that Mr Mackartney wounded the Duke? He answer'd, that he could not be positive, for he unbutton'd his Grace's Breast, and felt neither Blood nor Wound there; that is, as near as I can possibly remember, what pass'd between Colonel Hamilton and me upon that Subject.

And whereas some scandalous and insolent Person or Persons have lately affix'd the following Libel on the Doors of several Coffee-houses near St. James's, and elsewhere, in these Words, and in the same Spelling, "whereas it has been industriously reported that the Lord Southerland in a Visit to Col. Hamilton as a Relation now sick upon questioning the Col. had received Answers very much to the Advancement of General Mackartnis Character as to the Duel. Note so far to the contrar I askt Col. Hamilton no Questions but as to his Health and they are Rogues and Sons of whores that says so being damb'd Lyes.

SOUTHERLAND."

I do hereby declare the aforesaid Libel to be a spurious Forgery, and whosoever shall discover the infamous Actor or Actors, Contriver or Contrivers of the same, so as he or they be convicted and punish'd as the Law in such Cases directs, shall receive of me a handsom Gratuity, and be sav'd harmless, and indemnify'd from all Trouble and Costs that shall arise in the Prosecution thereof.

SOUTHERLAND.

From my Lodging in *Blooms-
bury*, Feb. 12, 1712/13.

III

The *Post Boy*, February 17–19, 1712/3

Upon what I read in the Flying Post on Saturday the 14th instant, said to be inserted by the Earl of Sutherland's Order; I think my self oblig'd to publish this. First, to declare that the Advertisement in the Post-Boy of the 10th, and the Gazette of the 14th, with Relation to the Murder of his Grace the Duke of *Hamilton*, were sign'd by me, and inserted in both those Papers at my Desire, and are true in every Part and Circumstance, as many that were in the Park at the time the Murder was committed, can bear witness: For I saw several on Horseback there, which I thought somewhat unusual at that early Hour in the Morning. Some seem'd to be Grooms watering their Horses; but those who surpriz'd me with their early being abroad, were some Gentlemen on Horseback and one in particular in brownish Cloaths, mounted on a very fine bay Gelding; who, when I had led my Lord Duke a little way, and his Grace began to faint and sink down, I heard the said Gentleman, mounted on the bay Gelding,

APPENDICES

say these Words, *By G—d it is done; he's dead, I'll warrant him.*[1] For my saying I never had any Discourse upon this Subject, with the E. of Sutherland, I again declare, I never had, during the time of my Illness, as was lately reported; but I'll do that Justice to his Lordship, as to acknowledge the Honour he did me, to make me a Visit, when in the Messengers Hands, and stood by me some part of the time, while my Wound was a dressing; during which time, I don't believe all I said to him amounted to six Words upon the Subject of the Duke's Murder. And, as to my saying, That Mr. Mackartney made a Poke at the Duke of Hamilton, I declare I never heard the Word, nor read of any such Word, till I read it in the *Flying-Post* of the 14th; nor know not what Language it is. I solemnly declare, all that's above-written is true, and inserted here at my Desire.

JOHN HAMILTON.

[1] This exclamation — if Hamilton ever really heard it — may have been a perfectly innocent, although profanely emphatic, assertion of the hopeless condition of the Duke. There is no mention of this gentleman in brown in Hamilton's previous accounts of the affair.

INDEX

INDEX

A., J. P., 272.
Addison, Joseph, 69, n. 2; 71, n. 4; 73, n. 2; 175; 266, n. 6.
"Aimes, Mr." (see also under Amy, Henry, and "Aymé, Mr."), 75, 104.
Aitken, G. A., 69, n. 2; 107, n. 1; 135, n. 3; 174, n. 2; 199, n. 2; 271.
Altham, Altham first Baron, 19, n. 1.
Ambassador, French (Camille d' Hostun, Duc de Tallart), 93.
Amy, Henry (see also under "Aimes, Mr.," and "Aymé, Mr."), 79, n. 2; 88; 89, n. 1; 104; 105; 220, n. 2; 225, ns. 2, 3, 4; 226, ns. 1, 3.
Ancaster, Robert first Duke of, 144, n. 1.
Anglesey, Arthur first Earl of, 6; 7; 8; 9, n. 2; 10, ns. 1, 3, 4; 11, n. 1.
Anglesey, James third Earl of, 19, n. 1; 55.
Annandale, William first Marquis of, 156.
Anne, Princess and Queen, 5, n. 3; 10, n. 5; 47; 59, n. 1; 78, n. 4; 93; 105; 109; 112; 134; 135; 142, n. 2; 144; 152; 153; 154; 162; 163; 165, ns. 1, 2; 166; 167; 168; 170; 171; 172; 173; 174; 181, n. 4; 183; 188; 192, n. 2; 223, n. 2; 227, n. 3; 228; 229; 236, n. 1; 241, n. 3; 248, n. 4; 255; 259; 260; 270; 272; 273; 275; 276; 278.
Annesley, Hon. Arthur, 19, n. 1.
Annesley, Hon. Charles, 19, n. 1.
Annesley, Lady Frances (see also under Haversham, Frances Lady), 60, n. 1.
Annesley, Dean the Hon. Richard, 19, n. 1.
Applegate, Robert, 82, n. 2; 83, ns. 1, 3; 87; 88, n. 1; 105, n. 3.
Arbuthnot, Dr. John, 188, n. 2.
Argyll, John first Duke of, 182; 242, n. 2.
"Arran, Earl of," 179.
Arran, Charles first Earl of, 180, n. 2.
Arran, James Earl of (see also under Hamilton, James fourth Duke of, and under Brandon, James first Duke of), 181.
Aston, Anthony, 24, n. 1.
Athenry, Francis twelfth Baron, 9, n. 1.
Atterbury, Dr. Francis, 186; 188.
Atwood, William, 95.
"Aymé, Mr." (see also under "Aimes, Mr." and Amy, Henry), 188.

INDEX

B., H., 228, n. 1.
Bacon, Sir Edmund, 213, n. 1.
Baden, Louis Margrave of (see also under Baden, Prince of), 50.
Baden, Prince of (see also under Baden, Louis Margrave of), 4; 49.
Baker, J., 130, n. 3; 241, n. 2; 271.
Baker, Sir Richard, 5, n. 2; 6, n. 1. 141, n. 2; 192, n. 1; 203, n. 2; 210, n. 4; 269; 270; 271.
Baldwin, A., 115, n. 1; 131, n. 2;
Ball, Rev. J. Elrington, 95, n. 1; 164, n. 2.
Bancroft, John, 31, n. 4; 40, n. 2.
Bankham, Capt. Richard (see also under "Bingham, Captain"), 53, n. 2.
Barry, Mrs. Catherine, 24, n. 1.
"Barsina," 134.
Bassett, James, 30, n. 2; 39, n. 4.
Bath, William third Earl of, 148.
Beaufort, Henry second Duke of, 181, n. 4.
Behn, Mrs. Aphra, 24, n. 1.
Bellamont, Earls of, 77, n. 2.
Bendish, Mr., 158.
Bentinck, William (see also under Portland, William first Earl of), 38, n. 1.
Berkeley, Charles second Earl of, 119, n. 1.
Berkeley of Stratton, John third Baron, 48.
Bertie, Peregrine, 144, n. 1.
Besant, Sir Walter, 69, n. 2; 73, n. 1.

Best, Mr., 139, n. 4.
Betterton, Thomas, 23, n. 3; 100, n. 1; 118.
Bickerstaff, Isaac, 69, n. 2.
"Bingham, Captain," (see also under Bankham, Capt. Richard), 53; 81, n. 2.
Biographia Dramatica, 25, n. 1; 33, n. 3; 40, n. 2; 73, n. 2.
Birkenhead, Frederick first Earl of, 24, n. 1; 34, n. 1; 43, n. 5; 44, n. 1; 80, n. 2; 84, n. 3; 85, n. 1. 86, n. 2; 91, n. 2; 96, ns. 2, 3.
Birmingham, Hon. Edward (see also under "Brummingham"), 9, n. 1.
Birrell and Garnett, 40, n. 2.
Blissett (or Bissett), Col. Andrew, 94.
Boconnoc, 19, n. 1; 139; 170.
Bolingbroke, Henry first Viscount (see also under St. John, Henry), 185; 236; 239; 242, ns. 1, 2; 262.
Bolton, Charles second Duke of, 172.
Booth, Barton, 119, n. 1.
Bouffier, Paul (see also under "Bussiere, Mr."), 216; 224; 225; 226, n. 1.
Boyer, Abel, 10, n. 5; 135, n. 2; 182, n. 2; 194, n. 4; 209, n. 1; 230, ns. 1, 2; 237, n. 3; 261; 263, n. 2; 264, n. 1; 267, n. 6.
Bracegirdle, The, 47, n. 2.
Bracegirdle, Mrs. Anne, 13; 23; 24, n. 1; 26; her abduction attempted by Capt. Richard

INDEX 287

Hill, 27; 28; 30; 31; 32; 34; 35; 36; 37; 39; 47, n. 2; 67, n. 1; 72; 100; 117.

Bracegirdle, Hamlet, 27.

Bracegirdle, Justinian, 23, n. 3.

Bracegirdle, Mrs. Martha, 27.

Brachiano, —, 255.

Bradshaigh, Sir Richard, 245, n. 3.

Bradshaigh, Sir Roger, 110, n. 1.

Brandon, Charles first Baron Gerard of (see also under Macclesfield, Charles first Earl of), 113, n. 3.

Brandon, Charles Lord (see also under Gerard, Charles Lord, and Macclesfield, Charles second Earl of), 194.

Brandon, James first Duke of (see also under Hamilton, James fourth Duke of, and Arran, James Earl of), 183.

Bray, W., 15, n. 3.

Brest, Battle of, 48; 49; 54;, n. 1.

Brewer, Mrs., 32, n. 1.

Bridgewater, Scroop fifth Earl of, 172.

Britton (or Breton), Col. William, 258.

Brodrick, Thomas, 59, n. 1; 109, n. 3; 119, n. 2; 135, n. 2; 158, n. 1; 177, n. 1; 178, n. 2; 258, n. 4; 259, ns. 6, 7; 266, ns. 1, 2.

Brown, ——, 223, n. 1.

Brown, Thomas, 24, n. 1; 25, n. 1; 26, n. 3; 53, n. 4; 71, n. 4; 73, n. 1.

Browne, Mrs. Dorothy, 26, ns. 2, 4; 28, ns. 2, 4; 29; 30; 31, n. 4; 32, n. 1.

Browne, Thomas, 83, ns. 1, 3; 84; 85, ns. 1, 2, 3; 86; 87, n. 1; 104.

"Brummingham" (see also under Birmingham, Hon. Edward), 9.

Brydges, Sir Egerton, 181, n. 3.

Bull, the Druggist, 247, n. 1.

Burgess, Col. Elizeus, 73, n. 2.

Burke, Sir Bernard, 5, n. 3; 8, n. 2; 16, n. 3; 19, n. 1; 20, n. 3; 63, n.2; 77, n. 2; 135, n. 3; 180, ns. 2, 3; 4, 6; 191, n. 1; 214, n. 4; 235; 244, n. 2.

Burnett, Gilbert (see under Salisbury, Bishop of).

Burnett, Thomas, 219, n. 3; 243, n. 1; 247, n. 1.

Bussiere, Mr. (see also under Bouffier, Paul), 270.

C., G. E. (see under C[okayne], G. E.).

C., J. B., 29, n. 1.

Cadogan, Gen. William (afterward first Earl Cadogan), 97, n. 1; 178, n. 2; 258; 268.

Caermarthen, Peregrine Marquis of, 49.

Caermarthen, Thomas first Marquis of (see also under Leeds, Thomas first Duke of), 43; 45; 49.

Camelford, Thomas second Baron, 139, n. 4.

Cannon, R., 128, n. 2.

Cardonnel, Adam de, 178, n. 2.

Carlyle, E. Irving, 110, n. 1.

INDEX

Cassilis, John seventh Earl of, 22.

Cassilis, Susan Countess of, 22, n. 2.

Castlewood, 3; 4; 65; 66; 67; 68; 69; 107, n. 1; 184, n. 1.

Castlewood, Francis fifth Viscount (see also under Esmond, Hon. Frank), 107; 117, n. 3; 118; 120; 176; 178; 184, n. 1; 189.

Castlewood, Francis fourth Viscount, 4; 65; 66; 67; 68; 69; 70; 71; 72, ns. 1, 3; 74; killed by Lord Mohun, 75; 76; 97; 98; 99; 101; 102; 104; 105; 106; 109, n. 3; 117; 119; 128; 176; 188; 238, n. 1.

Castlewood, Isabel Dowager Viscountess, 71, n. 1; 109, n. 3; 184, n. 1.

Castlewood, Rachel Viscountess, 65; 67; 68; 71; 73, n. 2; 106; 107; 179; 184, n. 1; 186; 188.

Cato, 73, n. 2.

Catro, Peter, 83, n. 1; 87; 88, n. 1.

Cavendish, William Lord (see also under Devonshire, William Earl of, and afterward first Duke of), 8; 9; 10.

Cawthorne, Samuel (or Joseph?), 78, n. 2; 79, n. 2; 81; 82; 103.

Cecil, Ensign William, 123.

Chabiner, Charles, 213, n. 3; 214.

Chancellor, E. Beresford, 71, n. 4; 73, n. 1; 83, n. 2; 98, n. 2; 233, n. 2; 244, n. 2.

Chargneau, Peter, 124, n. 4.

Charles II, King, 8, n. 2; 10, n. 5; 121, n. 1; 135, n. 2; 165; 181.

Chaworth, Grace Lady, 8, n. 2; 9, n. 2; 10, n. 4.

Chesterfield, Phillip fourth Earl of, 242, n. 2; 243; 248, n. 4.

Chevenix, Richard (Bishop of Waterford), 242, n. 2; 244, n. 1.

Cheyne, Dr. George, 69.

Chichester, H. Manners, 209, n. 1; 228, n. 1; 229, n. 4; 230, n. 5; 248, n. 4; 257, n. 1; 259, ns. 3, 4, 7.

Cholomondeley, F., 245, n. 3.

Christian Hero, The, 107, n. 1.

Churchill, Lieut. Gen. Charles, 266, n. 1.

Churchill, Col. Joseph, 207; 213; 246.

Cibber, Colley, 23, n. 3; 24, n. 1; 25, n. 1; 29, n. 3; 73, n. 2; 118, n. 4.

Cibber, Theophilus, 25, n. 1; 35.

Civelle, Jeanne de, 113, n. 3.

Clark, Andrew, 217; 227; 231.

Clarke, George, 174.

Clydesdale, James Marquis of, 180, n. 2.

Cobbett, William, 10, n. 5; 51, n. 3; 52, n. 1; 98, n. 2; 143, n. 1; 161, n. 2; 168, ns. 1, 3; 172, n. 1; 259, ns. 1, 2, 4, 5.

Coffin, Richard, 37, n. 1.

C[okayne], G. E., 5, n. 2; 6, n. 1; 9, n. 1; 10, n. 1; 22, n. 2; 113, n. 3; 135, n. 3; 140, ns. 2, 3; 179, n. 3; 180, n. 6; 181, ns. 1, 2, 4;

INDEX

182, n. 2; 183, ns. 1, 3, 5; 223, n. 2; 256, n. 1.
Coke, John, 193, n. 1.
Coke, Thomas, 193, n. 1.
Collins, Arthur, 135, n. 3; 140, ns. 1, 2, 4; 142, n. 2; 144, n. 1; 181; 193, n. 2; 214, n. 4; 244, n. 2; 260, n. 5; 261, n. 2.
Coloony, Barons Coote of, 77, n. 2.
Congreve, William, 5, n. 3; 23, n. 3; 175.
Conway, Francis first Baron, 160.
Cook, Richard, 105, n. 1; 213; 214.
Cooke, Sir Thomas, 40, n. 2; 147.
Coote, Col., 55.
Coote, Lieut. Col. Chidley, 55, n. 4.
Coote, Richard, jun., 77, n. 2.
Coote, Capt. Richard, 66; 74, n. 2; 76; 77; 79, n. 2; 80; 81; 82; 83; 84; killed by Richard French, 85; 86; 87, n. 2; 89; 90; 91; 92; 93; 94; 95; 97; 98; 99; 101; 102; 103; 104; 105; 106; 130; 131; 146; 238, n. 1.
Coote, Col. Richard, 55, n. 4.
Coote, Ensign Richard, 77, n. 2.
Coote, Sir Richard, 77, n. 2.
Couch, Reynold, 63, n. 2.
Coward, William, merchant, 10, n. 5.
Coward, Serjeant William, 10; 63, n. 2.
Cowper, Mary Lady, (afterward Countess Cowper), 139; 255, n. 2; 256, n. 1.
Coxe, Rev. William, 143, n. 4.

Cranstoun, Maj. J., 257, n. 4; 268, n. 3.
Crattle, James, 73, n. 1; 88, n. 1.
Crippes, William, 84; 86; 87, n. 1; 104.
Crowe, Eyre, 97, n. 1.
Crowne, John, 25, n. 1.
Cunningham, Robert, 257, n. 4; 268, n. 3.
Curll, E., 81, n. 2; 218, n. 1; 269; 270.
Cutts, John first Baron, 5, n. 3; 48; 107, n. 1; 124, ns. 2, 3; 125, n. 3.

Dalton, Charles, 12, n. 2; 23, n. 2; 47, ns. 1, 2; 48, ns. 1, 3; 49, ns. 3, 4; 53, n. 2; 55, ns. 4, 5; 59, n. 3; 71, n. 2; 72, n. 1; 77, ns. 1, 2; 78, ns. 1, 4; 79, n. 1; 80, n. 1; 89, n. 2; 94, ns. 1, 2, 3; 95, n. 1; 107, n. 1; 109, ns. 1, 2; 110, n. 1; 115, n. 3; 116, n. 2; 121, ns. 1, 2, 3, 4, 5; 123, ns. 4, 5, 7; 124, ns. 1, 4; 125, n. 1; 126, ns. 1, 2, 23, 4, 5; 127, n. 2; 158, n. 1; 202, n. 1; 209, n. 1; 228, n. 1; 230, ns. 3, 5; 237, n. 3; 257, n. 3; 258; 261; 264, n. 3; 265; 266, ns. 3, 5, 10; 268.
Dartmouth, William second Baron and afterward first Earl of, 144; 159; 270.
Davenant, Mr., 141; 142; 249, n. 1.
Davenant, Dr. Charles, 141.
D'Avenant, Henry, 141.
Davenport, John, 30; 40, n. 1.

INDEX

Davenport, Maj. Gen. Sherington, 94, n. 1.
Davis, Mary, 24, n. 1.
Dawson, "Bully," 24, n. 1.
De Coverley, Sir Roger, 31, n. 2.
Defoe, Daniel, 271.
Dennis, John, 73, n. 2.
Denton, Dr. W., 9, n. 2.
Devonshire, William fourth Earl of and afterwards first Duke of (see also under Cavendish, William Lord), 45; 162, n. 1; 164; 174.
Devonshire, William second Duke of (see also under Lord Steward, the), 142; 259, n. 9.
Dickens, Serjeant Surgeon, 188, n. 2.
Dillon, Lieut. Gen. Arthur, 256, n. 2.
Disney (or Desaulnois), Ensign Henry, 95.
Dixon, William, 26, n. 2.
Doble, C. E., 14, n. 2; 249, n. 1.
Dockwra, Mr., 78, n. 4.
Dockwra, Capt. George, 78; 79, n. 2; 80; 81; 82; 83; 85; 88; 89; 90; 102; 103, n. 3; 104; 107; 188.
Dockwra, William, 78, n. 4.
Doneraile, Arthur first Viscount, 20, n. 3.
Doneraile, Arthur second Viscount (see under St. Leger, Hon. Arthur).
Doneraile, Arthur third Viscount (see under St. Leger, Hon. Arthur Mohun).

Dormer, Capt. (and afterwards Col.) James, 126; 127.
Dorset, Charles sixth Earl of, 45.
Douglas, Lieut. Gen. the Hon. James, 258, n. 1.
Dryden, John, 100, n. 1.
Duckenfield, Mrs. Elenor, 89, n. 2.
Duckenfield, Capt. Loftus, 89.
Duckenfield, Col. William, 89, n. 2.
Duckett, George, 219, n. 3; 243, n. 1; 247, n. 1.
Dudley, Robert, 255.
Dudley, Sir Robert, 256, n. 1.
Duffett, Thomas, 73, n. 1.
Dunmore, Charles first Earl of, 12, n. 2.
Duppa, Sir Thomas, 42.
Durfey, Thomas, 29, n. 3.
Durham, Bishop of (Nathaniel third Baron Crewe of Stene), 6.
Dursley, James Lord, 119, n. 1.
Dyer, John, 52.

Ebsworth, Rev. J. W., 244, n. 2; 272.
Edward III, 40, n. 2.
Edward VI, King, 93.
Edwards, Richard, 82, n. 1; 84, n. 2.
Elizabeth, Queen, 255.
Elrington, John, 195, n. 1.
"Ephelia," 132; 134.
Erle, Lieut. Gen. Thomas, 47.
Esmond, Beatrix, 3; 5, n. 3; 67; 68; 69, n. 2; 107; 179; 184, n. 1; 186; 188; 189; 235; 236; 240.
Esmond, Hon. Frank (see also un-

INDEX

der Castlewood, Francis fifth Viscount), 68.

Esmond, Henry, 3; 65; 66; 68; 69; 70; 71; 72; 73, n. 2; 74; second to Lord Castlewood, 75; 99; 102; 104; 105; 106; 107; 109; 116; 117; 118; 119; 120; fights Lord Mohun, 176; 178; 179; 180; 184; 185; 186; 187; 188; 189; 236; 238, n. 1; 239; 240; 241; 244; 246; 247; 248; 249; 250.

Esmond, The History of Henry, 3; 4, ns. 1, 2; 15, n. 1; 23; 33, n. 1; 37, ns. 4, 5; 50, n. 3; 63; 66, n. 3; 68, n. 2; 71, n. 2; 72, n. 1; 73, n. 2; 75, n. 1; 76; 97, n. 1; 98; 99; 101, n. 4; 102; 103; 104, ns. 1, 2; 105; 106, n. 2; 107, n. 1; 109, n. 3; 117, ns. 1, 5; 118, ns. 1, 2; 120, n. 1; 176, ns. 1, 2; 177, n. 5; 178, n. 2; 179, ns . 1, 2; 180, ns. 1, 5; 181, ns. 1, 3; 183, ns. 1, 2, 3, 4; 184, ns. 1, 2; 185, n. 1; 187, ns. 1, 2; 188, ns. 1, 2; 189; 190; 201; 207, n. 2; 208, n. 1; 233; 236, n. 1; 240, ns. 3, 5; 241, n. 3; 246, n. 2; 247, n. 2; 248; 250; 251.

Essex, William Anne fourth Earl of, 180, n. 4.

Evelyn, John, 15; 43, n. 1.

Faber, J., 4, n. 3; 174, n. 3.
Fairfax, Ferdinand, 228, n. 1; 245, n. 3.
Farington, Joseph, 139, n. 4.
Fennell, Thomas, 30, n. 1.
Fenwick, Sir John, 12, n. 2.

Ferguson, 216; 221; 224.
Ferguson, Maj. Gen. James, 258.
Firebrace, Lord, 3.
Firth, Sir, C. H., 63, n. 1.
Flanders, 4; 48, n. 2; 49; 259.
Fletcher, —, 219, n. 3.
"Florella" (see also under Griffith, or Griffin, Mrs. Elizabeth), 137.
Forbes, George Lord, 94, n. 1.
Fountain, Sir Andrew, 110.
Foxcroft, H. C., 44, n. 1.
France, 4; 62; 66, n. 1; 89; 109, n. 2; 151; 152; 153; 170.
Freind, Dr. John, 125, n. 4.
French, Richard, 78; 79, n. 2; 80; 81; 82; 83; kills Capt. Coote, 85; 87; 88; 89; tried for murder, convicted, and pardoned, 90; 93; 95; 98; 99; 101, n. 4; 102; 103; 104; 105; 106; 107; 188; 238, n. 1.
Fuller, William, 159.
Funeral, The, 107, n. 1.

Galway, Henry first Earl of, 125; 169; 258, n. 5.
Garth, Sir Samuel, 59, n. 1; 175.
Gawseworth Hall, 139; 193.
Gay, John, 95.
Genest, Rev. John, 23, n. 3; 24, n. 1; 73, n. 2; 100, ns. 3, 4; 118, n. 4; 119, n. 1.
George I, King (see also under Hanover, George Lewis Elector of), 94, n. 2; 110, n. 1; 141; 173, n. 1; 194, n. 4; 209, n. 1; 230,

n. 3; 237, n. 3; 256; 260; 261, n. 1; 264; 265; 267; 268.

George II, King (see also under Hanover, George Electoral Prince of), 213, n. 1.

George, Prince, of Denmark, 93; 107, n. 1; 135, n. 3; 152; 168.

"Gerard, Lord," 184; 186.

Gerard, Hon. Elizabeth (see also under Hamilton, Elizabeth Duchess of), 190, 191.

Gerard of Brandon, Charles Lord (see also under Brandon, Charles Lord, and Macclesfield, Charles second Earl of), 41; 194.

Gerard of Bromley, Digby fifth Baron, 190; 191; 234; 235.

Gerard of Bromley, Elizabeth Lady, 190; 191; 192; 193; 197; 198; 202; 235.

Gery, Capt. Phillip, 122, n. 1.

Gibbs, Rev. V., 9, n. 1; 22, n. 2.

Gibson, John, 88, n. 1.

Gibson, Col. John, 47.

Gilbert, Davies, 5, n. 1; 20, n. 2; 135, n. 3; 139, n. 4; 193, n. 3.

Gildon, Charles, 5, n. 3; 24, n. 1.

Gloucester, William Duke of, 93; 161.

Godolphin, Sidney first Baron, and later first Earl of, 45; 175.

Goodall, Mrs., 88, n. 2.

Googene, Capt. Vincent, 23, n. 2.

Grafton, Charles second Duke of, 174.

"Gratian" (see also under Mohun, Charles fourth Lord), 137; 138.

Greenwich Park, 25, n. 1.

Gresham, Sir Thomas, 148.

Grew, Edwin and Marion S., 25, n. 1; 38, n. 1.

Grew, Marion E., 37; 38, n. 1.

Griffith (or Griffin), Anne (see also under Stanhope, Mrs. Anne, afterward Harrington, Anne Countess of), 140.

Griffith (or Griffin), Col. Edward, 135; 136; 137; 138.

Griffith (or Griffin), Mrs. Elizabeth (see also under "Florella" and Mohun, Elizabeth Lady), 132, n. 1; 135.

Grosvenor, Ensign John, 122, n. 1.

Grosvenor *v.* Coy, 159.

Grove, Joseph, 4, n. 4; 8, n. 2; 130, n. 3; 151, n. 4; 259, n. 9.

Gwyn, Eleanor, 24, n. 1.

Gwyn, Francis, 35, n. 2; 51, n. 3.

Haile, Martin, 15, n. 4; 109, n. 3; 241, n. 3.

Halifax, Charles first Baron, and afterward first Earl of (see also under Montague, Charles), 151; 161; 172; 175.

Halifax, George first Viscount, and afterward first Marquis of, 7; 44, n. 1; 45; 55.

"Hamilton, Col. Andrew," 244, n. 2.

Hamilton, Lord Anne, 180.

Hamilton, Anne Dowager Duchess of, 181; 209, n. 1.

Hamilton, Anne Duchess of, 179.

Hamilton, Charles, 183, n. 1.

INDEX

Hamilton, Elizabeth Duchess of (see also under Gerard, Hon. Elizabeth), 179; 182; 186; 190; 191; 193; 194; 195, n. 1; 196; 197; 198; 228; 235; 240; 276.

Hamilton, J. A., 8, n. 2.

Hamilton, James first Duke of, 22, n. 2.

Hamilton, James fourth Duke of (see also under Arran, James Earl of, and Brandon, James first Duke of), 6, n. 1; 13, n. 1; 22, n. 2; 65, n. 1; 73, n. 2; 76, n. 1; 81, n. 2; 98; 101; 104; 105; 115, n. 1; 128, n. 3; 130, n. 3; 131, n. 2; 141, n. 2; 142, n. 2; 165; 179; 180; 181; 182; 183; 184; 185; 186; 187; 188; 190; 191; 192; 193; 194; 196; 197; 198; 199, n. 1; 201; quarrels with Lord Mohun, 202; 203; 204; 205; 206; 207; challenges Lord Mohun, 208; 209, n. 1; 210; 211; 212; 215; 216; 217; 218; fights Lord Mohun, 219; 220; 221; 222; kills Lord Mohun, 223; dies of his own wounds, 224; 225; 226; 227; 228; 230; 231; 233; 234; 235; 236; 237; 238; 239; 240; 241; 242; 243; 244; 245; 249; 250; 260; 261; 262; 263; 264; 268; 269; 270; 271; 272; 273; 274; 276; 277; 278; 279; 280; 281.

Hamilton, Col. John, 104; 105, n. 1; 201, n. 4; 202, n. 2; 203, n. 1.; 204, n. 1; 206, n. 1; 207, ns. 1, 2; 209; 210; 211; 212; 213; ns. 1, 2; 214, ns. 1, 2, 3, 4, 5; 215; 216; 217; 218; acts as the Duke of Hamilton's second in his duel with Lord Mohun and is wounded by Gen. Maccartney, 219; 220; 221; 222; 223; 224; 227, n. 1; gives himself up, 231; is tried for murder and acquitted, 232; 233, n. 2; 242; 243; 244; 245; 246, n. 1; 262; 263; 264; 269; 274; 277; 278; 279; 280; 281.

Hanover, Prince Christian of, 260, n. 3.

Hanover, Prince Ernest Augustus of (afterward Duke of York), 260, n. 3.

Hanover, George Augustus Electoral Prince of (see also under George II, King), 260, n. 4.

Hanover, George Lewis Elector of (see also under George II, King), 109; 111; 112; 115; 131; 229; 260, n. 4.

Hanover, Prince Maximilian William of, 260, n. 3.

Harley, Edward, 245, n. 3.

Harley, Sir Edward, 35, n. 2; 44, n. 1; 49, n. 2; 71, n. 4.

Harley, Robert (see also under Oxford and Mortimer, Robert first Earl of), 35; 44, n. 1; 49, n. 2; 51, n. 3; 54, n. 4; 55, ns. 1, 6; 71, n. 4; 127, n. 1; 173.

Harrington, William first Earl of (see also under Stanhope, William), 135, n. 3; 140.

Harris, C. A., 139, n. 5.

INDEX

Harris, John, 63, n. 2.
Harris, Dame Theophila, 63, n. 2.
Harte (or Hartus), Capt. Henry, 124.
Hatton C., 10, n. 2; 44, n. 1; 83, n. 3; 98, n. 2.
Hatton, Christopher second Baron, and afterward first Viscount Hatton, 10, n. 2; 44, n. 1; 85, n. 3; 98, n. 2.
Haversham, Frances Lady (see also under Annesley, Lady Frances), 60, n. 1.
Haversham, John first Baron, 60, n. 1; 164; 166.
Hawles, Sir John, 43; 86, n. 3; 92; 93.
Hearne, Thomas, 14, n. 2; 249, n.1.
Henry II, 40, n. 2.
Heyward, William, 156.
Hide, Lady, 5, n. 3.
Hill, Capt. Richard, 13, n. 2; 23; 24; 26; attempts to abduct Mrs. Bracegirdle, 27; 28; 30; 31; slays William Mountford, 32; 33; 34; 35; 36; 38; 39; 40; escapes from justice, 46-47; 63; 67, n. 1; 72, n. 2; 101.
Hill, Capt. William, 19, n. 1; 51; 53, n. 4; is killed by Lord Mohun, 54; 56; 60; 62, n. 2; 63; 66, n. 1; 77, n. 1; 128, n. 3; 129; 145.
Hipsley, Joseph, 212, n. 2; 239.
Historical Manuscripts Commission Reports: MSS. of
    Annesley, Lieut. Gen. L., 6, n. 1; 10, n. 4.

Bath, Marquess of, 173, n. 2; 194, n. 1.
Cowper, Earl, 193, n. 1.
Dartmouth, Earl of, 144, n. 2; 202, n. 2; 216, n. 4; 218, ns. 1, 2; 219, n. 1; 220, n. 1; 221, n. 1; 223, ns. 1, 3; 227, n. 3; 228, n. 1; 231, ns. 4, 6.
Downshire, Marquess of, 260, n. 3.
Egmont, Earl of, 9, n. 2.
Fortesque, J. B., 139, n. 4.
Frankland - Russell - Astley, Mrs. 124, n. 3; 126, n. 2.
Hodgkin, J. Eliot, 5, n. 2; 20, n. 3; 138, n. 2.
House of Lords, 12, ns. 1, 2; 41, n. 3; 42, ns. 1, 4; 43, n. 3; 46, n. 1; 92, ns. 4, 6; 93, n. 3; 96, n. 3; 151, ns. 4, 5; 159, ns. 1, 2; 160, n. 1; 164, n. 3; 196, n. 1; 197, n.1.
Kenyon, Lord, 245, n. 3.
King of Great Britain, Stuart MSS. of the, 20, n. 3; 256, n. 2; 264, n. 4.
Laing MSS of the University of Edinburgh, 257, n. 2.
Le Fleming, S. H., 9, n. 2.
Manchester, Duke of, 266, n. 6.
Mar, Earl of, 199, n. 1.
Marlborough, Duke of, 127, n. 2; 196, n. 2.
Orlebar, Richard, 201, n. 2.
Ormonde, Marquess of, 122, n. 1; 123, ns. 2, 3; 124, n. 2; 125, n. 3.

INDEX

Pine-Coffin, J. R., 37, n. 1.
Portland, Duke of, 35, n. 2; 44, n. 1; 49, n. 2; 51, n. 3; 54, n. 4; 71, n. 4; 124, n. 5; 127, n. 1; 182, n. 1; 228, n. 1; 245, n. 3; 257, n. 4; 258, ns. 1, 2, 3; 264, n. 4; 268, n. 3.
Rutland, Duke of, 8, n. 2; 9, n. 2; 10, n. 4.
Townshend, Marquess, 265, n. 1; 266, n. 9.
Verney, Sir Harry, 9, n. 2; 10, n. 1.
Webb, Rev. T. W., 232, n. 1; 263, n. 1.
Hoare, Sir Richard, 201, n. 4; 269; 276.
Holland, Edward third Earl of (see also under Warwick, Edward sixth Earl of), 60, n. 2.
Holt, Chief Justice Sir John, 41; 55; 56; 248, n. 4.
Honeywood, Charles, 237, n. 3.
Honeywood, Brig. Gen. Phillip, 237; 247, n. 2; 248; 259; 267.
Hopkins, Charles, 5, n. 3.
"Horatio" (see also under Peterborough, Charles third Earl of). 136.
Horden, Hildebrand, 73, n. 2.
Howard, Mrs. Henrietta, (see also under Suffolk, Henrietta Countess of), 138, n. 3.
Howard of Escrick, Charles fourth Baron, 155.
Howe, Hon. Anne, 140, n. 2.

Howe, Scrope first Viscount, 140, n. 2.
Howell, T. B., 66, n. 2; 73, n. 1; 74, n. 2; 78, ns. 1, 2, 3; 79, n. 2; 80, n. 2; 81, ns. 1, 3, 4; 82, ns. 1, 2, 3; 83, ns. 1, 3; 84, ns. 1, 2; 85, ns. 1, 2, 3; 86, ns. 1, 2, 3; 87, n. 2; 88, ns. 1, 2; 89, ns. 1, 3, 4; 90, n. 6; 91, ns. 1, 3; 92, ns. 2, 7; 96, ns. 1, 3; 103, n. 3; 105, n. 3; 130, n. 2.
Hudson, John, 26, n. 1.
Hunt, F. K., 52, n. 2.
Hunt, William, 31, n. 4.
Hutchinson, Charles, 22, n. 2.
Hutchinson, Elizabeth, 22, n. 2.
Hutton, Edward, 256, n. 1.

"Ianthe," 134.
Inese, L., 264, n. 1.
Injur'd Lovers, The, 180, n. 6.
Ireland, William, 165.
Irvine, Rev. John, 178, n. 2.
Irving, H. B., 37.

Jackson, 84, ns. 1, 2.
James, Capt. Roger, 79; 80; 81; 82; second to Richard French, 83; 85; 88; 89; tried and convicted of manslaughter, 90; 98, n. 2; 102; 103; 104; 107; 188.
James II, King (see also under York, James Duke of), 15; 16, n. 1; 109, n. 3; 181; 241, n. 3.
Jeffreys, John second Baron, 159.
Jenkins, Burris, 47, n. 2.
Jennings, Miss, 135, n. 3.

INDEX

Jersey, Edward first Earl of, 167; 173.
Johnson, Esther (or "Stella"), 220, n. 2; 224, n. 1; 228, n. 1; 229, ns. 1, 2, 3; 239; 240; 242, n. 2.
Johnson, J., 77, n. 1.
Jones, Anne, 31, n. 4; 32, n. 1.
Jones, Edward, 26, n. 1.
Juckes, Capt. Edward, 122, n. 1.
Juckes, Ensign, George, 122, n. 1.
Judge Jeffreys, 37.

Keeting, Capt. Edmund, 78; 79, n. 2; 80.
Kennedy, John Lord, 22; 23; 28.
Kennett, White, Bishop of Peterborough, 52, n. 2; 272.
Kent, Henry first Duke of, 181, n. 4.
Kenyon, George, 245, n. 3.
Kildare, John eighteenth Earl of, 149.
King, Gregory, Lancaster Herald, 111; 112.
King's Bench, The Marshal of the, 56.
Kingston-upon-Hull, Evelyn first Earl of (afterward first Duke of Kingston-upon-Hull), 45.
Kinoull, Thomas sixth Earl of, 245, n. 3.
Kit-Cat Club, 4, n. 3; 5, n. 2; 14, n. 1; 36; 69, n. 2; 174; 223, n. 1.
Kneller, Sir Godfrey, 4; 174.
Knevett, Anne, 28, n. 3.
Knight, Mr., 35.
Knight, Mrs. Anne, 26, n. 1.

Knight, Joseph, 23, n. 3; 24, n. 1; 25, n. 1; 29, n. 3; 118, ns. 3, 4, 5.
Koenig, Dr. W. F., 38, n. 1.

La Fage, Mr., 226, n. 3; 270.
Lake, Thomas, 26, n. 2; 31, n. 4; 32, n. 1.
Lauder, Maj. Gen. George. 266, n. 2.
Lawrence, Sir Thomas, M.D., 135.
Lee, Anthony, 71, n. 4.
Lee, Sir Sidney, 177, n. 5; 178, n. 1; 178, n. 1; 256, n. 1.
Leeds, Thomas first Duke of (see also under Caermarthen, Thomas first Marquis of), 49.
Leicester, Robert Earl of, 255.
Leighton, Col. Baldwin, 152; 202, n. 2.
Lesly (or Lesley), John, 212, n. 2; 216; 217, n. 1; 227; 230; 231, n. 1.
Levada, David, 124, n. 4.
Lewis, E., 127, n. 1.
Lexington (or Lexinton), Robert second Baron, 173.
Lindsey, Robert third Earl of, 144, n. 1.
Lisburne, Viscounts, 89, n. 2.
Lodge, John, 9, n. 1; 89, n. 2.
Lodge, Sir R., 50, n. 1; 51, n. 1.
Loftus, Sir Dudley, 89, n. 2.
London, Bishop of (Henry Compton), 160.
Lord Steward, the (see also under Devonshire, William second Duke of), 158.

Lothian, William second Marquis of, 156.
Louis XIV, King, 8, n. 2; 15; 151; 154.
Love, Anne, 10, n. 4.
Love in a Wood, 71; 100.
Lowe, Coroner Charles, 274.
Lowe, R. W., 100, ns. 1, 2.
Lowther, Robert, 245, n. 3.
Lucas, Robert third Baron, 58.
Luttrell, Narcissus, 5, n. 3; 12, n. 2; 16, n. 2; 23, n. 1; 33, n. 2; 35; 41, n. 1; 42, n. 3; 43, n. 1; 44, n. 1; 46, ns. 2, 5; 48, n. 2; 49, n. 2; 50, n. 2; 51, n. 3; 53, ns. 1, 2; 54, ns. 4, 5; 55, ns. 1, 2; 56, ns, 1, 3, 5; 57, n. 3; 58, ns. 1, 4; 59, n. 1; 60, n. 2; 63, n. 2; 71, n. 4; 77, ns. 1, 2; 78, n. 1; 90, ns. 1, 2, 3, 4; 93, n. 2; 96, n. 3; 107, n. 1; 112; 113, ns. 1, 2, 3; 115, n. 2; 116, n. 3; 1̇, n. 4; 123, ns. 1, 5; 124, n. 4; 126, n. 4; 135, ns. 2, 3; 169, n. 5; 171, n. 1; 192; 193, n. 5; 194, ns. 1, 2, 3; 196, n. 3; 197, n. 1; 198, ns. 1, 3, 4; 199, n. 1; 255, n. 1; 256, n. 1; 257, n. 3; 258; 259, ns. 6, 9; 266; 267, ns. 2, 3, 4.
Lying Lover, The, 107, n. 1.
Lyte, Sir H. C. Maxwell, 5, ns. 2, 3; 6, n. 1; 10, n. 5; 12, n. 3; 19, n. 1; 44, n. 1; 77, n. 1; 135, n. 3; 139, n. 5.

Macartney, Captain" or "Colonel" (see also under Macartney, Lord, and Maccartney, Lieut. Gen. George), 71; 74, n. 1; second to Lord Mohun in his duel with Lord Castlewood, 75; 76, n. 1; 102; 107; 115; second to Lord Mohun in his duel with the Duke of Hamilton, and is accused of killing the latter, 185; 186; 187; 244.
Macartney, Lord (see also under "Macartney, Captain" and Maccartney, Lieut. Gen. George), 76, n. 1.
Macaulay of Rothley, Thomas first Baron, 12, n. 2; 24, n. 1; 36; 38, n. 2; 41, n. 4; 44, n. 1; 49, n. 1; 53, n. 3; 62, n. 1; 66, n. 1.
Maccartney, Lieut. Gen. George (see also under "Macartney, Captain," and Macartney. Lord), 52, n. 2; 72, n. 1; 73, n, 2; 74, n. 1; 101; 105; 115; 116; 124, n. 5; 126, n. 3; 203, n. 2; 204; 205; 206; bears Lord Mohun's message to the Duke of Hamilton, 207; meets the Duke at the Rose Tavern, 208; 209; arranges the duel, 210; 211; 212; 213; 214; 215; 216, n. 4; 218; acts as Lord Mohun's second in his duel with the Duke of Hamilton, 219; is accused of stabbing the Duke, 220; 221; 222; 223; 226; escapes to Belgium, 227; returns to England, 229; is tried for murder and convicted of manslaughter, 230; 231; 233, n. 2; 234, n. 1; 237; 238; 239; 242;

243; 244; 245; 246; 247; 248; 249; memoir of, 257-265; 267; 271; proclamation regarding him, 273-275; Duchess of Hamilton's advertisement concerning him, 276; 277; 278; 279; 281.

Maccartney, George, the elder, 257.

Maccartney, Mrs. George, 258.

Macclesfield, Anne Countess of, 113, n. 1.

Macclesfield, Charles first Earl of (see also under Brandon, Charles first Baron Gerard of), 15, n. 2; 16; 45; 121, n. 1; 127, n. 3; 140, n. 2; 190; 193; 195; 235.

Macclesfield, Charles second Earl of (see also under Gerard, Charles Lord), 13; 15, n. 2; 18, n. 1; 48; 55; 65; 109; goes to Hanover as a special envoy, 110; 111; 112; death, 113; 115; 117; 120; 121; 127; 131; 140; 174; 190; 191; leaves his fortune to Lord Mohun, 192; 193; 194; 195; 197; 198; 199; 202; 235; 260.

Macclesfield, Fitton third Earl of, 15, n. 2; 190; 192; makes Lord Mohun his heir, 193; 195; 196; 235.

Mackinnon, Col. Daniel, 54, n. 1; 78, n. 4; 79, n. 1; 258, n. 5.

Macky, John, 5, n. 1.

Maclean, Sir John, 169.

Macpherson, James, 12, n. 2; 181, n. 1.

Maggs Brothers, 273.

Mailáth, Count N. J., 50, n. 3.

Manchester, Charles fourth Earl of, 172; 266, n. 6.

Manley, Mrs. Mary de la Rivière, 3, n. 3; 4, n. 3; 5, n. 1; 16, n. 4; 17; 18; 19; 24, n. 1; 69, n. 2; 119, n. 1; 130, n. 3; 132; 134; 135, n. 3; 136; 138, n. 2.

Manwaring, Charlotte (see under Mohun, Charlotte Lady).

Manwaring, Lady Charlotte (see also under Orby, Lady Charlotte), 16; 140, n. 2; 235.

Manwaring, James, 16; 234.

Mar, John first Duke of [Jacobite creation] (see also under Mar, John sixth Earl of), 20, n. 3; 256, n. 2; 264, n. 4.

Mar, John sixth Earl of (see also under Mar, John first Duke of), 199, n. 1.

Maria Christina, Queen, of Sweden, 255.

Marlborough, John first Duke of (see also under Marlborough, John first Earl of), 120; 124, n. 5; 127, n. 2; 142; challenges Earl Poulet, 143; is prevented from fighting, 144; 172; 175; 178, n. 2; 181, n. 1; 187; 207; 228; 242, n. 2; 246; 247; 248; 249; 257; 259; 260, ns. 1, 2; 267, n. 1; 268.

Marlborough, John first Earl of (see also under Marlborough, John first Duke of), 45, 97, n. 1.

INDEX

Marlborough, Sarah Duchess of, 135, n. 3; 138, n. 3.
Marriage à la Mode, 29, n. 3.
Mary II, Queen, 5, n. 3; 25, n. 1; 37; 44, n. 1; 46; 62.
Mary, Queen (of Modena), 15, n. 4; 161; 241, n. 3.
Masham, Mrs. Abigail (afterward Lady Masham), 134, 188, n. 2; 267, n. 1.
Masham, Samuel, afterward first Baron, 267, n. 1.
Mason, Gawin, 202, n. 2; 207.
Mason, Sir Richard, 113, n. 3.
May, Capt. Griffin, 122, n. 1; 123.
May, T. E. (afterward first Baron Farnborough), 52, n. 2.
Maycock, F. W. O., 119, n. 2; 177, n. 1.
Maynwaring, Arthur, 175.
"Melville, Lewis," 38; 73, n. 2; 97, n. 1; 100, n. 3; 139, n. 2; 173, n. 1; 178, n. 2; 244, n. 2; 256, n. 1.
Memoirs of Europe towards the Close of the Eighth Century, 3, n. 3; 69, n. 2; 135, n. 3; 138, n. 1.
Menzies, J., 264, n. 3.
"Meredith, Colonel" (see also under Meredyth, Lieut. Gen. Thomas), seconds Lord Mohun in his duel with the Duke of Hamilton in *Esmond*, 185; 186; 187.
Meredyth, Arthur, 265.
Meredyth, Lieut. Gen. Thomas (see also under "Meredith, Colonel"), 237; 238; 239; 247; 248; 249; 258; 259; memoir of, 265–268.
Merry, William, 30, n. 2.
Middleton, Charles second Earl of, 12, n. 2.
Midwinter, Edw., 130, n. 3; 240, n. 6; 268.
Millington, Sir Thomas, M.D., 59; 135, n. 2.
Minshall (or Minshull), Alice, 200.
Minshall (or Minshull), Elizabeth 199, 200.
Minshall (or Minshull), Jane, 199, 200.
Minshall (or Minshull), Thomas, 200.
Minshall (or Minshall), 119, n. 1.
Minshull, Mr., 119, n. 1.
Minshull, Edward, 199, n. 2.
Minshull (or Minshall), Peter, 119, n. 1; 199; 200.
Mock-Tempest, The, 73, n. 1.
Mohocks, 31, n. 2.
Mohun, Charles third Baron, 5; 6; 8; is killed in a duel, 9; 11; 12; 13; 19; 45; 170; 192.
Mohun, Charles fourth Baron (see also under "Gratian"), 3; 4; 5; birth, 6; 7; 8; 9, n. 1; early life, 10–15; first marriage, 16; 17; 18; 19; 20; 22; duel with Lord Kennedy, 23; 25, n. 1; aids Capt. R. Hill in his attempt on Mrs. Bracegirdle, 26–28; 29; 30; present when Hill killed Mountford, 31–32; 33; 34; 35; 36; 37; 38; 39; 40, n. 2; 41;

tried for Mountford's murder and acquitted, 42–44; 45; 46; military experience, 48–51; in a brawl in Pall Mall, 51; cudgels Dyer, the newsletter writer, 52; duel with "Captain Bingham," 53; kills Capt. William Hill, 54; arrested, 55; imprisoned in the Tower, 56–59; released on bail, 59; pardoned, 60; takes his seat in the House of Lords, 61; 62; 63; intimacy, quarrel, and duel with Lord Castlewood, in *Esmond*, 65–75; 76, n. 1; at Locket's tavern, 77; 78, ns. 1, 3; 79, n. 2; 80; attempts to prevent a duel, 81–83; 84, n. 1; 85, ns. 1, 2; 86, n. 3; 87; is probably present when Mr. French kills Capt. Coote, 90–91; surrenders himself, 92; 93, n. 1; is tried for Capt. Coote's murder, and acquitted, 95–96; 97; 98; 99; 101; 102; 103, ns. 1, 3; 105; 106; 107; 108; accompanies the Earl of Macclesfield to Hanover, 110–115; 117; 119; 120; military career, 121–127; 128; 129; his reformation, 130–131; an intrigue, 132–134; second marriage, 135; anecdote of Lord Mohun and Mrs. Griffith, 136–138; 140; quarrel with Mr. Davenant, 141–142; carries the Duke of Marlborough's message to Earl Poulet, 143–144; political career, 145–175; duel with Esmond, in *Esmond*, 176; 177; 179; 180; 184; fatal duel with the Duke of Hamilton, in *Esmond*, 185; 186; 187; 188; 189; 190; origin of his trouble with the Duke of Hamilton, 191–193; lawsuits with the Duke and Duchess, 193–199; 200; meeting with the Duke at a Chancery hearing, 201; exchanges words with the Duke, 202–203; 204; 205; 206; sends the Duke a message, 207; 208; 209, n. 1; 210; 211; 212; 213; 214; 215; 218; fatal duel in Hyde Park with the Duke of Hamilton, 219–222; death, 223; his wounds, 226, 231, 233; his last duel not political, 234; 235; 236; 237; 238; n. 1, 239; 241; 243; further indication of the personal character of the last duel, 244–246; 247; 248; 249; 250; 258; 260; 261, n. 1; 262; 263; 265; 268; 269; 270; 271; 272; 273; 274; 278; 279.

Mohun, Charlotte Lady, 13; marriage to Lord Mohun, 16; unfaithfulness, and separation from him, 17–18; 19; her death, 20; 48; 55; 67, n. 1; 109; 120; 121; 128; 131; 135; 140, n. 2; 186; 190, n. 1; 191; 193; 194, n. 4; 198, n. 1; 234; 235.

Mohun, Elizabeth Lady (see also under "Florella" and Griffith, Mrs. Elizabeth), 119, n. 1; marriage to Lord Mohun, 135; anecdote of her and Lord Mo-

INDEX

hun, 136–138; inherits Lord Mohun's property which she sells, 139; marries Charles Mordaunt, 139; 194; 195; 200; anecdote told of her, 223, n. 1.

Mohun, Hon. Elizabeth (sister of the fourth Lord), 5, n. 3; 11.

Mohun, Hon. Elizabeth (daughter of the fourth Lord), 20; 195, n. 1.

Mohun, Capt. James (see also under Mohun Sr. Sa.: and Mohun, James, of Polmangan)

Mohun, James, of Polmangan, 18; 19, 59; 60, n. 2.

Mohun, John, first Baron, 5, n. 2; 12, n. 3; 63, n. 2.

Mohun, Hon. John, 5, n. 2.

Mohun, Katherine Lady, 63, n. 2.

Mohun, Phillippa Lady, 6; her second marriage, 10; 13; 14; 41, n. 4; 43, n. 3; 55, n. 2; 63, n. 2.

Mohun, Mrs. Philippa, 8.

Mohun, Sr. Sa.: (see also under Mohun, James of Polmangan), 60, n. 2.

Mohun, Hon. Theo, hila, 63, n. 2.

Mohun (afterwards Ha. s), Theophila, 63, n. 2.

Mohun, Warwick, 77, n. 1.

Mohun, Warwick second Baron, 5, n. 2; 11; 19, n. 1; 77, n. 1; 192.

Molton-Hindmarsh, 6, n. 1.

Monmouth, James first Duke of, 113, n. 1; 121, n. 1.

Montagu, Ralph first Duke of, 172.

Montague, Charles (see also under Halifax, Charles first Baron), 41.

Mordaunt, Col. Charles, 140.

Mordaunt, John first Viscount, 140, n. 2.

Mordaunt, Lewis, 140, n. 2.

Morphew, John, 115, n. 1; 216, n. 4; 270.

Mountford, Capt., 25, n. 1.

Mountford, Susannah (daughter of the actor), 119, n. 1.

Mountford, Mrs. Susannah (wife of the actor), 24, n. 1; 25, n. 1; 29; 31; 46; 108; 118.

Mountford, William, 13, n. 2; 23, n. 2; 24, n. 1; 25; 26, ns. 1, 3; 28; 29; 30; 31; is killed by Capt. Richard Hill, 32; 33; 34; 35; 36; 37; 38; 39; 40; 41; 44, n. 1; 45; 47; 51, n. 3; 63; 67, n. 1; 72; 98, n. 2; 101; 118; 128; 180, n. 6.

Mountrath, Earls of, 77, n. 2.

Mudge, I. G., 76.

Mulgrave, John third Earl of (afterward first Duke of Buchinghamshire), 45.

Murray, Gen. G., 127, n. 2.

Newburgh, Charles second Earl of, 12, n. 2.

Newton, Maj. Gen. William, 267, n. 6.

Nicholas, Sir H., 140, n. 1; 180, n. 4.

Nichols, J., 53, n. 4.

Nicholson, Joseph, 215; 221; 222; 242; 262.

Nicoll, A., 24, n. 1; 73, n. 2.
Norris, William, 221; 242.
North and second Baron Grey, William sixth Baron, 126, 157; 158.
Norwich, Bishop of (John Moore) 148, n. 3.
Nottingham, Anne Countess (afterward Countess of Winchelsea), 6, n. 1.
Nottingham, Daniel second Earl of (afterward seventh Earl of Winchelsea), 23; 45; 149; 166; 167; 169.

Oglethorpe, Fanny, 20, n. 3.
Oldfield, Mrs. Anne, 23, n. 3.
Oldmixon, John, 271.
Orange, William Prince of (see also under William III, King), 12, n. 2; 121, n. 1.
Orby, Sir Charles, 12; 16; 59; 198, n. 1.
Orby, Lady Charlotte (see also under Manwaring, Lady Charlotte), 191; 194, n. 4; 195, n. 1; 198; 235.
Orby, Sir Thomas, the elder, 12, n. 2.
Orby, Sir Thomas, the younger, 16; 60, n. 2; 198.
Orleans, Phillippe Duc de, 139.
Orlebar, Mr., 201; 202, n. 2; 203; 204.
Orlebar, Richard, 201, n. 2.
Ormerod, G., 265, n. 2.
Ormonde, James second Duke of, 47; 115; 122, n. 1; 123; 124, n.
2; 125, n. 3; 142; 170; 172; 180, n. 2.
Orrery, Charles fourth Earl of, 264; 267.
Osler, Mrs. A. May, 60, n. 3.
Ossulstone, Charles second Baron, and afterward first Earl of Tankerville, 160.
Otway, Capt. Charles, 124.
Oxford, Audrey [De Vere] eleventh Earl of, 151; 161.
Oxford and Mortimer, Robert [Harley] first Earl of (see also under Harley, Robert), 173; 181, n. 4; 182; 245, n. 3.
Oxford, and Mortimer, Sarah Countess of, 228, n. 1; 245, n. 3.

Page, Gawen, 27; 31, n. 4; 32, n. 2.
Page, Mrs. Mary, 28, n. 4; 29; 30; 32, n. 2.
Paleotti, Marchese Andrea, 255.
Paleotti, Marchesa Cristina, 255.
Paleotti, Marchese Ferrante, 255; 256.
Palmer, John, 83, n. 1; 84, ns. 1, 2.
Palmes, Lieut. Gen. Francis, 258.
Panizzi, Sir Anthony, 97, n. 1; 178, n. 2.
Paris, 65; 69; 70.
Parker, Lord Chief Justice Sir Thomas (afterward Earl of Macclesfield), 261; 263; 264, n. 1.
Parnell, Col. A., 125, ns. 4, 5; 258, n. 4.
Payne, Dr. J. F., 69, n. 1.

INDEX

Pengelly, Serjeant Thomas, 232, n. 1; 263, n. 1.
Pennington, John, 214; 215; 221; 223; 242.
Perceval, Sir Philip, 9, n. 2.
Perceval, Susannah (see under Mountford, Mrs. Susannah).
Perceval, Thomas, 29, n. 3; 46.
Peter I, Czar, 260.
Peterborough, Charles third Earl of (see also under "Horatio"), 125, n. 4; 135, n. 3; 136; 138, n. 3; 140; 172.
Petit, Lieut. Col. Isaac, 125, 126.
Phillips, Lieut. William, 124.
Pickering, Miss Elizabeth (afterward Lady Cutts), 5, n. 3.
Pitt, Robert, 139, n. 5.
Pitt, Thomas, 139.
Pomfret, Henry, 79, n. 2; 89, n. 1.
Poole, Ensign Thomas, 122, n. 1.
Pope, Alexander, 95.
Portland, Henry second Earl of, 217.
Portland, William first Earl of (see also under Bentinck, William), 45; 62, n. 1; 151; 161.
Poulet, Lord Anne, 142, n. 2; 180, n. 4.
Poulet, Bridget Countess, 144.
Poulet, John first Earl, 142; challenged by the Duke of Marlborough, 143; 144; 180, n. 4; 181, n. 4; 248.
Powell, George, 26, n. 1; 31, n. 4.
Power, John, 8; 9.
Power, Pierce, 8, n. 2.

Power, Richard sixth Baron (afterward first Earl of Tyrone), 8, n. 2.
Powis, Sir Thomas, 43; 93.
Pratt, Miss Anne S., 271.
Pretender, Old, 109, n. 3; 151; 154; 161; 164; 185; 189; 241, n. 3; 256.
Price, Mr., 43.
Prideaux, Dean Humfrey, 36.
Prior, Matthew, 53, n. 4.
Prior, Samuel, 53, n. 4.
Public Records Office, 62, n. 2.
Pulteney, William, 175.

Raby, Thomas second Baron (afterward first Earl of Strafford; see also under Stratford, Thomas Earl of), 173.
Radnor, Charles second Earl of, 172.
Raleigh, Sir Walter, 63, n. 1.
Ramsey, Lieut. Col. John, 258, n. 4.
Rapin, Capt. (afterwards Maj.) Solomon, 122, n. 1; 125, n. 4.
Rapin de Thoyras, Paul, 35, n. 3; 122, n. 1; 143, n. 3; 164, n. 1; 174, n. 1; 207, n. 2; 227, n.2; 259, n. 9; 267, n. 2; 272.
Read, J., 101, n. 3; 130, n. 3; 269.
Redding, Cyrus, 139, n. 3.
Regiments:
  Allen's Foot, 125, n. 2.
  Sir R. Atkin's Foot, 53, n. 2.
  Earl of Bath's Foot, 53, n. 2; 59, n. 3.
  Brudenal's Foot, 125, n. 2.

INDEX

Gen. Cadogan's Horse, 110, n. 1.
Cameronian, 257.
Toby Caulfield's Foot, 125, n. 2.
Chudleigh's Foot (see also under Col. Hans Hamilton's Foot), 178.
Earl of Clanricarde's, 9, n. 1.
Coldstream Guards, 54; 78, n. 4; 79; 94, n. 1; 107, n. 1; 258, n. 5.
Col. Richard Coote's Foot, 23, n. 2; 80, n. 1.
Earl of Denbigh's Dragoons, 123; 126, n. 2.
Earl of Donegal's Foot, 80, n. 1.
Col. Thomas Erle's Foot, 23; 47; 156.
Farrington's Foot, 125, n. 2.
First Carabiniers, 265.
First Troop of Horse Grenadier Guards, 126, n. 6.
Foot Guards, 51; 78, n. 4; 94, ns. 2, 3; 95, n. 1; 126; 158, n. 1.
Prince George of Denmark's Foot, 95, n. 1.
Grenadier Guards, 213, n. 1.
Col. Hans Hamilton's Foot (see also under Chudleigh's Foot), 177; 178.
Col. Thomas Handasyde's Foot, 128, n. 2; 156; 177, n. 5; 178.
"Handyside's Regiment," 120; 128; 176; 178.
Honeywood's Horse, 237, n. 3.
Earl of Huntingdon's Foot, 77, n. 2; 237, n. 3.
"Independent Companies at New York in America," 156.
King's Dragoon Guards, 237, n. 3.
Duke of Leinster's Horse, 265.
Life Guards, 121, n. 1; 127, n. 3.
Viscount Lisburne's Foot, 23, n. 2; 55, n. 4; 89, n. 2.
Col. John Livesay's Foot, 156.
Lord Lucas's Foot, 107, n. 1.
"Lucas's Fusileers," 107, n. 1; 117.
Col. George Maccartney's Foot, 116; 257; 258; 259.
Earl of Macclesfield's Horse, 48; 49; 110, n. 1; 120; 202, n. 1.
"Lord Macclefield's Regiment of the Horse Guards," 120.
Col. Thomas Meredyth's Foot, 265.
Lord Mohun's Foot, 49; 121; 122; 123; 124; 125; 202, n. 1.
Maj. Gen. William Newton's Foot, 267.
Lord North and Grey's Foot, 158, n. 1.
Sir Thomas Pendergasse's Foot, 259.
Queen's Foot, 12, n. 2; 16, n. 1.
Queen's Horse, 71, n. 4.
Queen's Troop of Horse Guards 12, n. 2.
"Quin's Fusileers," 109.
Col. Henry Rowe's Foot, 80, n. 1.
Royal Fusiliers, 237, n. 3.
Royal Scots Fusiliers, 116; 264; 267.

INDEX

Duke of Schomberg's Foot, 55, n. 4.
Scots Foot Guards, 72, n. 1; 115; 209, n. 1; 248, n. 4; 257.
Stanley's Foot, 237, n. 3.
Gen. Sybourg's Foot, 123, n. 5.
Sir J. Talbot's Dragoons, 12, n. 2.
Sir R. Temple's Foot, 89, n. 2.
Third Troop of Life Guards, 12, n. 2.
Townshend's Foot, 237, n. 1.
Twenty-second or Cheshire Foot, 128, n. 2.
Col. James Tyrrell's Dragoons, 110, n. 1.
Col. James Tyrrell's Foot, 110, n. 1.
Lord Vaughan's Foot, 77, n. 1.
Renaudot, Eusébe, 15.
Reynolds, John, 215; 221; 222; 223; 242; 262.
Rich, Lady, 132, n. 1; 135, n. 3; 213, n. 1.
Rich, Sir Robert, 135, n. 3; 207; 213.
Richmond, Charles first Duke of, 174; 213; 219, n. 3; 227; 263; 272.
Rigg, J. M., 113, n. 3; 121, n. 1; 142, n. 2.
Rivers, Richard fourth Earl, 172; 173.
Rochester, Bishop of (Thomas Sprat), 12, n. 2.
Rochester, Laurence first Earl of, 45; 57; 58.

Rochford, William first Earl of, 110.
Roffeni, Count Alessandro, 255.
Rogers, J. E. Thorold, 36; 168, ns. 1, 3; 169, ns. 2, 4, 5; 170, n. 1.
Rogers, John, 27.
Rooke, Admiral Sir George, 159.
Roos, John Lord (afterward ninth Earl and first Duke of Rutland), 8, n. 2; 9, n. 2; 10, n. 4.
Roscoe, Thomas, 122, n. 1.
Roujat, Mr., 224, n. 1; 225; 226, n. 1.
Rowe, Nicholas, 23, n. 3; 71, n. 4.
Russell, Constance, 260, n. 4.
Ryswick, Treaty of, 66.

Sacheverell, Rev. Henry, 62, n. 2; 157; 160; 165.
"St. Girrone, M. de," 136.
St. John, Henry (see also under Bolingbroke, Henry first Viscount), 118; 119, n. 1; 183.
St. Leger, Hon. Arthur (afterward second Viscount Doneraile), 20, n. 3.
St. Leger, Hon. Arthur Mohun (afterward third Viscount Doneraile), 20, n. 3.
Salisbury, Bishop of (Gilbert Burnet), 164; 272.
Salmon, William, 86, n. 3.
Sanders, Mary F., 37.
Sandys, Rev. Dr., 110.
Sandys (or Sands), Mrs. Elizabeth, 13, n. 2; 26, ns. 1, 4.
Sark, Lady, 3.

INDEX

Savery, Thomas, 146.
Savoy, Prince Eugene of, 51; 187.
Say and Sele, Nathaniel fourth Viscount, 110; 114.
Scarsdale, Nicholas fourth Earl of, 165.
Scarsdale, Robert third Earl of, 12, n. 2.
Scobell, Francis, 51; 146, n. 2.
Scott, Temple, 5, n. 1; 220, n. 2; 224, n. 1; 228, n. 1; 239, ns. 1, 2; 240, ns. 1, 2, 4, 6; 242, n. 2; 244, n. 1; 248, n. 4; 256, n. 1; 259, n. 9; 267, ns. 2, 5.
Scourers, The, 73, n. 2.
Sears, M. E., 76.
Seccombe, T., 4, n. 4; 5, n. 2; 6, n. 1; 22; 23, n. 1; 53, n. 4.
Secret Memoirs .... from the New Atalantis, 3, n. 3; 4, n. 3; 16, n. 4; 18, n. 2; 24, n. 1; 119, n. 1; 130, n. 3; 132, n. 1; 134, n. 3; 138, n. 2.
Sertorius, 40, n. 2.
Shadwell, Thomas, 73, n. 2.
Shaen, Sir Arthur, 149.
"Shan," Lieut., 124.
Sheperd, Thomas, 195.
Shepherd, Sir Fleetwood, 56; 58.
Sherburn, Prof. G. W., 277, n. 1.
Shorter, Sir John, 29; 33, n. 3.
Shrewsbury, Adelaide Duchess of, 132; 133; 134; memoir of, 255–256.
Shrewsbury, Charles first Duke of, 133; 173; 255; 256.
Shrimpton, Maj. Gen. John, 258.
Sidney, W. C., 233, n. 2.

Simmonds, John, 47.
Sisson, Isaac, 210; 211.
Smith, D. Nichol, 219, n. 3.
Snow, T. C. and W., 4, n. 2; 6, n. 1; 38; 50, n. 3; 73, n. 2; 74, n. 2; 98, n. 2; 106, n. 1; 107, n. 1; 109, ns. 1, 3; 117, n. 1; 118, n. 1; 121, n. 1; 183, ns. 1, 3; 188, n. 2; 190, n. 1.
Snowe, W., 54, n. 4; 55, ns. 1, 6.
Solly, E., 229, n. 5; 233; 243, n. 2; 260, n. 5.
Somers, John first Baron (see also under Somers, Sir John), 92; 93; 96; 107; 148, n. 3; 151; 161; 166; 170, n. 1; 173; 175.
Somers, Sir John (see also under Somers, John first Baron), 43.
Somerset, Charles sixth Duke of, 47; 127, n. 2; 172; 174; 232, n. 1; 266.
Sophia, Electress Dowager of Hanover, 109; 112; 115; 131; 172; 173.
Southwell, Sir Robert, 9, n. 2.
Spectator, 31, n. 2.
Stamford, Thomas second Earl of, 159; 172.
Stanhope, Mrs. Anne (afterward Harrington, Countess of; see also under Griffith, or Griffin, Anne), 132, n. 1; 135, n. 3.
Stanhope, James, first Earl (see also under Stanhope, Col. James) 175.
Stanhope, Col. James (see also under Stanhope, James first Earl), 94.

INDEX

Stanhope, Phillip fifth Earl, 242, n. 2.

Stanhope, William (see also under Harrington, William first Earl of), 135, n. 3; 140.

Steele, Mrs. Mary, 135, n. 3.

Steele, Sir Richard, 53, n. 4; 69, n. 2; 71, n. 2; 73, n. 2; 94, n. 1; 107, n. 1; 135, n. 3; 174, n. 2; 175; 199, n. 2.

"Stella" (see under Johnson, Esther).

Stephen, H. L., 5, n. 3; 6, n. 1; 23, n. 1; 76, n. 1.

Stephen, Sir L., 260, n. 1; 267, n. 1.

Stepney, George, 175.

Sterne, Rev. Lawrence, 177.

Sterne, Mary, 177, n. 5.

Sterne, Capt. (or Lieut.) Roger, 176; 177; 178; 184, n. 1.

Stratford, 267.

Stratford, Thomas Earl of (Strafford, Thomas first Earl of; see also under Raby, Thomas second Baron), 181, n. 4.

Stratford, Dr. William, 245, n. 3.

Suffolk, Henrietta Countess of (see also under Howard, Mrs. Henrietta), 139, n. 2.

Summers, Rev. Montague, 39; 46, n. 5; 73, n. 1.

Sunderland, Robert second Earl of, 45; 181, n. 1.

Sunderland, Charles third Earl of, 172; 196, n. 2.

Sutherland, John sixteenth Earl of, 220, n. 1; 245, n. 2; 277; 278; 279; 280; 281.

Swaine, John, 165.

Swift, Dean Jonathan, 4; 5, n. 1; 73, ns. 1, 2; 95; 122, n. 1; 129, n. 2; 141; 164, n. 2; 185; 202, n. 2; 214, n. 3; 220, n. 2; 224, n. 1; 228, n. 1; 229; 236; 239; 240; 242, n. 2; 244, n. 1; 248, n. 4; 249, n. 1; 256; 259, n. 9; 260, n. 2; 267; 270; 272; 273.

Sydney, Henry first Viscount (afterward first Earl of Romney), 40, n. 2.

Szalankemen, Battle of, 50.

Talbot, Robert, 216; 221; 224.

Talmash, Lieut. Gen. Thomas, 48.

Tangiers, Lieutenant Governor of, 135, n. 2.

Tatler, The, 69, n. 2; 94, n. 1; 107, n. 1.

Taverns:
 Cross Keys, 83, n. 1.
 Globe, 206.
 Grayhound (Locket's), Charing Cross, 73; 78; 80; 84; 88; 91, n. 2; 93; 95; 102; 103; 105.
 Half Moon, Cheapside, 231.
 Queen's Arms, Pall Mall, 204; 206; 212; 213, n. 2.
 Rose, Covent Garden, 73, n. 1; 208, 210, 211, 212.
 Rose, Holborn, 231.
 Rummer, Charing Cross, 51; 53.

INDEX

Rummer, Gray's Inn Passage, 53, n. 4.
Rummer, Soper Lane, Queen Street, City, 53, n. 4.
Ship and Castle, Cornhill, 89.
Standard, Leicester Square, 74; 83; 84; 103, n. 3.
"Trumpet, in the Cockpit, Whitehall," 69.
Trumpet, Sheer Lane, 69, n. 2.
White Horse, 31; 32.
White's Chocolate House, 204; 206.

Thackeray, W. M., 3, n. 3; 4; 5; 33, n. 1; 37, 38; 48; 49; 50, n. 3; 51; 63; 65; 67, n. 2; 68, n. 1; 71; ns. 2, 4; 72, n. 3; 73, ns. 1, 2; 74, n. 1; 76; 83, n. 2; 97; 98; 99; 100; 103, n. 1; 104; 105; 106, n. 1; 107; 109; 115; 116; 118; 119, n, 1; 120; 121. n. 1; 127; 128; 129, n. 2; 130; 156; 177, n. 5; 178, n. 2; 180; 181; 183; 189; 190; 201; 233; 234; 235; 236; 237; 238; 240; 241; 246; 247; 248; 249; 250; 251.

Theatres:
Dorset Gardens, 23, n. 3; 100, n. 1.
Duke's, 29, n. 3; 99; 100, n. 1.
"Duke's Playhouse," 71.
Haymarket, 23, n. 3; 118; 119.
"Theatre in Duke Street," 71; 99.
Little Lincoln's Inn Fields, 100.

Theatre Royal, 23, n. 3; 26; 29, n. 3; 100, ns. 1, 3; 101; 118.
Thompson, —, 135, n. 3.
Thornhill, Mr., 202, n. 2.
Tilson, George, 266, n. 9.
Tindal, Nicholas, 35; 48, n. 3; 143, n. 3; 164, n. 1; 174, n. 1; 207, n. 2; 227, n. 2; 259, n. 9; 267, n. 2; 272.
Tisdale, Rev. W., 164, n. 2.
Toland, John, 55, n. 5; 111; 112; 114; 130, n. 3.
Tomson, Serjeant, 43.
Tomson, J., 150.
Tonson, Jacob, 35; 40, n. 2; 175.
Trent, Prof. W. P., 271.
Tressam, Mrs., 8.
Trevor, Sir Thomas, 43; 92; 93, n. 1.
Tuck, Capt. Thomas, 122, n. 1.
"Tucks, Mr.", 122, n. 1.
Tully, —, 98, n. 2.
Tunbridge, William Viscount, 110; 111; 114.
Turberville, A. S., 38; 63.
Turks, 4; 49; 50.
Turner, Stephen, 86.
Tyrawley, Charles first Baron, 169.
Tyrrell (or Tyrrel), Capt. James, 55, n. 5; 110.
Tyrrell, James the elder, 110, n. 1.
Tyrrell, Sir Robert, 55; 110, n. 1.

Vanbrugh, Sir John, 175.
Venice, 65.
Verbruggen, John, 29, n. 3; 118.
Verney, John, 10, n. 1.

INDEX

Verney, Margaret, 53, n. 4; 113, n. 3.
Verney, Sir R., 9, n. 2; 10, n. 1.
Vian, A., 180, n. 6; 209, n. 1.
Vienna, 4; 49; 50; 65.

Wales, Caroline Princess of, 256.
Walker, Elizabeth, 31, n. 4; 32, n. 1.
Wallop, Mr., 43, n. 3.
Walpole, Horatio, 266, n. 9.
Walpole, Sir Robert, 29; 175; 273.
Walpoliana, 29, n. 1; 37.
Walsh, William, 175.
Ward, Sir A. W., 109, n. 3; 255, n. 1; 256, n. 1.
Ward, Edward, 100, n. 1; 231, n. 3.
Warrington, Edward, 31, n. 3.
Warwick, Charlotte Countess of, 71, n. 4.
Warwick, Edward sixth Earl of (see also under Holland, Edward third Earl of), 23, n. 1; 38; 48, n. 2; 49, n. 2; Lord Mohun arrested at his house, 55; bondsman for Lord Mohun, 59; 60, n. 2; 66; 71; 73, n. 1; 74, n. 2; second of Lord Mohun in his duel with Lord Castlewood in *Esmond* and wounds Henry, 75; at Locket's, 76; 77, ns. 1, 2; 78, ns. 1, 2, 3; 79, n, 2; 80; 81; 82; 83, n. 1; 84, ns. 1, 2; 85, ns. 1, 2, 3; 86, ns. 1, 2, 3; wounded acting as Mr. French's second in his duel with Capt. Coote, 87; 88; 89; 91; tried for the murder of Capt. Coote, 92; found guilty of manslaughter, 93; 94; 95; 97; 98, n. 2; 101; 102; 103, ns. 1, 3; 104; 105; 106; 107; death, 116; 188; 213, n. 1.
Warwick, Edward seventh Earl of, 71, n. 4.
Webb, Lieut. Gen. John Richmond, 97, n. 1; 178; 184; 237.
Westbury, Col. 14; 71; 75; 102; 105; 107.
Wharton, Thomas fifth Baron, first Earl, and first Marquis of, 122, n. 1; 148, n. 3; 164; 173; 175.
White, J., 13, n. 1; 270.
White, Coroner Robert, 56, n. 1; 57; 60, n. 3.
Whitmore, Lieut. Col. George, 125, n. 4; 126.
Whitworth, Charles first Baron, 202, n. 1.
Whitworth, Ensign Edward, 202, n. 1.
Whitworth, Richard, the Elder, 202; 204, n. 2.
Whitworth, Cornet Richard, the Younger, 202, n. 1.
Wightman [or Whiteman], Col. Joseph, 66, n. 2; 89, n. 5; 91, n. 3; 94.
William III, King (see also under Orange, William Prince of), 5, n. 3; 10, n. 5; 16, n. 1; attempts to prevent a duel between Lord Mohun and Lord Kennedy, 22; 37; 38; refuses to pardon Lord Mohun for Mountford's murder, 41, n. 4; is present at Lord

INDEX

Mohun's trial, 42; 43, n. 1; 44, n. 1; 46, n. 5; 54, ns. 2, 5; 58; 59, n. 1; pardons Lord Mohun for Capt. William Hill's murder, 60; his probable reasons therefor, 62; 63; pardons Mr. French for Coote's murder, 90; 91; attends Lord Warwick's trial, 93; 107; 109; 111; 112; 113; 135, n. 2; 151; 152; 161; 163; 166; 181; 224, n. 1; 248, n. 4.

William King, and Mary, Queen 54, n. 5; 56, ns. 2. 5; 57, n. 3; 58, ns. 1, 2, 4; 60, n. 2.

Williams, Rice, 101, n. 2; 201, n. 4; 202, n. 2; 203, n. 1; 204; 205, n. 2; 206; 207, ns. 1, 2; 212, n. 5; 213, n. 2; 222; 223; 242, n. 2; 246, n. 2.

Williams, W. R., 213, n. 1.

Williamson, Sir Joseph, 58, n. 4.

Willoughby de Broke, Richard eleventh Baron, 149.

Windham, John, 60, n. 1.

Windham, Thomas, 60.

Windsor of Blackcastle, Thomas first Viscount, 121.

Wishart, Sir James, 174.

Woodward, Mr., 231.

Worcester, Bishop of (William Lloyd), 152.

Wren, Sir Christopher, 92, n. 3.

Wright, Serjeant, 92.

Wycherley, William, 71; 100.

York, Archbishop of (John Sharp), 172.

York, James Duke of (see also under James II, King), 113, n. 3.

Young, Robert, 12, n. 2.

Zenta, Battle of, 50; 51.